Popular Cultures in England 1550–1750

THEMES IN BRITISH SOCIAL HISTORY

edited by John Stevenson

This series covers the most important aspects of British social history from the Renaissance to the present day. Topics include education, poverty, health, religion, leisure, crime and popular protest, some of which are treated in more than one volume. The books are written for undergraduates, postgraduates and the general reader, and each volume combines a general approach to the subject with the primary research of the author.

Currently available

THE ENGLISH FAMILY 1450–1700 *Ralph A. Houlbrooke*
POVERTY AND POLICY IN TUDOR AND STUART ENGLAND *Paul Slack*
CRIME IN EARLY MODERN ENGLAND 1550–1750 *J.A. Sharpe*
POPULAR CULTURES IN ENGLAND 1550–1750 *Barry Reay*
GENDER IN ENGLISH SOCIETY, 1650–1850: The Emergence of Separate Spheres? *Robert Shoemaker*
LITERATURE AND SOCIETY IN EIGHTEENTH-CENTURY ENGLAND *W.A. Speck*
CRIME AND SOCIETY IN ENGLAND 1750–1900 (Second Edition) *Clive Emsley*
THE LABOURING CLASSES IN EARLY INDUSTRIAL ENGLAND 1750–1850 *John Rule*
POPULAR DISTURBANCES IN ENGLAND 1700–1832 (Second Edition) *John Stevenson*
SEX, POLITICS AND SOCIETY: The Regulation of Sexuality since 1800 (Second Edition) *Jeffrey Weeks*
THE WORKING CLASS IN BRITAIN 1850–1939 *John Benson*
THE RISE OF THE CONSUMER SOCIETY IN BRITAIN 1880–1980 *John Benson*
HEALTH AND SOCIETY IN TWENTIETH-CENTURY BRITAIN *Helen Jones*
LAND AND SOCIETY IN ENGLAND 1750–1980 *G.E. Mingay*

Popular Cultures in England 1550–1750

BARRY REAY

Longman
London and New York

Addison Wesley Longman Limited
Edinburgh Gate,
Harlow, Essex CM20 2JE, United Kingdom
and Associated Companies throughout the world.

Published in the United States of America by Addison Wesley Longman, New York.

First published 1998

ISBN 0-582-48954-7 PPR
ISBN 0-582-29296-4 CSD

Visit Addison Wesley Longman on the world wide web at
http://www.awl-he.com

British Library Cataloguing in Publication Data

A catalogue entry for this title is available from the British Library

Library of Congress Cataloging-in-Publication Data
Reay, Barry.
Popular cultures in England, 1550–1750 / Barry Reay.
p. cm. — (Themes in British social history)
Includes bibliographical references (p.) and index.
ISBN 0-582-29296-4. — ISBN 0-582-48954-7 (pbk.)
1. Popular culture—England—History—17th century. 2. Popular
culture—England—History—16th century. 3. Popular culture—
England—History—18th century. 4. England—Social life and
customs—17th century. 5. England—Social life and customs—16th
century. 6. England—Social life and customs—18th century.
I. Title. II. Series.
DA320.R43 1998
306'.0942—dc21   98–16046
                                                          CIP

Set by 35 in 10/12pt Baskerville
Produced by Addison Wesley Longman Singapore (Pte) Ltd.,

Printed & bound by Antony Rowe Ltd, Eastbourne
Transferred to digital print on demand 2003

To University of Auckland history students:
past, present, and future

Contents

Acknowledgements

This book has had an unusually long gestation but a rather short, and not too uncomfortable, birth. Both processes were eased by the support networks of family, friends, and colleagues. You know who you are; and I would like to start by thanking you warmly.

Popular Cultures was created in a relatively short period of time: I wrote Chapter 1 in the summer (the southern hemisphere summer) of 1995–6, Chapter 4 at the end of 1996, and the bulk of the book in the first half of 1997. However, I have been reading, researching, teaching, and thinking its subject matter for well over a decade. Indeed, I first conceived of a text of this type in the early 1980s. I am glad that I waited until the late 1990s to write it, however. Any earlier, and I would not have had the benefit of the scholarship of many of those whose insights are crucial to my analysis – the work of Tessa Watt and Ronald Hutton, for example, which is used in several chapters. Some of the most important research in early modern social and cultural history has been a product of this decade; so much so, that the making of *Popular Cultures* has been a rather precarious exercise. The chapter on sexualities was written and rewritten as books by Fletcher, Gowing, and Hitchcock appeared. Five major texts on witchcraft (Briggs, Barry et al., Sharpe, Purkiss, and Clark) were published either during or just after the 'completion' of Chapter 4. David Cressy's new work on ritual and the life-cycle came out as I finished the 'final' draft! I am greatly in debt, then, to the work of other scholars. This book could never have been written without their labours.

My thanks also go to the editor of this series, John Stevenson, and to the publisher's editorial director, Andrew MacLennan, for their persistence, patience, and good humour.

Finally, I am immensely grateful to the history students of the University of Auckland. Not just to the waves of undergraduates who have studied and engaged with early modern history, and kept me on my toes, but the graduates – not just early modernists – who make the job seem so worthwhile. In appreciation, this book is dedicated to them.

Auckland
September 1997

Introduction

Stuart Hall once said that he had many problems with the term 'popular' and even more with the word 'culture': 'When you put the two terms together, the difficulties can be pretty horrendous.'[1] Past popular cultures are best known through description and example, by the historically crafted fiction of experience, rather than by crude definition. However, it is necessary to provide readers with at least a working definition lest I suffer the fate of the editors of a book called *Rethinking Popular Culture*, whose reviewer, having read the 'compendious volume', remarked that he was 'no clearer about what popular culture is'.[2] 'Popular cultures' refers to widely held and commonly expressed thoughts and actions. We will be exploring what have been termed structures of feeling and systems of meaning: attitudes and values expressed performatively, symbolically, orally, and in writing. We will be covering both belief and behaviour. While the focus is necessarily on those below the level of England's social elite in rural and urban early modern England, the bulk of the population, it is only a focus. Common cultural values spill across tidy social demarcations. The term popular cultures is not intended to imply some firm, exclusive division between popular and elite, high and low, great and little, or learned and unlearned. Nor is it to be taken to indicate cultural homogeneity among the subordinate: the 's' in cultures represents the subcultural splinterings (or segmentation) of locality, age, gender, religion, and class. The key-words for this history are: ambiguous, complex, contradictory, divided, dynamic, fluid, fractured, gendered, hybrid, interacting, multiple, multivalent, overlapping, plural, resistant, and shared.

We will return to definitions and different approaches to popular cultures in the final chapter (Chapter 7), for this book can be

1. S. Hall, 'Notes on deconstructing "the popular"', in R. Samuel (ed.), *People's History and Socialist Theory* (London, 1981), p. 227.
2. E. Weber, 'PC? Rethinking popular culture: contemporary perspectives in cultural studies', *Contention* 2 (1993), 5.

1

seen as an extended investigation of both the utility of the term 'popular culture' and the problems of representing long-lost cultural worlds. My reason for not concentrating on definitions now is to steer the reader away from habitual approaches to popular culture. (The act of discussing entrenched ideas has a danger of embedding them further.[3]) But it should be said that the intellectual point of departure for what follows goes against the logic of an influential tendency in British social history to begin with a social group or groups (those below the gentry or upper-bourgeois level) and then to seek a cultural correspondence to that position in the social structure (popular culture). My aim is to reverse this order and start instead with popular culture itself. This is not to deny the role of power or social hierarchy in the shaping of ideas and behaviour, to reject notions of domination and subordination, or to preclude any correspondence between society and culture. It is purely to make the point that the ordering principle of analysis will *not* be that culture corresponds to social status in some unproblematic, predetermined manner.[4]

The aim of this book is not to provide a complete cultural history of the early modern world – the generality of such a survey would lose all analytical meaning – but to explore some of the more important aspects of early modern popular cultures. I have deliberately chosen areas where there is a sophisticated historiography: the selection of topics indicates the richness of historians' work as much as any personal choice of what the important topics are. I have attempted to combine secondary and primary sources to give readers a feel (mediated, of course) for early modern languages of description. Hence the detailed document analysis or evocation with which most chapters begin. While the end product is a textbook synthesis, I have tried to give a different twist to each chapter. Individual chapters could therefore stand on their own, as essays, although together they provide a sustained examination of early modern popular cultures. In fact they can be seen as demonstrating different facets of early modern culture. Chapter 1, on sexuality, illustrates the importance of gender. Chapter 2 explores the complex mix of cultural forms – in this case, orality and literacy. Chapter 3, on religion, deals with cultural change. Chapter 4, the witchcraft chapter,

---

3. Of course I am aware that there is nothing to stop you – as active readers – reading the last chapter first.

4. Miri Rubin makes similar points, far more eloquently, in the introduction to her book, *Corpus Christi: the Eucharist in Late Medieval Culture* (Cambridge, 1991), pp. 7–9.

covers the difficulties in explaining alien belief systems. Chapter 5 argues for the ubiquity and the multiple meanings of ritual in early modern England. Chapter 6 focuses on repertoires of protest. Chapter 7 (the concluding chapter) returns to definitions and approaches. My brief is the period 1550–1750. Although historians of the sixteenth and eighteenth centuries will complain that my lens favours the middle part of the early modern period (the seventeenth century is my area of expertise), I trust that this has not provided too much of a distorting focus. The time-spans covered vary from chapter to chapter, but I have attempted to range over the three centuries (and earlier and later, where appropriate). Readers should remain relaxed about this: popular cultures do not follow the tight chronologies of political history.

CHAPTER ONE

Sexualities

I

The Somerset quarter sessions rolls for 1657 contain a series of
complaints against a woman called Mary Coomb, the wife of an
innkeeper from a small village near Axbridge in central Somerset.
A wheelwright, John Barber, alleged all-night drinking sessions which
disturbed people in the community, and also some rather outra-
geous sexual behaviour. Barber deposed that Coomb had lain on
the Axbridge road, calling out to passers-by 'wishing all good fellows to come & occupie wth her', 'spreading of her leggs abroad,
saying come play wth my Cunt and make my husband a cuckwalld'.
She put her hand down the codpiece of Barber's apprentice. She
told Barber that his wife was 'fucking with William Fry, wch [Barber
complained] caused a debate for a long time betweene me & my
wife and likewise he and his wife'. On one occasion, when Barber
went to her house, 'shee shut ye door and would force me to be
naught with her spreading of her legs & shewing her comoditie
saying come rouge look thee here wt thou shalt play withall'. She
said 'come & thrust thy pricke in my Cunt and there shalbe an end
to all bussiness'.[1]

Here was a woman who was promiscuous in both speech and
sexuality. As we shall see, there was an early modern correspondence between the mouth and genitals: a woman with a loose mouth
was a woman with a loose vagina. Indeed, there was a belief that the
umbilical cord linked the tongue and the sexual organs. Hence it

---

1. Somerset Record Office, Q/SR 95 ii/41: Somerset Quarter Sessions Rolls, 1657.
G.R. Quaife first drew attention to this document in his *Wanton Wenches and Wayward
Wives: Peasants and Illicit Sex in Early Seventeenth Century England* (London, 1979),
pp. 156–7.

4

was to be cut long in men to provide them with long tongues and penises, and cut short in women to give them short tongues and tight vaginas.[2]

Of course there are several readings of this text, and it is important to realise that we are hearing only one mediated voice. One response might be that the woman was mad, but it is significant that this was not alleged in the deposition. Barber does complain that Coomb's behaviour was animal-like, 'tumbling herselfe in the highway more liker to a swine than a christian'. He does not impute madness.

When we are confronted with a cultural extract such as this, our immediate reaction is to seek the familiar: we recognise the 'cunt' and the 'fucking'. Yet it is the differences which are more important to the cultural historian: the significance of the mouth/vagina correspondence, for example, or the use of the words 'cuckold' and that freighted term 'commodity'. The meanings of sex are inconstant. The history of sex acts, as Lawrence Stone once observed, 'is a somewhat boring topic' given the human body's rather limited repertoire.[3] What are far more interesting are the taboos and the attempts to control such sexual activities, the meanings attached to sex acts. Sexuality is a social, cultural, and temporal construct. Concepts of pornography – to take just one example – have changed over time. Pornography, as we know it, certainly existed in the early modern world, but was presented primarily as a subtext of biological reproduction, or was there to make a religious or political point. Pornography as an end in itself is a recent construct.[4]

Thus we have to be prepared to encounter sexual worlds different from our own.[5] It is a simple point to make, if often missed by

2. R.A. Erickson, ' "The books of generation": some observations on the style of the British midwife books, 1671–1764', in P.-G. Bouce (ed.), *Sexuality in Eighteenth-century Britain* (Manchester, 1982), p. 80; G. Williams, *A Dictionary of Sexual Language and Imagery in Shakespearean and Stuart Literature* (London, 1994), pp. 918–19, 1402.

3. L. Stone, 'Sex in the west', *New Republic*, 8 July 1985.

4. See L. Hunt, 'Introduction: obscenity and the origins of modernity, 1500–1800', in L. Hunt (ed.), *The Invention of Pornography: Obscenity and the Origins of Modernity, 1500–1800* (New York, 1993), pp. 9–45; R. Darnton, 'Sex for thought', *New York Review of Books*, 22 December 1994.

5. See R.A. Padug, 'Sexual matters: on conceptualizing sexuality in history', *Radical History Review* 20 (1979), 3–23; A.I. Davidson, 'Sex and the emergence of sexuality', *Critical Inquiry* 14 (1987), 16–48; J. Weeks, *Sex, Politics and Society: the Regulation of Sexuality since 1800* (London, 1989), ch. 1; J. Weeks, 'Sexuality and history revisited', in L. Jamieson and H. Corr (eds), *State, Private Life and Political Change* (London, 1990), ch. 2; B.R. Smith, *Homosexual Desire in Shakespeare's England: a Cultural Poetics* (Chicago, 1991), ch. 1. See also, the useful collection of essays: D.C. Stanton (ed.), *Discourses of Sexuality from Aristotle to Aids* (Ann Arbor, 1992).

those who ransack the past to locate the familiar or to chart some logical progression towards the present. Indeed, our very categorisation, our privileging of sex, is a current preoccupation, a product of our culture. Sex is central to our identity and self-definition. It is, in the words of Jeffrey Weeks, 'a unified domain', a 'thing in itself' (like politics or religion), 'a continent of knowledge with its own rules of exploration and its own expert geographers'.[6] We must not assume – in fact it is extremely unlikely – that this was so in the past.

The historian must also look for dissonance, for cultural jarring. Anyone who has studied the early modern conduct books or household manuals, in which ministers of the church dispensed advice on marriage and the family, is certain to be taken with the aggressiveness of Mary Coomb's behaviour. The advice literature of the time assumed female modesty, chastity, and obedience, teaching that 'the ornament of a woman consisted in chaste and honest conditions' and that men were 'stronger and more able to beare and support the infirmities and weaknesses of their wives'.[7] But Coomb is aggressive in her sexuality; she is active, not passive. Her husband, John, is a shadowy figure in the depositions. He is there at the beginning of the document to establish the legal identity of Mary, but thereafter appears only as the putative cuckold – indeed holds her clothes for her as she lies in the highway. The case of Mary Coomb provides an entry into the subject matter of this chapter: the contours of sexual worlds recognisable yet different from our own.

II

The sociologist Anthony Giddens has characterised the sexuality of modern western societies, relatively free from the bonds of reproduction, as 'decentred' or 'plastic sexuality'.[8] If modern sexuality is indeed 'plastic', early modern sexuality could be described as married or procreative sexuality, for the matrices of marriage and reproduction dominated the meanings, languages, and practices of

6. Weeks, *Sex, Politics and Society*, p. 12.
7. See K.M. Davies, 'Continuity and change in literary advice on marriage', in R.B. Outhwaite (ed.), *Marriage and Society* (London, 1981), ch. 3; A. Fletcher, 'The Protestant idea of marriage in early modern England', in A. Fletcher and P. Roberts (eds), *Religion, Culture and Society in Early Modern Britain* (Cambridge, 1994), ch. 7. The quotes come from R. S[nawsell], *A Looking-Glasse for Married Folkes* (London, 1631), pp. 33, 122.
8. A. Giddens, *The Transformation of Intimacy: Sexuality, Love and Eroticism in Modern Societies* (Cambridge, 1992), p. 2.

early modern sex.[9] Premarital sex occurred, and was even tolerated – but within boundaries. The dominant framework was intention to marry.

People married at widely varying ages. Most married in their twenties, but from 20 to 25 per cent of women and 25 to 30 per cent of men were aged 30 or over when they first married. Although many London-born women, of all classes, married while still in their teens, national reconstitutions show that only 3 or 4 per cent of men and 11 to 13 per cent of women were married under the age of 20; indeed, more couples were marrying in their late thirties and forties.[10] This meant that for large numbers of women and men there were years of sexual maturity, and presumably sexual desire, before marriage. And not all did marry: demographers have calculated that in the seventeenth century some 25 per cent of men and women in their early forties had never married.[11]

Illegitimacy ratios (the number of illegitimate births per 100 registered births) were low: from about 1.0 to 4.4 over the whole period 1550–1750, with peaks from 1590 to 1610 and after 1750, and low rates in the second half of the seventeenth century. The period from 1570 to 1640 had rates of from 2.9 to 4.3, but these were 'composites' of lower levels in the south and east and higher rates in the north and west. Individual parishes and periods had higher (and lower) ratios. Colyton, for example, reached 9.5 in the 1720s; in Terling the illegitimacy ratio was only 0.8 during the period 1650–99.[12] But this measurement is a misleading gauge of a community's

---

9. J. D'Emilio and E.B. Freedman refer to the 'reproductive matrix' in their discussion of sexuality in colonial America: *Intimate Matters: a History of Sexuality in America* (New York, 1989), pp. xv, xix. See also M. Foucault, *The History of Sexuality: Volume 1: An Introduction* (London, 1978), p. 37; R. Porter and L. Hall, *The Facts of Life: the Creation of Sexual Knowledge in Britain, 1650–1950* (New Haven, 1995), pp. 125, 277; T. Hitchcock, *English Sexualities, 1700–1800* (New York, 1997), ch. 3.

10. Calculated from E.A. Wrigley and R.S. Schofield, 'English population history from family reconstitution: summary results 1600–1799', *Population Studies* 37 (1983), Table 2, p. 162, Table 3, p. 164.

11. See E.A. Wrigley and R.S. Schofield, *The Population History of England 1541–1871* (Cambridge, 1989), Table 7.28, p. 260.

12. See the tables in P. Laslett, 'Introduction: comparing illegitimacy over time and between cultures', in P. Laslett, K. Oosterveen, and R. Smith (eds), *Bastardy and its Comparative History* (Cambridge, Mass., 1980), p. 14; K. Oosterveen, R. Smith, and S. Stewart, 'Family reconstitution and the study of bastardy: evidence from certain English parishes', in Laslett, Oosterveen, and Smith (eds), *Bastardy*, pp. 96–7; D. Levine and K. Wrightson, 'The social context of illegitimacy in early modern England', in Laslett, Oosterveen, and Smith (eds), *Bastardy*, p. 159; R. Adair, *Courtship, Illegitimacy and Marriage in Early Modern England* (Manchester, 1996), p. 50. Adair, *Courtship*, ch. 2, modifies the earlier figures of Laslett et al., and shows the pre-1640 variations between the regions.

experience of the phenomenon of illegitimacy. If estimated as a percentage of first births rather than all births (a more realistic measurement), the figures would be higher. At an extreme, with illegitimacy ratios of from 10 to 12 per cent, it has been suggested that up to a half of first births in mid-eighteenth-century London were illegitimate.[13] A family reconstitution study of a nineteenth-century rural parish in Kent found that although the illegitimacy ratio was only 5.0, over a third of the households in that community contained family members who had direct experience of illegitimacy.[14] We may need to make such upward mental adjustments when considering the local impact of childbirth outside of marriage. Nonetheless, it is significant that the ages of those women bearing illegitimate children were about the same as those marrying, suggesting that childbirth outside wedlock reflected interrupted intended marriage rather than blatant disregard for the institution.[15]

Although historians have spent much time measuring the phenomenon, illegitimacy is something of a blunt classification which most probably obscures complex social scenarios and human relationships. Bastardy, as David Levine and Keith Wrightson have observed, was a 'compound phenomenon'.[16] Attitudes must have varied according to the type of illegitimacy. The woman who bore a single illegitimate child to an unmarried man, and the woman who was in a long-term relationship (even if she had several children), were no doubt treated differently to those who fell pregnant to married men or who had a variety of liaisons. Peter Laslett has argued for the existence of 'bastard-bearing sub-cultures', 'a series of bastard-producing women, living in the same locality, whose activities persisted over several generations, and who tended to be related by kinship or marriage'.[17] Yet detailed local studies suggest that the neat demarcation between legitimate and illegitimate implied by Laslett's influential typology has little value in understanding the context or meaning of illegitimacy. 'Bastard bearers' included a few families which could perhaps be described as 'deviant', but for the

13. A. Wilson, 'Illegitimacy and its implications in mid-eighteenth-century London: the evidence of the Foundling Hospital', *Continuity and Change* 4 (1989), 104, 136.

14. B. Reay, 'Sexuality in nineteenth-century England: the social context of illegitimacy in rural Kent', *Rural History* 1 (1990), 242.

15. For the age of women bearing illegitimate children, see Levine and Wrightson, 'Social context of illegitimacy', p. 161; Oosterveen, Smith, and Stewart, 'Family reconstitution', pp. 92, 107–8.

16. Levine and Wrightson, 'Social context of illegitimacy', p. 169.

17. P. Laslett, 'The bastardy prone sub-society', in Laslett, Oosterveen, and Smith (eds), *Bastardy*, p. 217.

most part illegitimacy should be seen as part of the normal sexual culture of the hamlets of the past.[18] Anthea Newman's charting of the linkages between families who produced illegitimate children in eighteenth- and early-nineteenth-century Ash-next-Sandwich has demonstrated the way in which illegitimates and unmarried mothers were scattered amongst conventional unions and legitimate progeny. Many of the mothers of illegitimates eventually married in church, and we would not have our figures and tables if 'bastards' had not been baptised in the first place.[19] This is not to argue for a widespread tolerance of illegitimacy, nor to claim that attitudes to unmarried mothers and children born out of wedlock were as benign as those towards pregnant brides. But (as was hinted earlier) many families in a village or hamlet must have had kin who had directly experienced unmarried motherhood. Illegitimacy was a risk that virtually all women confronted.

Another quantitative marker of sexuality explored by demographers is the rate of bridal (or prenuptial) pregnancy. Roughly 20 to 25 per cent of brides were pregnant when they entered the church in the early modern period, but in some parishes the figure was as high as 30 or even 50 per cent.[20] Clearly these figures represent the mere tip of a hidden number of actual acts of sexual intercourse, not to mention heterosexual activity which stopped short of coitus.[21] The statistics hint at two types of prenuptial intercourse: that where sexual activity resulting in pregnancy led to marriage (marriage which was 'courtship-led') and that where anticipation of marriage led to sexual activity and pregnancy (courtship which was 'marriage-led'). From just under 50 per cent to nearly 70 per cent of pregnant brides in the period 1550–1750 were at least three months pregnant when they stood in front of the minister, indicating sexual activity some time before marriage. The remainder – from a half to a third – presumably had intercourse once marriage had been agreed. Adrian Wilson has suggested that rural England had a courtship pattern that was marriage-led, whereas in early modern London marriage was decided as a solution to pregnancy

---

18. See the critiques by Levine and Wrightson, 'Social context of illegitimacy', pp. 158–75; and Reay, 'Sexuality in nineteenth-century England', pp. 219–47.

19. A. Newman, 'An evaluation of bastardy recordings in an east Kent parish', in Laslett, Oosterveen, and Smith (eds), *Bastardy*, ch. 4.

20. See the tables in Laslett, Oosterveen, and Smith (eds), *Bastardy*, pp. 23, 109; Adair, *Courtship*, ch. 3.

21. R.M. Smith, 'Marriage processes in the English past: some continuities', in L. Bonfield, R.M. Smith, and K. Wrightson (eds), *The World We Have Gained* (Oxford, 1986), p. 92.

(it was courtship-led). The interesting shift in the period before 1750 was the drop in the proportion of more heavily pregnant brides during the second half of the seventeenth century (a period when illegitimacy ratios were also at a low point), combined with a rise in the proportion of brides who had obviously waited until marriage had been arranged before they had intercourse. The eighteenth century saw rural England move towards the London pattern. But for most of our period of interest both patterns of courtship existed; even during the seventeenth-century high point of marriage-led courtship, pregnant brides were evenly divided between the two types.[22]

In other words, either marriage would be promised or agreed upon and sexual intercourse would commence, or couples would have sex and the spoken or unspoken assumption was that if the result was a pregnancy they would get married. In the words of the female character in a seventeenth-century ballad,

> Therefore we will embrace a while,
> and afterwards we'l marry.[23]

A Somerset woman said that a fuller had been 'a suiter to her' for more than a year. The woman's brother (a weaver) and her widowed mother had been present when the man had promised to marry her, and 'upon assurance that he would pforme his promise she did consent to let him have the carnall knowledge of her Body on the Sunday after Michelmas day last, at her Mothers house'. The man had visited the woman at all hours of the night; he 'was with her alone in the Chamber often times'; 'her Mother did once see him in Bed with her and asked him what he meant by it, who sayd that he did intend to Marry with this Examinate'. The fuller referred to the young woman as 'his wife', and said 'that she was his'.[24] There was a recognition that sexual intercourse carried certain responsibilities, and providing these responsibilities were not avoided sex was permissible. As one woman put it, 'after a couple have talked of matrimony it is lawful for them to have carnal copulation'.[25] Lawrence Stone has discovered some remarkable examples

---

22. Wilson, 'Illegitimacy', pp. 138–9; Smith, 'Marriage processes', Table 3.2, p. 86 (the calculations of percentages are mine).

23. W.G. Day (ed.), *The Pepys Ballads*, 5 vols (Cambridge, 1987), Vol. 3, p. 6.

24. Somerset Record Office, Q/SR 95 ii/40.

25. Quoted in S.D. Amussen, *An Ordered Society: Gender and Class in Early Modern England* (Oxford, 1988), p. 110.

of freedom in this type of sexual courtship among upper to middling groups.[26] Contemporaries were more tolerant of bridal pregnancy than they were of illegitimacy. Indeed, when early modern women took action against slanderers to protect their honour, their 'sexual credit', they rarely did so over bridal pregnancy.[27] It is likely that from a quarter to more than a third of pregnant brides in the early modern period were visibly with child when they entered the church.[28]

Given the general frame of anticipated marriage, there was, as I have already suggested, considerable room for manoeuvre. We know from the court records that couples had intercourse in meadows, in ditches, under hedges, up against stiles, in barns and dairies, in their masters' houses (many were servants), in the woods, at the backs of inns and alehouses, in churchyards, in the homes of the women's parents.[29] Women and men mixed freely at work and at play; only at church were they segregated.[30] There is growing evidence of a tolerance of sexual activity other than heterosexual sexual intercourse. References to kissing, mutual fondling and groping suggest that unmarried couples may well have limited their sexual activity within that frame, and that intercourse may not have had the centrality in people's desires that it has (for many) today.[31] The future excise officer, John Cannon, from a middling-sort Somerset family, engaged in 'highly physical but non-penetrative sex' with a series of female partners.[32] And Samuel Pepys certainly had a repertoire of mutual (and self-) gratification which did not involve actual

26. See L. Stone, *Uncertain Unions: Marriage in England 1660–1753* (Oxford, 1992), esp. ch. 3.

27. M. Ingram, *Church Courts, Sex and Marriage in England, 1570–1640* (Cambridge, 1987), p. 230.

28. That is, those whose children were baptised 0–3 months after marriage: Smith, 'Marriage processes', Table 3.2, p. 86.

29. See Quaife, *Wanton Wenches and Wayward Wives*; and J. Addy, *Sin and Society in the Seventeenth Century* (London, 1989).

30. R.A. Houlbrooke, *The English Family 1450–1700* (London, 1984), pp. 72–3; Ingram, *Church Courts, Sex and Marriage*, p. 156.

31. Ingram, *Church Courts, Sex and Marriage*, pp. 225–6, 240–2. See also, P. Griffiths, *Youth and Authority: Formative Experiences in England 1560–1640* (Oxford, 1996), ch. 5, especially his comments on p. 237. It has been argued recently that the second half of the eighteenth century saw a privileging of sexual intercourse, a shift towards a penetrative sexual culture: H. Abelove, 'Some speculations on the history of sexual intercourse during the long eighteenth century in England', *Genders* 6 (1989), 125–30; T. Hitchcock, 'Redefining sex in eighteenth-century England', *History Workshop* 41 (1996), 73–90; Hitchcock, *English Sexualities*, esp. p. 2, and ch. 3.

32. Hitchcock, *English Sexualities*, pp. 28–37 (quote on p. 34).

penetration: there is no reason to assume that he was particularly innovative in this respect.[33]

Diaries give some idea of the relative freedom for courtship at the middling level. Leonard Wheatcroft, a tailor/farmer, stayed overnight at his future bride's home; and although Elizabeth Hawley was only a teenager, she was permitted some freedom of movement once their courtship was well established. They went to a fair and wakes together. Roger Lowe stayed up all night 'a wooing' one young woman and the pair secretly agreed 'to be faithful to death'. Yet he lined up another prospective partner in case the relationship faltered, kept company with a variety of 'wenches', and eventually married a third. Lowe's bride, Emm Potter, was likewise involved with others: the young mercer recorded his concern when he saw her out with another man. These diaries convey the impression of a world where there were numerous opportunities for the sexes to meet; where networks of friends, brothers and sisters, servants and apprentices interacted and interceded on one another's behalf; where young people talked of love and marriage and sent and received love letters.[34]

This was not, however, a world without rules. The community was an important locus of restraint and control upon the sexual behaviour of the unmarried. It was a world, it needs to be emphasised, which lacked our rigid separation between private and public and where family and community overlapped. Courting couples came under neighbourhood scrutiny, as is clear from the number of witnesses able to comment on the courtship practices and liaisons of those who appeared before the courts. There was a framework of moral vigilance. Couples were also constrained by the feelings and reactions of friends and parents.[35] A third party was often present during the initial stages of courtship, and there could be a degree of formality and preliminary negotiation. Diana O'Hara has outlined the complex range of influences from family, friends, and community which lay behind marriage formation in the early modern period. As a Canterbury woman put it in 1564, 'I must be

---

33. R. Latham and W. Matthews (eds), *The Diary of Samuel Pepys*, 11 vols (London, 1970–83). Pepys is discussed in M. George, *Women in the First Capitalist Society* (Urbana, Ill., 1988), ch. 12: 'The enjoyment of sex?' See also the interesting piece by J.G. Turner, 'Pepys and the private parts of monarchy', in G. MacLean (ed.), *Culture and Society in the Stuart Restoration: Literature, Drama, History* (Cambridge, 1995), ch. 5.
34. W.L. Sachse (ed.), *The Diary of Roger Lowe* (New Haven, 1938); G. Parfitt and R. Houlbrooke (eds), *The Courtship Narrative of Leonard Wheatcroft* (Reading, 1986).
35. L. Gowing, *Domestic Dangers: Women, Words, and Sex in Early Modern London* (Oxford, 1996), pp. 146–59.

ruled by my freends . . . as well as by myself'.[36] David Cressy has pointed out that we are witnessing the 'unwritten rules of a deeply patterned activity' which cut across all social groups – 'the workings of a common culture'.[37]

There has been some rather curious discussion about whether or not people of the past were capable of love before they were taught the concept by romantic novelists. Yet there are numerous indications that love was an important ingredient in popular culture. The making of love charms was a common form of popular magic.[38] Romantic love was an important theme of both chapbook and ballad, the main forms of popular literature in the early modern period.[39] And we know that unrequited love, romantic passion, and lovers' quarrels were common causes of mental anguish among the numerous patients of the physician astrologer Richard Napier: 'troubled courtship' was the most important of the four main categories of stress reported by those who consulted him.[40]

Leonard Wheatcroft was certainly enthusiastic in his 'warblings':

O my Dearest,
Must I still be alone from those glorious looks of thine? You know my love is real unto you. O how oft must I tell you I love you ere you will believe me?

Sweet Betty,
. . . dear Love, the secrets of my love is sealed up here in my heart, which none can see but those starlike eyes of yours . . . O let me not then languish in the lingering hopes of my desires . . .

He wrote of 'unchangeable love', of absences which broke his heart, of 'loving expressions' which passed between him and the object of his desire, of 'sweet relapse of love', 'discourse of love', 'many sweet expressions' of love. He was as firm in his love 'As the turtle dove'.[41] We need to be somewhat wary of the use of the word 'love';

36. D. O'Hara , ' "Ruled by my friends": aspects of marriage in the diocese of Canterbury, c. 1540–1570', *Continuity and Change* 6 (1991), 14.
37. D. Cressy, *Birth, Marriage, and Death: Ritual, Religion, and the Life-cycle in Tudor and Stuart England* (Oxford, 1997), ch. 10 (quotes on p. 234).
38. K. Thomas, *Religion and the Decline of Magic* (London, 1973), pp. 277–8, 292.
39. M. Spufford, *Small Books and Pleasant Histories: Popular Fiction and its Readership in Seventeenth-century England* (London, 1981), ch. 7; J.A. Sharpe, 'Plebeian marriage in Stuart England: some evidence from popular literature', *Transactions of the Royal Historical Society* 36 (1986), 69–90.
40. M. MacDonald, *Mystical Bedlam: Madness, Anxiety, and Healing in Seventeenth-century England* (Cambridge, 1981), pp. 75, 89.
41. Parfitt and Houlbrooke (eds), *Courtship Narrative of Leonard Wheatcroft*, pp. 42, 44, 45, 47, 49, 51, 52, 58.

Roger Lowe used it of male friends and acquaintances in contexts which suggest friendship or friendliness rather than passion.[42] But even allowing for these different meanings, and for what Ralph Houlbrooke has described as the gap between experienced feeling and literary convention, Wheatcroft's representation of his courtship 'was highly romantic'.[43] This is not to deny the role of material considerations in such deliberations. Wheatcroft and Hawley were well aware that their marriage was an economic as well as an emotional transaction.[44] Parents at a middling level had vested interests in making the right match for sons or daughters and may well have exercised 'control' over their choice of partners. At the lower levels of society controls were somewhat freer.[45]

This focus upon contexts of illegitimacy, types of bridal pregnancy, and courtship practices should not divert attention from the fact that some 70 per cent of brides in the sixteenth century and around 80 per cent in the seventeenth and early eighteenth centuries were not pregnant when they married.[46] Even allowing for all the physiological barriers to pregnancy, and for the possibility of sexual activity excluding intercourse, these figures suggest that for large numbers of women sex came after marriage. There must have been many for whom fear of pregnancy – 'fear of the rising of the Apron' as one woman put it – was an effective contraceptive.[47] Fear of pregnancy, the linkage of premarital heterosexual sex with pregnancy, and unmarried pregnancy as the visible badge of lack of chastity, were recurring refrains in the early modern ballad.[48]

III

The centrality of the matrix of marriage does not mean that extramarital sex did not exist; indeed, as many as 30 per cent of illegitimacies in some studies were the result of a liaison with a

42. Sachse (ed.), *Diary of Roger Lowe*, pp. 47, 66.
43. Parfitt and Houlbrooke (eds), *Courtship Narrative of Leonard Wheatcroft*, p. 23.
44. Ibid., pp. 53, 54, 59, 79.
45. B. Hill, *Women, Work, and Sexual Politics in Eighteenth-century England* (Oxford, 1989), ch. 10.
46. Calculated from Laslett, Oosterveen, and Smith (eds), *Bastardy*, Table 1.3, p. 23.
47. The quote comes from P. Crawford, 'The construction and experience of maternity in seventeenth-century England', in V. Fildes (ed.), *Women as Mothers in Pre-industrial England* (London, 1990), p. 16.
48. This claim is based on my reading of *Pepys Ballads*.

married man.[49] The conduct books certainly urged marital chastity. Marital sex – 'matrimonial meetings' as William Whately's wedding sermon coyly termed them – 'must be cheerfull' but not performed 'as brute creatures . . . through the heate of desire'. Adultery represented the quintessential loss of control: it was unlawful, poisonous, filthy, forbidden.[50] 'Matrimoniall chastitie', wrote William Gouge, avoided defilement 'with strange flesh'.[51] Yet adultery and fear of adultery were important themes of the popular ballad literature.[52] The case books of the Elizabethan doctor astrologer Simon Forman and the diary of the bureaucrat Pepys certainly imply that at the upper levels of society adultery was commonplace and that servants and the wives of subordinates were considered to be almost there for the taking.[53] When one of Forman's nurses became pregnant, he was able to compile a list of men (including himself) who had 'had' or 'used' her.[54] Forman regularly had intercourse with his female patients, many of whom were married. Lawrence Stone has argued that fear of pregnancy drove such men to seek out married women so that mistakes would be hidden.[55] Of course this is sexuality through male eyes; we do not know the combinations of power and desire on the female side of these liaisons.

A sexual double standard operated. In effect, ecclesiastical justice permitted separation on the grounds of the wife's rather than the husband's adultery. As Laura Gowing has put it, 'Men sued their wives for adultery; women sued their husbands for extreme cruelty.'[56] Female adultery was far worse than male adultery, for the woman, in this one transgression, defiled her body, damned her

---

49. M. Ingram, 'The reform of popular culture? Sex and marriage in early modern England', in B. Reay (ed.), *Popular Culture in Seventeenth-century England* (London, 1985), p. 151.

50. W. W[hately], *A Bride-bush or a Wedding Sermon* (London, 1617), pp. 43–4; W. Whately, *A Care-cloth: or a Treatise of the Cumbers and Troubles of Marriage* (London, 1624), pp. 37–9.

51. W. Gouge, *Of Domesticall Duties* (London, 1622), p. 216.

52. E. Foyster, 'A laughing matter? Marital discord and gender control in seventeenth-century England', *Rural History* 4 (1993), 5–21.

53. Latham and Matthews (eds), *Diary of Samuel Pepys*; A.L. Rowse, *The Case Books of Simon Forman: Sex and Society in Shakespeare's Age* (London, 1976); L. Stone, *The Family, Sex and Marriage in England 1500–1800* (London, 1977), pp. 545–61. See also, B. Hill, *Servants: English Domestics in the Eighteenth Century* (Oxford, 1996), ch. 3; T. Meldrum, 'London domestic servants from depositional evidence, 1660–1750: servant–employer sexuality in the patriarchal household', in T. Hitchcock, P. King, and P. Sharpe (eds), *Chronicling Poverty: the Voices and Strategies of the English Poor, 1640–1840* (London, 1997), ch. 2.

54. Rowse, *Case Books of Simon Forman*, pp. 91–2.

55. Stone, *Family, Sex and Marriage*, p. 554.

56. Gowing, *Domestic Dangers*, pp. 180–206 (quote on p. 180).

soul, robbed her husband of 'his right' and potentially imposed an illegitimate line upon his posterity, dishonoured her family, and destroyed her sex's prime virtue: honesty. This was the proscription of the cleric Matthew Griffith.[57] Upper-class daughters were told that adultery was unacceptable in a wife but tolerable in a man.

> Remember, that next to the danger of committing the fault yourself, the greatest is that of seeing it in your husband. Do not seem to look or hear that way: If he is a man of sense, he will reclaim himself . . . if he is not so, he will be provok'd, but not reformed . . . Such an undecent complaint makes a wife much more ridiculous than the injury that provoketh her to it.[58]

We do not find such statements at the lower levels of society, but actions betray attitudes. The defamation suits of the early modern period represented the double standard at the popular level. Women and not men had to preserve their sexual honour, their sexual credit. There was no male equivalent of the (loosely defined) 'whore'.[59]

As we saw with courting couples, much of the control of popular sexuality was through community regulation. In the eighteenth-century west country, a mock court held every year after the Wells fair – 'time out of mind' – elected mock officials, drew up obscene bills of indictment, and read out a list of 'lewd' persons and crimes committed. Those mentioned as taking part in the revel in 1784 included a baker, a woolcomber, a dealer in horses, and a shoe-maker; there was drinking, and young males seem to have been disproportionately involved. One of the targets of their proceedings was a tradesman's daughter. Like most of this sort of informal regulation, control was gendered. One of the men accused of immorality was a self-accuser, drawing up the indictment himself, presumably as a form of sexual bragging. The woman involved was the true object of ridicule; we only know about the case because she took action in the church court to protect her name.[60] Mocking rhymes and ballads, rough music (the beating of pots and pans),

---

57. A. Fletcher, *Gender, Sex and Subordination in England 1500–1800* (London, 1995), p. 109.

58. K. Thomas, 'The double standard', *Journal of the History of Ideas* 20 (1959), 196.

59. See L. Gowing, 'Gender and the language of insult in early modern London', *History Workshop* 35 (1993), 1–21; L. Gowing, 'Language, power, and the law: women's slander litigation in early modern London', in J. Kermode and G. Walker (eds), *Women, Crime and the Courts in Early Modern England* (London, 1994), ch. 2; and Gowing, *Domestic Dangers*, a marvellous book.

60. P. Morris, 'Defamation and sexual reputation in Somerset, 1733–1850' (University of Warwick, Ph.D., 1985), pp. 443–55.

crude pictures, the iconography of sexual insult, were all used to patrol the borders of acceptable morality.[61] While men were mocked as cuckolds, their offence was their lack of control over their wives: the cuckold rather than the male adulterer was the primary focus of ridicule.

Actions in the church courts against defamation and sexual slander open a window into notions of shame and sexual honour at the popular level in early modern England. Gossip, moral evaluation, and insult were the means by which women – particularly married women – wielded power, although the targets of these weapons were more likely to be female than male. Women, Laura Gowing has written, 'were at the pivotal centre of the circulation of blame and dishonour for sex: responsibility was channelled entirely through them.'[62] Gossip could be used by women who felt that they had no other recourse against men who had wronged them, but it was a risky means of retribution. The domestic servant Margaret Knowsley took this gamble in 1625 when she was sexually harassed by the minister Stephen Jerome. Steven Hindle has traced the networks of gossip as Knowsley publicised her employer's attempted rape: she talked to women while hay making, walking in the streets and fields, and knitting at the fireside; she even told her midwife as she went into labour. (Knowsley was present at at least forty conversations, many of which were limited exclusively to women.) Others relayed her allegations in gossip – in agreement and denial – as they talked to neighbours, visited a sick friend, and argued in the churchyard. Knowsley was prosecuted for slander and sentenced to a public shaming and whipping.[63]

Suits for sexual slander show how important reputation was for married women at the popular level. Most of those who took action in the church courts were from the middling sort: those from the families of yeomen, husbandmen, craftsmen, and shopkeepers.[64] The very poor rarely took action, but this does not mean that they

61. M. Ingram, 'Ridings, rough music and the "reform of popular culture" in early modern England', *Past and Present* 105 (1984), 79–113; M. Ingram, 'Ridings, rough music and mocking rhymes in early modern England', in Reay (ed.), *Popular Culture*, ch. 5; A. Fox, 'Ballads, libels and popular ridicule in Jacobean England', *Past and Present* 145 (1994), 47–83.

62. Gowing, 'Language, power, and the law', p. 30.

63. S. Hindle, 'The shaming of Margaret Knowsley: gossip, gender and the experience of authority in early modern England', *Continuity and Change* 9 (1994), 391–419.

64. J.A. Sharpe, *Defamation and Sexual Slander in Early Modern England* (York, 1980), p. 17; Ingram, *Church Courts, Sex and Marriage*, p. 304; Gowing, 'Gender and the language of insult', p. 3.

had no sense of sexual honour. As a humble Yorkshire woman put it in defence of another who was being slandered, 'they might as well take her life as her good name from her'.[65]

IV

Although the word 'freedom' is often used by historians in their descriptions of early modern sex, it is a somewhat inappropriate description of a problematic situation. There is much evidence of exploitative sex, male violence, and a degree of meanness of spirit and predatoriness in male sexuality. Young men as well as women were the objects of this aggressive sexuality. The court records are full of references to men exposing themselves, forcing, grabbing at genitalia.[66] Even the innocuous Wheatcroft saw courtship as a siege – it is a central metaphor in his narrative. 'I at last advanced towards . . . this forenamed town called Woman.' 'I mustered up all my man forces, and close siege to her, which siege lasted for the space 23 months and more, before she would yield I should enter, etc.'[67] Other young men likewise saw courtship in terms of siege warfare and martial combat.[68]

Nor have historians been sensitive to the languages of sex. '[S]trived with her', 'had his pleasure of her', 'had the knowledge of her body', 'would punch [i.e. penetrate] her', 'strived and struggled', 'occupied her as oft as he liked', 'have the use of her body in the day time as her husband did at night': these are hardly the languages of mutuality. One man referred to a woman who 'stood as quietly to be done as his own wife'. Men talked of riding mares and bulling cows. They referred to lovers as their whores. They had their will of women, their pleasure of them, the use of their bodies.[69] When the minister harassed Knowsley, he told her that he had a 'burning in his body' and could not be satisfied without 'the use of a woman'.[70] In the popular medical guides and

---

65. Sharpe, *Defamation and Sexual Slander*, p. 3.

66. See (for women) Quaife, *Wanton Wenches and Wayward Wives*; and Addy, *Sin and Society*; and (for men) R. Trumbach, 'Sodomitical assaults, gender role, and sexual development in eighteenth-century London', in K. Gerard and G. Hekma (eds), *The Pursuit of Sodomy: Male Homosexuality in Renaissance and Enlightenment Europe* (New York, 1989), pp. 407–29.

67. Parfitt and Houlbrooke (eds), *Courtship Narrative of Leonard Wheatcroft*, pp. 36, 41.

68. Cressy, *Birth, Marriage, and Death*, p. 235.

69. These examples are from Quaife, *Wanton Wenches and Wayward Wives*; and Addy, *Sin and Society*.

70. Hindle, 'Shaming of Margaret Knowsley', p. 400.

early modern conduct books too the female body was often defined in terms of male pleasure.[71]

The terms for sexual intercourse and the sexual organs are wearingly repetitious in their obsession with violent male dominance. The metaphors used were mainly those of war and work. To fuck was to 'bang', 'beat', 'charge', 'drill', 'grind', 'hit', 'knock', 'mount', 'pierce', 'poke', 'punch', 'ram', 'ride', 'stab', 'strike', 'stuff', 'thresh', 'thrum' [beat], or 'thump'. The penis was an 'arrow', 'awl', 'blade', 'bolt', 'club', 'engine', 'flail', 'gun', 'hammer', 'hanger', 'instrument', 'knife', 'ladle', 'lance', 'loom', 'mast', 'may pole', 'oar', 'pestle', 'pistol', 'plough', 'pole', 'rod', 'rolling pin', 'rudder', 'shuttle', 'sickle', 'spade', 'stake', 'standard', 'stick', 'sword', 'tool', 'truncheon', 'weapon', 'whip', and 'yard'.[72] More than 100 Shakespearean terms, we are told, 'portray intercourse as an act of male dominance'.[73] Such was the imagery of ballad as well as theatre. Punching was a common ballad term for sexual intercourse.[74] 'Morgan Rattler' was a street song of the eighteenth century, sung in the public house owned by the father of the young Francis Place:

> First he niggled her, then he tiggled her
> Then with his two balls he began for to batter her.
> At every thrust, I thought she'd have burst
> With the terrible size of his Morgan Rattler.[75]

The vagina was there to be stormed or occupied: it was a 'box', 'cabinet', 'cage', 'castle', 'cave', 'cellar', 'chamber', 'corner', 'fishpond', 'fort', 'gap', 'gash', 'gate', 'glove', 'gulf', 'hive', 'mark', 'mouth', 'nick', 'oven', 'pit', 'port', 'pot', 'premises', 'pulpit', 'purse', 'quagmire', 'quiver', 'room', 'ruff', 'scabbard', 'shoe', 'slit', 'socket', 'trench', 'tub', 'well', and 'wound'.[76] The reader will have noticed that some of the metaphors for the female anatomy are somewhat capacious and doubtless indicate male insecurities about satisfying female desire. There is no escaping the misogynistic general tone. These languages of sex make it very difficult to accept a recent claim that 'sexual assault and conquest were not a central part of male identity'.[77]

71. M. Fissell, 'Gender and generation: representing reproduction in early modern England', *Gender and History* 7 (1995), 433–56.
72. These are all from Williams, *Dictionary of Sexual Language*.
73. Fletcher, *Gender*, p. 93.
74. E.g. Day (ed.), *Pepys Ballads*, Vol. 3, pp. 184, 287.
75. M. Thale (ed.), *The Autobiography of Francis Place (1771–1854)* (Cambridge, 1972), p. 59.
76. Williams, *Dictionary of Sexual Language*.
77. S.D. Amussen, ' "The part of a Christian man": the cultural politics of manhood in early modern England', in S.D. Amussen and M.A. Kishlansky (eds), *Political Culture and Cultural Politics in Early Modern England* (Manchester, 1995), p. 219.

Women were objects possessed, legally or illegally, by men. It is significant that 'commodity' was a common word for women's genitals, that 'tenure' was used to indicate sexual possession, and that adultery and rape were considered theft.[78] One manual of advice for married couples compared a male adulterer to a thief 'that having store of Deere in his owne Parke, would yet needs steale a Buck out of his neighbours ground'.[79] A woman's reputation and honour depended upon her protection of her commodity.

Sexuality must therefore be seen in the context of configurations of power. As Susan Amussen has explained, 'the core values' of early modern popular culture were 'profoundly misogynistic'.[80] Women were 'subordinate', the 'weaker vessell'. The man was 'God's immediate officer, and the King in his family'. Whately's advice to brides was short: 'The whole duty of the wife is referred to two heads. The first is, to acknowledge her inferiority: the next, to carry her selfe as inferiour.' And the rule that wives had to observe was equally simple: '*Mine husband is my superior, my better*; he hath authority and rule over mee: Nature hath given it him, having framed our bodies to tendernes, mens to more hardnesse.' To disobey a husband was to 'strive against GOD and nature'. A wife had to practise reverence and obedience, and her demeanour should reflect her subordination; women should be 'meeke, quiet, submissive' in speech and gesture. A dutiful wife, wrote Whately, 'submits her-selfe with quietnesse, cheerfully, even as a wel-broken horse turnes at the least turning, stands at the least check of the riders bridle, readily going and standing as he wishes that fits upon his backe'. (The metaphor of horse-riding was a favourite with Whately.[81]) Ballads promoted similar values:

> Your Husbands are your Lords & heads,
> you ought them to obey.[82]

Patient Griselda, the obedient wife in Boccaccio, Petrarch, Chaucer, and seventeenth-century chapbook, ballad, and play, who endured

78. For tenure, see Williams, *Dictionary of Sexual Language*, p. 1374; for adultery, see A. Macfarlane, *Marriage and Love in England 1300–1840* (Oxford, 1986), p. 242; for rape, see M. Chaytor, 'Husband(ry): narratives of rape in the seventeenth century', *Gender and History* 7 (1995), 378–407.

79. Whately, *Care-cloth*, p. 39.

80. S.D. Amussen, 'The gendering of popular culture in early modern England', in T. Harris (ed.), *Popular Culture in England, c. 1500–1850* (London, 1995), p. 50.

81. Whately, *Bride-bush*. See also Gouge, *Domesticall Duties*, pp. 270, 281, 285.

82. Day (ed.), *Pepys Ballads*, Vol. 1, p. 121.

loss of children and humiliation at the hands of her husband, was the archetypal submissive woman. She was a lesson to others; a pattern for all virtuous women, as a chapbook put it in 1682, 'how Wives by their Patience and Obedience, may gain much Glory'.[83] Her husband, the marquis, in Henry Chettle, William Haughton, and Thomas Dekker's drama, *The Pleasant Comodie of Patient Grissill* (1603), saw himself as training Griselda to be pliable:

> I tride my Grissils patience when twas greene,
> Like a young Osier, and I moulded it
> Like ware to all impressions: married men
> That long to tame their wives must curbe them in,
> Before they need a bridle, then they'll proove
> All grissils full of patience, full of love,
> Yet that olde tryall must be tempered so,
> Least seeking to tame them they master you.[84]

There were no neat demarcations between household politics and sexuality. The unruly wife (in patriarchal logic) slid quickly into female dominance and harlotry. Unruliness and female adultery went hand in hand. Charivaris – a public shaming ritual aimed at rebellious women – worked often on the assumption that a woman who wore the breeches was likely to seek extramarital sex: a man beaten by his wife was also a man cuckolded.[85] The female tongue, woman's unruly member, proclaimed this inversion of the natural order, the axis of insubordination and adultery.[86] 'This impudencie, this unwomanhood tracks the way to the harlots house.'[87] Karen Newman has referred to the early modern woman's 'two mouths': 'An open mouth and immodest speech are tantamount to open

83. *The True and Admirable History of Patient Grissel* (London, 1682), title page. This book is in the library of Samuel Pepys at Magdalene College Library, Cambridge: Vulgaria Collection, Vol. 4, no. 2. For the recasting of the Griselda story over the centuries, including a sado-masochistic, early-twentieth-century German version, see J. Bronfman, *Chaucer's Clerk's Tale: the Griselda Story Received, Rewritten, Illustrated* (New York, 1994).
84. H. Chettle, W. Haughton, and T. Dekker, *The Pleasant Comodie of Patient Grissill* (London, 1603) (AMS Press reprint, New York, 1970), sig. L1v.
85. D.E. Underdown, 'The taming of the scold: the enforcement of patriarchal authority in early modern England', in A. Fletcher and J. Stevenson (eds), *Order and Disorder in Early Modern England* (Cambridge, 1985), p. 127.
86. L.E. Boose, 'Scolding brides and bridling scolds: taming the woman's unruly member', *Shakespeare Quarterly* 42 (1991), 179–213. This focus on the female tongue was still to be found in the nineteenth century in connection with women's suffrage. A joke in *Punch* asked: 'Why is Mr Mill like a tongue?' The answer was: 'Because he is the Ladies' Member'. See *Punch*, 30 March 1867, p. 128.
87. Whately, *Bride-bush*, p. 38.

genitals and immodest acts.'[88] At her worst, the rebellious wife took a lover, succumbed to lust, and killed her husband: fears of domestic insubordination were represented in the pamphlet narratives of murderous wives.[89]

V

This stress on male definitions is not to ascribe a purely passive role to women. As Frances Dolan has argued, the stories of husband murder also reflected contradictions and tensions in the realm of domestic power, for the home 'was an arena of female power as well as subordination'.[90] Charivaris clearly bore witness to the slippage between patriarchal ideals and the realities of gender relations in cottage and community. Ritual mockery reinforced the gender order, but if there had been no cracks in the male power structure there would have been no need for charivaris.[91] While enjoining female submissiveness, the conduct books were fully aware that many women did not adhere to the ideal. Robert Snawsell's *A Looking-Glasse for Married Folkes* (1631) is shot through with a recognition that there were women who stood up to their husbands. It was written, the author tells us, in response to the 'unquiet living betweene man and wife' in 'many places'.[92] One of his female characters protests against female subjection: 'Here are fetters for the legs, and yokes for the necks of women: must they crouch on this manner to their currish and swinish husbands? . . . Are you a woman, and make them such dishclouts and slaves to their husbands? Came you of a woman, that you give them no prerogative, but make them altogether underlings?'[93] William Gouge's *Of Domesticall Duties* (1622) also recognises that many wives do not follow his precepts of subjection; some may acknowledge the superiority of husbands in general, but 'when the application commeth to themselves they faile'.[94] In the wider world of English popular literature, whatever the preferred readings of the authors, female characters were frequently portrayed as strong and rebellious – even in the story of

88. K. Newman, *Fashioning Femininity and English Renaissance Drama* (Chicago, 1991), pp. 11, 134.
89. F.E. Dolan, *Dangerous Familiars: Representations of Domestic Crime in England 1550–1700* (Ithaca, NY, 1994).
90. Ibid., p. 31.
91. Ingram, 'Ridings, rough music and the "reform of popular culture"', pp. 97–8.
92. Snawsell, *Looking-Glasse*, sig. A3.   93. Ibid., p. 55.
94. Gouge, *Domesticall Duties*, pp. 269, 273, 339.

Patient Griselda! In the dramatic version of the tale, there are sub-plots involving other women set up as alternatives to Griselda. There is a former widow who represents a household where the woman is in control, and who says 'tis not fid that poore womens should be kept alwaies under'. There is Griselda's sister-in-law, who is put off marriage both by Griselda's patience and the widow's turbulent relationship with her spouse. She wants her freedom, referring to the 'war of marriage', and invoking proverbial wisdom: 'those that goe to wooe, goe to woe'.[95] Griselda herself attains a sort of empowerment through her strength in extreme adversity. To quote Joy Wiltenburg, 'marriage in the popular texts is presented primarily as a struggle for power between the sexes'.[96]

A conduct book might hold forth on the gendered body; the tenderness of women versus the hardness of men, the stern facial imprint of the governor versus the delicate visage of the ruled.[97] Yet this cloistered class view seems widely at variance with a popular culture where the work of women – women's hard physical toil – was central to the economic order. Working women were not delicate and fragile. It was not until the nineteenth century that Arthur Munby recorded his fascination with the contrast between the soft and tiny (feminine) hand of a gentleman and the large rough (masculine) hands of a working woman, but similar contrasts must have existed in earlier periods.[98] There were contradictions and complexities in the subordination of women.[99]

The contradictions were nowhere stronger than in the sphere of sexuality. As we have seen, marital chastity was an important (though not uncontested) tenet in popular culture. But this was a culture with a powerful recognition of the strength of female desire.[100] This spirit is captured perfectly in the refrain of a fictional west-country

95. Chettle, Haughton, and Dekker, *Patient Grissill,* sigs I2, L2, L2v.

96. J. Wiltenburg, *Disorderly Women and Female Power in the Street Literature of Early Modern England and Germany* (Charlottesville, Va., 1992), p. 95.

97. Whately, *Bride-bush,* pp. 18, 36.

98. 'Are the relations of the sexes really inverted when three men sit at table, with hands delicate and jewelled, and a woman stands behind and waits, offering the dishes with so large coarse a hand that makes her master's look almost lady-like . . . ?' Quoted in L. Davidoff, 'Class and gender in Victorian England', in J.L. Newton, M.P. Ryan, and J.R. Walkowitz (eds), *Sex and Class in Women's History* (London, 1983), p. 62.

99. See A. Fletcher, 'Men's dilemma: the future of patriarchy in England 1560–1660', *Transactions of the Royal Historical Society* 4 (1994), 61–81; Amussen, 'Gendering of popular culture'; Fletcher, *Gender.* The best recent summary of early modern women's work is to be found in Fletcher, *Gender,* ch. 12.

100. Amussen makes this contrast too: 'Gendering of popular culture', p. 50. See also, Fletcher, *Gender,* ch. 1: 'Prologue: men's dilemmas'.

servant who carried her lover over her shoulders up to her room so that her employers, if listening, would only hear one pair of footsteps:

> ... I first mean to try him, and if bad's his Gear,
> I'd not have him, if he had ten Thousand a Year.[101]

Ballad after ballad told of single women craving married sex:

> My fancy it is set on fire,
> As Love-sick as another,
> I love to taste of Married joys,
> as well as did my Mother:
> you are the Engine that must quench
> the flames of my affection,
> If you will be my Husband dear,
> I'le follow your direction.[102]

> You see how my visage
> is grown pale and wan,
> You well may perceive
> 'tis for want of a man:
> my Pulses do beat,
> and my body doth sweat,
> And my sences are all at great strife
> my belly doth ake
> and my heart-strings will break,
> If I cannot be made a wife.[103]

And of married women craving more sex:

> For he lyes by me like a cold stone in the Wall,
> And will do a poor woman no kindness at all.[104]

> [G]ive me a Lord, if he can be had,
> that will do it at Night and Noon.[105]

As Anthony Fletcher has expressed it, women were perceived as 'possessing a powerful and potentially destructive sexuality which made them naturally lascivious, predatory and, most serious of all, once their desire was fully aroused, insatiable'.[106] The conduct books wrote of the 'unsatiablenesse' of a bedfellow – of either sex – as a cause of disruption in marriage, but also made it clear that marital intercourse, 'due benevolence', a mutual debt, was pleasurable in

---

101. Day (ed.), *Pepys Ballads*, Vol. 5, p. 161.   102. Ibid., Vol. 3, p. 6.
103. Ibid., p. 94.   104. Ibid., p. 87.   105. Ibid., p. 190.
106. Fletcher, *Gender*, p. 5.

itself and not merely for the purpose of conception ('for it is to be rendred to such as are barren').[107] It was believed that female orgasm was necessary for conception to occur; and so there was an emphasis on female pleasure and upon foreplay as a means of achieving this arousal.[108] *The Practice of Physick* (1658) wrote of the woman's womb 'skipping as it were for joy' to meet her husband's sperm, drawing it in, 'graciously and freely', to 'withal bedew and sprinkle it with her own Sperm, and powered forth in that pang of Pleasure, that so by the commixture of both, Conception may arise'.[109]

This recognition of female pleasure was not without its penalties. It formed part of the male violence mentioned earlier, for the logic was that a woman's protests could be ignored, and that if the male persevered the female body would respond. *Faint Heart never won fair Lady*, a particularly nasty ballad in Samuel Pepys's collection, sung to the tune of Lillibullero, gave advice on courtship which amounted to rape:

> Tickle her Knees, and something that's high'r,
> kissing and feeling go hand in hand;
> No Flesh and Blood but what will take fire,
> tho' she may seem at first to withstand . . .

> When the Outworks they fairly are won,
> enter the Fort, it now is your own;
> Plunder and Storm it from Sun to Sun,
> Revel and Sport until weary grown:
> Fie Sir, why Sir, I'll sooner dye Sir,
> now are exchang'd for another Tone . . .[110]

Moreover, rape victims who became pregnant were assumed to have consented to the violence. Presumably also – if the logic of the link between pleasure and procreation was followed – those who wished to avoid conception, particularly unmarried women, would attempt to *avoid* orgasm. This is a suggestion that has been made of the nineteenth century, when the belief in the reproductive role of the female orgasm was still commonly held, but early modern historians have been slow to consider this penalty. Michael Mason has

107. Gouge, *Domesticall Duties*, pp. 222, 223, 224.
108. A. Eccles, *Obstetrics and Gynaecology in Tudor and Stuart England* (London, 1982), ch. 5; A. McLaren, *Reproductive Rituals: the Perception of Fertility in England from the Sixteenth Century to the Nineteenth Century* (London, 1984), ch. 1; T. Laqueur, *Making Sex: Body and Gender from the Greeks to Freud* (Cambridge, Mass., 1990).
109. Quoted in McLaren, *Reproductive Rituals*, p. 20.
110. Day (ed.), *Pepys Ballads*, Vol. 5, p. 21.

raised the possibility that large numbers of women in England's past feared or avoided sexual pleasure because they associated it with the likelihood of pregnancy.[111] Popular medical advice from the Restoration held that the spread of syphilis was associated with female sexual excitement; so once again a premium was placed on the avoidance of female satisfaction.[112]

VI

We have focused so far on heterosexual sex, but this presents a very partial picture. Some of the most interesting recent work on early modern sexuality has been carried out by scholars 'queering the Renaissance'.[113] Yet it is a book dealing with a later period of gay history which has been the most challenging in its findings. In his study of early-twentieth-century gay New York, George Chauncey has revealed a world protean in its sexuality, far removed from the later strict division between deviant homosexuality and compulsory heterosexuality. It was the world of the fairy rather than the queer, where some men were seen as woman-like and effeminate but where the men who sought them out for sex were not considered homosexual or unmanly. It was a world in which the important classification or source of identity was gender (male/female) rather than sexual orientation (gay/straight). The penetrator, because penetration was associated with dominance, did not compromise his masculinity. A fairy was a fairy not because he engaged in what we would term homosexual activity but because he was the passive partner. The world of the fairy was firmly working-class, the culture of single men, immigrants, boarding houses, saloons and dance halls, and home of what Chauncey has called the 'phallocentric presumption that a man's sexual satisfaction was more significant than the gender or character of the person who provided that satisfaction'.[114] Men went with fairies much as they went with female prostitutes.

Clearly, early modern England is not *fin de siècle* New York, but there are intriguing similarities. We know that some early modern

---

111. M. Mason, *The Making of Victorian Sexuality* (Oxford, 1994), p. 203.
112. R. Davenport-Hines, *Sex, Death and Punishment: Attitudes to Sex and Sexuality in Britain since the Restoration* (London, 1991), pp. 46–7.
113. See J. Goldberg (ed.), *Queering the Renaissance* (Durham, NC, 1994); K. Thomas, 'As you like it', *New York Review of Books*, 22 September 1994; and S. Orgel, *Impersonations: the Performance of Gender in Shakespeare's England* (Cambridge, 1996).
114. G. Chauncey, *Gay New York: Gender, Urban Culture, and the Making of the Gay Male World* (New York, 1994), p. 85.

men sought out younger men to satisfy their sexual needs but did not distinguish between this desire and lust for women.[115] Both boys and women, Stephen Orgel has argued of the Renaissance public theatre, were 'objects of erotic attraction for adult men'.[116] Men came between the legs of other males, telling them that they gave as much pleasure as 'a woman'.[117] Aggressive sex, as has been intimated earlier, was part of the sexual culture of alehouse and street, and could surface when males drank together or (as was common practice) shared a bed.[118] It spanned what we would term heterosexual and homosexual behaviour; as in New York, men were as likely to turn to another man as to a whore. When a Somerset servant approached a mason in his master's hayloft, the mason told him to 'go to Bath and get a Whore'.[119] In elite culture, adult male libertines were men who were true libertines, enjoying the bodies of both male and female. Their sin – for those who saw it as sin – was in their excess rather than their attraction to men.[120] In other words, there was early modern homosexual behaviour but not early modern homosexuality. People were not accused in the courts of being homosexual; nor was homosexuality a cause of defamation or sexual slander. Men were punished for buggery and sodomy, but these were considered to be the excesses of mankind in general rather than the practices of a specific group.[121] A more identifiable male homosexual subculture – with its effeminate 'mollies' and young male prostitutes with female names – had emerged in London by the early eighteenth century, but it is debatable how exclusively homosexual this culture was and whether it qualifies as a genuine subculture or is best seen as part of the wider sexuality of the streets.[122]

Literary critics and cultural studies scholars have also alerted us to the strong vein of homosociality which runs through early

115. Davenport-Hines, *Sex, Death and Punishment*, ch. 3.

116. Orgel, *Impersonations*, p. 103.

117. Quaife, *Wanton Wenches and Wayward Wives*, p. 176.

118. Trumbach, 'Sodomitical assaults'.

119. P. Morris, 'Sodomy and male honor: the case of Somerset, 1740–1850', in Gerard and Hekma (eds), *Pursuit of Sodomy*, p. 391.

120. R. Trumbach, 'The birth of the queen: sodomy and the emergence of gender equality in modern culture, 1660–1750', in M.B. Duberman, M. Vicinus, and G. Chauncey (eds), *Hidden from History: Reclaiming the Gay and Lesbian Past* (London, 1991), pp. 129–40.

121. Smith, *Homosexual Desire*, pp. 11–12.

122. For the subculture, see R. Trumbach, 'London's sodomites', *Journal of Social History* 11 (1977–8), 1–33; Trumbach, 'Birth of the queen'. But for the overlap between the sodomitical subculture and alehouse sexuality, see Trumbach, 'Sodomitical assaults'. Margaret Hunt is critical of the subcultural thesis: 'Afterword', in Goldberg (ed.), *Queering the Renaissance*, pp. 370–1.

modern culture. Male bonding overrode ties to women; so much so, that at times male heterosexuality seemed merely to serve to reinforce homosocial ties.[123] Men hunted women together, competed for them, and poached from one another. It was a culture where it was acceptable for men to express open physical affection for one another and to use homoerotic language without the least aspersion of effeminacy.[124] (Curiously, in this culture effeminates were womanisers who spent too much time in the company of women.[125]) The canons of English literature are suffused with homoeroticism.[126] One of the criticisms of these studies is that they focus on elite rather than popular culture, but it is likely that homosociality was widespread. An eighteenth-century Quaker, Josiah Langdale, recounted his relationship with a fellow servant in husbandry in strikingly homoerotic terms. His workmate was blind but 'a young strong man' of about 30 years of age (Langdale was then in his teens). The two men became close friends. They would sit in a field while Langdale read aloud from the Bible, or they would discuss religion. As servants, they shared a bed. '[B]eing Bedfellows sweet Communion & Fellow Ship we had, yea more than ever'. '[I]ndeed we loved entirely'.[127] We are faced with what Bruce Smith has termed the 'startling ambiguity' of a culture where homoeroticism was commonplace but where sodomy was punishable by death.[128]

Lesbianism is more problematic. Although our concepts of lesbianism may have to be redefined to avoid what Martha Vicinus has termed a dependence upon the 'evidence of sexual consummation', it is generally assumed that female homosexuality played little part in early modern discourse.[129] What we do have evidence of is a recognition of woman-to-woman sexual contact in the form of tribades (those who enjoy sex through rubbing); a few instances of cross-dressing women who (as men) married other women; close

123. E.K. Sedgwick, *Between Men: English Literature and Male Homosocial Desire* (New York, 1985), ch. 3; A. Bray, 'Homosexuality and the signs of male friendship in Elizabethan England', *History Workshop* 29 (1990), 1–19.
124. Bray, 'Homosexuality and the signs of male friendship'; Smith, *Homosexual Desire*; Thomas, 'As you like it'.
125. Smith, *Homosexual Desire*, p. 171; P. Rackin, 'Foreign country: the place of women and sexuality in Shakespeare's historical world', in R. Burt and J.M. Archer (eds), *Enclosure Acts: Sexuality, Property, and Culture in Early Modern England* (Ithaca, NY, 1994), ch. 4.
126. Smith, *Homosexual Desire*; Thomas, 'As you like it'.
127. Friends House Library, London, 'Some Account of the Birth, Education . . . of Josiah Langdale' (1723).
128. Smith, *Homosexual Desire*, pp. 13–14.
129. The quote is from M. Vicinus, 'Lesbian history: all theory and no facts or all facts and no theory', *Radical History Review* 60 (1994), 59, who discusses the problems of writing a history of lesbianism.

female friendships which may (or may not) have included sexual activity; the potential of same-sex attraction at the theatre; and the possibility of mutual masturbation by women who shared beds in service, the workhouses, and houses of correction.[130] However, one is struck by the discursive silence – for whatever reason – about female homosexuality. A fascinating recent study of the marriage of two women in London in 1680 has raised the possibility of lesbian desire, but also shows the unwillingness of contemporaries to describe it as such.[131] As Valerie Traub has expressed it, historians and literary critics are faced with something of a conceptual quandry in trying to extrapolate a lesbian 'cultural *presence*' from this 'discursive *silence*'.[132]

VII

It is vital to remember that sexuality existed in an environment of church and state intervention. We need to distinguish here between the more strongly enforced moralities of the sixteenth and seventeenth centuries and the relative laxity of the eighteenth century, when, apart from cases involving provisions for illegitimacy and some prosecutions for sodomy, there was far less control of popular mores.[133] But for much of the period sexual behaviour was governed by a range of punishments. The church courts dealt with premarital sex and adultery, and this could involve public penance. (Defendants also faced court fees of more than a week's wages for a labourer.[134]) The secular courts punished women who bore children outside of marriage; offenders were either publicly whipped in the marketplace or imprisoned in a house of correction. (The men involved rarely suffered punishments of this type.) Magistrates

130. See J.C. Brown, 'Lesbian sexuality in medieval and early modern Europe', in Duberman, Vicinus, and Chauncey (eds), *Hidden from History*, pp. 67–75; R. Trumbach, 'London's sapphists: from three sexes to four genders in the making of modern culture', in J. Epstein and K. Straub (eds), *Body Guards: the Cultural Politics of Gender Ambiguity* (New York, 1991), ch. 5; E. Donoghue, *Passions between Women: British Lesbian Culture 1668–1801* (New York, 1993) (essentialist in approach); M. Vicinus, '"They wonder to which sex I belong": the historical roots of the modern lesbian identity', in H. Abelove, M.A. Barale, and D.M. Halperin (eds), *The Lesbian and Gay Studies Reader* (New York, 1993), ch. 29; Hitchcock, *English Sexualities*, ch. 6.
131. P. Crawford and S. Mendelson, 'Sexual identities in early modern England: the marriage of two women in 1680', *Gender and History* 7 (1995), 362–77.
132. V. Traub, 'The (in)significance of "lesbian" desire in early modern England', in Goldberg (ed.), *Queering the Renaissance*, pp. 62–83 (quote at p. 79).
133. Morris, 'Defamation and sexual reputation', p. 17; Stone, *Family, Sex and Marriage*, pp. 631–5.
134. Ingram, *Church Courts, Sex and Marriage*, p. 57.

had the power to order the bodily examination of suspected bastard bearers.[135] Midwives could interrogate an unmarried woman
during the agonies of childbirth – on pain of death and damnation
– in an effort to determine the father of her child.[136] An act of 1650
even instituted the death penalty for adultery and three months
imprisonment for fornication. The double standard was enshrined
in its definitions, for adultery was the adultery of the married woman:
married men who had intercourse with single women were liable to
the lesser charge of fornication. Although the act was riddled with
so many escape clauses that conviction for adultery was almost an
impossibility, its brief existence was a dramatic proclamation of the
will to enforce a gendered morality.[137]

We shall probably never be able to gauge the effects of the
interventions of church and state. Martin Ingram has argued that
the increased rigour of the church courts on matters sexual helped
to inculcate stricter attitudes during the seventeenth century. He
has written of adjustments in popular attitudes to extramarital
sexuality rather than any far-reaching cultural revolution.[138] But it
is likely, as we shall see elsewhere in this book, that the impact of
this acculturation was socially selective. This is not to advance the
thesis of two competing early modern discourses: Christian morality versus an amoral popular culture.[139] Nor is it to argue for an
'alternative plebeian morality' such as Anna Clark has implied for
the late eighteenth century.[140] Sexual cultures were far more complex than that. Early modern sexualities were heavily inscribed by
the matrices of marriage and procreation and shaped by the values
of law and church, yet they were also multiple and fragmented.

VIII

The boundaries of marriage and procreation have been discussed
at length in this chapter because they were so important. The

---

135. Quaife, *Wanton Wenches and Wayward Wives*, p. 89.

136. Ingram, *Church Courts, Sex and Marriage*, p. 263; Quaife, *Wanton Wenches and Wayward Wives*, p. 105.

137. For the act, see K. Thomas, 'The Act of 1650 reconsidered', in D. Pennington and K. Thomas (eds), *Puritans and Revolutionaries* (Oxford, 1978), pp. 257–82.

138. Ingram, 'Reform of popular culture', pp. 157–60; Ingram, *Church Courts, Sex and Marriage*, pp. 219, 230, 257, 280–1.

139. The interpretation of Quaife, *Wanton Wenches and Wayward Wives*, pp. 63, 179, 245.

140. A. Clark, *The Struggle for the Breeches: Gender and the Making of the British Working Class* (London, 1995), ch. 4.

wedding was central to English popular culture.[141] The tropes of marriage and procreation can be found in the most unlikely places. Tim Hitchcock has shown that the recorded erotic dreams of the (married) eighteenth-century excise officer, John Cannon, were fantasies of married sex: 'he could not dream of a sexual encounter without unconsciously linking it to courtship and marriage'.[142] Thomas Middleton's Jacobean witch, Hecate, could cause impotence and marital strife, but she could not break marriage:

> No, time must do't. We cannot disjoin wedlock.
> 'Tis of heaven's fostering. Well may we raise jars,
> Jealousies, strifes and heart-burning disagreements,
> Like a thick scurf o'er life, as did our master
> Upon that patient miracle, but the work itself
> Our power cannot disjoint.[143]

Warrior women, transvestites who donned male clothing to seek adventure at war and sea, and who were the subject of a whole genre of ballad literature, invariably found true love, returned to their female state, and settled down to marry someone of the opposite sex.[144] The chapbook heroine, Long Meg, wore men's clothing and fought with 'manly courage', but she married eventually, pledging obedience to her husband.[145] Male 'gay' subcultures in eighteenth-century London were even said to have mock marriages and births.[146]

And yet boundaries exist to be crossed. Not everyone married, married in church, or confined their sexuality to the marriage bed.[147] Women aborted unwanted children and used (ineffective) means of family limitation. They may well have read against the grain of medical advice: pointers on how to bring on menstruation slipped easily into hints for inducing a miscarriage; advice on increasing fertility was turned upside down to become information about

141. Ingram, 'Reform of popular culture'; J.R. Gillis *For Better, For Worse: British Marriages, 1600 to the Present* (Oxford, 1985).
142. Hitchcock, *English Sexualities*, p. 24.
143. P. Corbin and D. Sedge (eds), *Three Jacobean Witchcraft Plays* (Manchester, 1986), p. 96.
144. R.M. Dekker and L.C. van de Pol, *The Tradition of Female Transvestism in Early Modern Europe* (London, 1989); D. Dugaw, *Warrior Women and Popular Balladry, 1650–1850* (Cambridge, 1989).
145. *The Life of Long Meg of Westminster*: Pepys Chapbooks, Penny Merriments Collection, Vol. 2, no. 26. Meg is mentioned in the next chapter.
146. Trumbach, 'Birth of the queen', pp. 137–8.
147. J.R. Gillis, 'Conjugal settlements: resort to clandestine and common law marriage in England and Wales, 1650–1850', in J. Bossy (ed.), *Disputes and Settlements* (Cambridge, 1983), ch. 10; Hill, *Women, Work, and Sexual Politics*, ch. 11.

fertility control.[148] Vicious legal prohibitions existed alongside a working tolerance of such infractions. A dominant heterosexuality accommodated what we would term homosexual desire as well as homosexual acts short of anal penetration, in fact was part of a culture which actively valorised homosociality. Literary scholars have explored the 'multi-layered eroticism' of the early modern theatre.[149] Socially and sexually mixed audiences were able to watch a man fall in love with a boy (actor) dressed as a woman who was disguised as a boy! Women could encounter Shakespearean 'female' characters with dialogues 'as erotically compelling as anything spoken in the heterosexual moments in these comedies'.[150] Men could lust after the 'woman' in a play or after the boy whom they knew was underneath the dress. When Pepys saw Edward Kynaston acting a female part (at a time when women actresses were common on the English stage), he observed that the 'boy . . . made the loveliest lady that ever I saw in my life – only her voice not very good'.[151]

It is also important to realise that early modern discourses promoted sex while condemning it. Medical advice for the married has been described as 'concealed pornography'.[152] A New England adulterer, for example, used his knowledge of 'Arristottle' in his pursuit of a young Massachusetts woman, informing her of the areas of pleasure in her body, what to expect of marriage, telling 'filthy things that are too much and too troublesome to mention'.[153] Moralising tracts served a similar function. Phillip Stubbes's famous *Anatomie of Abuses* (1583) created a certain frisson with its lingering descriptions of 'notable vices and imperfections' and cataloguing of the terrible visitations of God upon the wicked.

148. McLaren, *Reproductive Rituals*, chs 3–4; Porter and Hall, *Facts of Life*, pp. 104, 107.

149. For the (mixed) erotic charge of the stage, see the essays in S. Zimmerman (ed.), *Erotic Politics: Desire on the Renaissance Stage* (London, 1992). The quote is from S. Zimmerman, 'Disruptive desire: artifice and indeterminacy in Jacobean comedy', in ibid., p. 55.

150. Smith, *Homosexual Desire*, p. 147; Traub, '(In)significance of "lesbian" desire', p. 71.

151. Quoted in Orgel, *Impersonations*, p. 33. Note the phrase: 'her voice'. The issue of cross-dressing has become rather complex, see L. Levine, *Men in Women's Clothing: Anti-theatricality and Effeminization, 1579–1642* (Cambridge, 1994); and Orgel, *Impersonations*.

152. R. Porter, 'The literature of sexual advice before 1800', in R. Porter and M. Teich (eds), *Sexual Knowledge, Sexual Science: the History of Attitudes to Sexuality* (Cambridge, 1994), p. 150.

153. R. Thompson, *Sex in Middlesex: Popular Mores in a Massachusetts County, 1649–1699* (Amherst, Mass., 1986), pp. 130–1.

Stubbes wrote of the excesses of women's fashion, with velvets, silks, and scarlets '[revealed] down the back wonderfully', fringed skirts, flaunted by the daughters of yeomen, husbandmen, and cottagers alike ('suche wanton attyre'). He condemned the degeneracy of the theatre with its 'wanton gestures' and 'bawdie speaches', 'such kissing and bussing: such clipping and culling: Suche winckinge and glancinge of wanton eyes'. He mentioned the festivities of May when the youth of the parish took to the woods to bring home a may pole: 'I have heard it reported . . . that of fortie, threescore, or a hundred maides going to the wood over night, there have scaresly the third part of them returned home againe undefiled'. He outlined the corrosive influences of dancing, 'smouching and slabbering one of another, what filthie groping and uncleane handling is not practised every wher in these dauncings'.[154] Such double-edged repression was promulgated from pulpit as well as print. The Massachusetts adulterer referred to earlier mentioned a minister who had 'taught out of Job thou hast poured mee out like milk & curdled mee like cheese, Hee said the women blushed at it & I asked him why they blushed & he answered because of the meaning of it for said Hee the mans seed is white like milk'.[155] As both Kathleen McLuskie and Lyndal Roper have argued (developing Foucault), early modern moralism could incite eroticism and sexualise the targets of its condemnations. 'Instead of seeing repression as a simple imposition of control, we need to see it as an active part of the formation of sexual identities.'[156]

Early modern sexuality was a mix of control and self-control, ambiguity and contradiction, fluidity and unruliness. In Michel Foucault's influential *History of Sexuality* it is situated somewhere between the assumed expressive unity of the Middle Ages and an explosion of discourses of the nineteenth century.[157] But I am arguing that we should push the Foucauldian notion of multiple expressions of sex back from the Victorians to the sixteenth and seventeenth centuries. The discourses of sex were diffused throughout early modern society and culture: in the courts; in the moral codes of the conduct books; in medical advice; in ballad, rhyme, chapbook, and play; in verbal exchange in street and lane; in

154. P. Stubbes, *The Anatomie of Abuses* (London, 1583).
155. Thompson, *Sex in Middlesex*, p. 131.
156. L. Roper, *Oedipus and the Devil: Witchcraft, Sexuality and Religion in Early Modern Europe* (London, 1994), p. 8 (for the quote), and ch. 7 for her argument. See also, the valuable piece by K. McLuskie in Zimmerman (ed.), *Erotic Politics*, ch. 7 (esp. p. 105).
157. Foucault, *History of Sexuality: Volume 1*.

everyday perceptions and actions; in official and unofficial rituals of control; and in astrology and witchcraft.

It is interesting that the division between elite and popular does not loom large on the sexual grid: any notion of a coherent plebeian sexual culture in opposition to something called elite (or even middling-sort) respectability makes little sense in this period. This is not to deny social configurations, or the impact of the reformation of manners on those of middling status. It is rather to claim that the shared sexual cultures of marriage and the assumption of reproduction, and divisions – of gender, in particular – were far more deeply etched in the social fabric.

The claim for multiple discourses or inscriptions does not mean that all were of equal value. In an influential book, Thomas Laqueur has proposed a basic division between what he has described as a pre-Enlightenment 'one-sex' perception of the body and the post-Enlightenment 'two-sex' model. Before the late eighteenth century, a woman was portrayed in the medical texts as a man with sex organs inverted: the vagina was an interior penis, the ovaries were testicles. The rigid, modern two-sex correlation between gender and sex, male and female as different sexes with different genitals, as 'organically one or the other of two incommensurable sexes' was not part of the early modern mindset.[158] But seductive though it is as a concept, influential though it is in gender studies, it is debatable how significant Laqueur's 'one-sex' theory really was. The medical texts may have seen women's bodies as variants on maleness – woman as inverted man – rather than as uniquely and separately female, but surgeons and physicians were a minority group in the world of early modern medicine, and we should not assume that their theories were part of a wider medical culture. At every turn, including that of (medical) humoral theory, which *was* widely shared, male–female difference was declared and gender, as we have seen, was impressed on early modern sexuality.[159]

The brank, an iron crown with metal gag, used sometimes against northern scolds and unruly women – women like our old acquaintance Mary Coomb – is a powerful signifier both of male anxieties and the gendering of sex. Instead of exalting and glorifying the wearer this mock crown humiliated her, binding her face with iron

---

158. Laqueur, *Making Sex*, pp. 8, 52, 124–5, 149.

159. G.K. Paster, *The Body Embarrassed: Drama and the Disciplines of Shame in Early Modern England* (Ithaca, NY, 1993); Fletcher, *Gender*, chs 2–3. Laura Gowing makes a similar point: Gowing, *Domestic Dangers*, pp. 6–7. See also, Hitchcock, *English Sexualities*, ch. 4.

avoid detection. His father, who could read a little but not write, claimed to be able to sing or recite over a hundred ballads, and was frequently called upon to sing from his repertoire at the public house. Clare was also exposed to a rich local store of stories of the supernatural. When he weeded with the women as a boy, 'the old womens memorys never faild of tales to smoothen our labour, for as every day came new Jiants, Hobgobblins, and faireys was ready to pass it away'.[3] The village shoemaker's shop was a meeting place for ploughmen and labourers on winter evenings. The shoemaker was a good teller of jokes and stories and was famous for the nicknames he bestowed on his neighbours.

Another friend had a cupboard full of chapbooks, and the youth of the village would gather in his cottage, scaring one another with tales of witches and ghosts. Clare wrote evocatively of the impact that this combination of folktale and chapbook had on his young imagination. Memories of stories of ghosts and evil spirits terrified the young farm servant as he passed reputedly haunted landmarks, so he coped by wielding the imaginative power of the chapbook narratives. He became the chivalric hero, travelling in search of adventure, finding 'a fine lady' and becoming a rich gentleman. He could become so lost in these fantasies that – as in an exciting dream interrupted by waking – 'I have often got to the town un-awares and felt a sort of dissapointment in not being able to finish my story tho I was glad of the escape from the haunted places'.[4] Clare said that the poetry of villagers resided in the broadsheet ballad and the stories of Cock Robin and the Babes in the Wood, known by every old woman and child.

Clare learned arithmetic, encouraged by his parents because they wanted him to get a trade. He learned to write, taught in the even-ings by a farmer's son. His descriptions provide a sense of the deter-mination needed to master the skill, the barriers created by the lack of writing materials in labouring households. Clare used his mother's food wrappers as writing paper because proper paper cost nearly a penny a sheet.

He was often introduced to literature by others. He borrowed *Robinson Crusoe* from a school friend but only managed to read parts of it. He dipped into the *Pilgrim's Progress*, possibly in a book shop. A farmer's son he worked with brought a newspaper into the fields and they would read from it. The friend introduced him to school books from his boarding school; he recited a warrior woman

3. Ibid., p. 4.   4. Ibid., p. 73.

ballad and chapbook story from memory, and exposed him to the world of the almanac and William Lilly's astrological prognostications, to Culpeper's herbal, and even to a book on alchemy. Clare also worked with a gardener whose only reading matter was a gardening book, graveyard epitaphs, and the Bible. The man had a prodigious memory and was able to recite whole chapters of scripture by heart.

Clare gradually built up a library. It was the library of the archetypal autodidact, containing chapbooks, a gardening manual (he was an apprentice gardener briefly), a jest book, hymns, sermons, religious guides, poetry, arithmetic, a battered copy of Milton's *Paradise Lost*, maths books, herbals, *Aesop's Fables*, *Hudibras*, and a spelling guide. Clare's descriptions of his reading practices are almost identical to what has been termed 'traditional literacy': dipping into a book 'here and there' and laying it aside; picking it up again at a later stage and sampling it again. ('I cannot and never coud plod thro every a book in a regular mecanical way.'[5]) He would go back to books repeatedly, the same ones, *The Vicar of Wakefield*, for example, which he read every year, and Milton. He read *Macbeth* 'about twenty times and it chains my feelings still to its perusal like a new thing it is Shakspears masterpiece'.[6] This does not mean that he never read from cover to cover: he said that he could not put down Shakespeare's *Henry V*. But when he kept a brief journal of his reading, his descriptions were very often 'read some of', 'began', 'read some of', 'read in', 'lookd over', 'have been dipping into', 'looked into', 'lookd again into'.[7]

We can see a mix of orality and literacy in the early stages of his poetry composition. Until a weaver showed him a poem in a book of poetry, the only rhyme and verse he had encountered was in ballads and in a romantic poem read aloud to him by his father. His very first verse was in imitation of popular balladry. Clare wrote the verse but would read it out loud to his parents at night while they were seated around the fire, and their reactions and questions helped him to refine his technique. Later he would draw on the songs and stories he learned as a boy, building them into his poetry. His poem 'The Lodge House' 'was a story of my mothers put into ryhme'. 'The Fate of Amy' was based on a story popular in his village, adapted in imitation of the *Ballad of Edwin and Emma*

---

5. Ibid., p. 56. For 'traditional literacy', see D.D. Hall, *Culture of Print: Essays in the History of the Book* (Amherst, Mass., 1996), p. 57.

6. Robinson and Powell (eds), *John Clare*, p. 194.   7. Ibid., pp. 171–219.

'as far as the ideas of it floated on my memory'. (Clare had heard *Edwin and Emma* read while working in the fields.[8])

These autobiographical fragments come from just outside the time-frame of this chapter, but they are a particularly appropriate introduction to our topic. The sketches show the influences of orality: repetition, proverbial lore, poor spelling, lack of punctuation, colloquial style, and digression around a central 'narritive'. But they are also artefacts of literacy, drawn from letters, a journal, and notes for an autobiography, and based on their author's literacy skills. For we are dealing with a society which was neither purely oral (such a culture had long vanished from England) nor fully literate (England would achieve mass literacy only at the end of the nineteenth century).[9] There were strong oral components to early modern society (hence the wording of the title of this chapter). There is also convincing evidence for a developing block or wedge of literacy at the popular level, a literate popular culture. But, as the case of John Clare suggests, it would be a mistake to view literacy and orality as two separate spheres.

II

The statistical structures of literacy are relatively easy to chart. Historians favour the use of the signature as a guide to literacy. That is, they look at court depositions to see whether those 'signing' sign their actual names or make a mark (usually a cross). They then count the numbers and percentages falling into each category. This functional definition of literacy and non-literacy therefore hinges on a person's ability to sign his or her name: those who write their own names are 'literate'; those who make a mark are 'illiterate'. The attraction of using this gauge is that it permits measurement over time, according to class, gender, occupation, and place.[10]

We know that the proportions of men able to write their own names rose from about 20 per cent in the sixteenth century and 30 per cent in the seventeenth century to just over 60 per cent in

8. Ibid., pp. 101, 109–10. 'The Lodge House: A Gossips Tale', is in E. Robinson and D. Powell (eds), *The Early Poems of John Clare 1804–1822*, Vol. 2 (Oxford, 1989), pp. 233–47; 'The Fate of Amy' is in Vol. 1, pp. 270–84.

9. For a nuanced analysis of this transition, see D. Vincent, *Literacy and Popular Culture: England 1750–1914* (Cambridge, 1989).

10. R.S. Schofield, 'Dimensions of illiteracy, 1750–1850', *Explorations in Economic History* 10 (1973), 437–54; D. Cressy, *Literacy and the Social Order: Reading and Writing in Tudor and Stuart England* (Cambridge, 1980).

TABLE 1   *Male signature literacy, c. 1580–1700*[11]

	East Anglia	North	West	South-East	London/Middlesex
Gentry	98	100	97	97	98
Professions	100	97	100	100	100
Yeomen	65	51	73	67	70
Trades/crafts	56	57	53	58	72
Husbandmen	21	25	21	27	21
Labourers	15	15	–	–	22

the mid-eighteenth century. Female signature literacy rates were considerably lower than those of males. Only 11 per cent of David Cressy's East Anglian sample of sixteenth- and seventeenth-century female witnesses were able to write their names; and under 40 per cent of those in Roger Schofield's national sample for the mid-eighteenth century were signature literate. Rab Houston's work on literacy in the north of England between 1640 and 1760 has shown that nearly 60 per cent of male assize deponents were able to sign their names yet less than 20 per cent of women were able to do so.[12]

The social profile of literacy is unsurprising. Signature literacy and illiteracy reflected social and occupational hierarchies, with the gentry and professionals almost totally signature literate, the yeomen and those employed in the crafts and trades in an intermediate position, and small farmers and labourers at the bottom. (See Table 1.)

Although historians are not always sensitive to social gradations in female literacy, Houston has demonstrated a hierarchy there too. (See Table 2.) The very low general female signature literacy figures therefore mask quite high percentages for women of the elite, but the rates for those at the middle and lower levels of society were considerably lower than for their male counterparts.

11. Based on Cressy, *Literacy*, pp. 119–21; Houston, *Scottish Literacy*, p. 33. For the dioceses of Norwich, Exeter, and London, and the Northern Assizes: that is, covering the counties of Cornwall, Devon, Norfolk, Suffolk, Cambridgeshire, Essex, Hertfordshire, the City of London, Yorkshire, Northumberland, Durham, Cumberland, Westmorland, and Lancashire.

12. W.B. Stephens, 'Literacy in England, Scotland, and Wales, 1500–1900', *History of Education Quarterly* 30 (1990), 555; Cressy, *Literacy*, p. 119; Schofield, 'Dimensions of illiteracy', p. 446; R.A. Houston, *Scottish Literacy and the Scottish Identity: Illiteracy and Society in Scotland and Northern England, 1600–1800* (Cambridge, 1985), p. 57.

TABLE 2 *Female signature literacy*[13]

	North, 1640–99
Professions/gentry	76
Trades/crafts	22
Farmers	12
Labourers	5

There were more subtle gradations, particularly within the trade and craft category. Merchants, grocers, and haberdashers had literacy rates of around 90 per cent and above. Weavers, tailors, blacksmiths, butchers, carpenters, and shoemakers were within the range of 60 to 40 per cent, whereas those who worked in what have been described as hard-labouring occupations with little call for education or book learning – miners, bricklayers, labourers, thatchers – had literacy levels of about 10 per cent and less.[14] The literacy of early eighteenth-century London women likewise reflected an occupational hierarchy, with less than 20 per cent of washerwomen, charwomen, and hawkers able to sign their names, but 70 per cent of the needle trades and over 80 per cent of shopkeepers signature literate.[15]

Geography was another variant. There was little significant difference between counties when parishioners set their signatures or marks to the Protestation in the early 1640s, but there was great parish-to-parish variation within counties. Cornish parish literacies ranged from over 50 per cent to just 8 per cent; Lincolnshire from 50 to a mere 6 per cent; Nottinghamshire from 73 to 7 per cent; and Sussex from 41 to 18 per cent.[16] However, it does seem that there was an urban bias towards literacy. The signature literacy rates for London and Chester in the 1640s sample (although admittedly the number of usable parish returns was tiny) were 78 and 48 per

13. Houston, *Scottish Literacy*, p. 60.

14. Houston, *Scottish Literacy*, p. 38; D. Cressy, 'Levels of illiteracy in England, 1530–1730', *Historical Journal* 20 (1977), 5; D. Cressy, 'Literacy in context: meaning and measurement in early modern England', in J. Brewer and R. Porter (eds), *Consumption and the World of Goods* (London, 1993), pp. 315–16; K. Wrightson and D. Levine, *The Making of an Industrial Society: Whickham 1560–1765* (Oxford, 1991), pp. 326–7.

15. P. Earle, 'The female labour market in London in the late seventeenth and early eighteenth centuries', *Economic History Review* 42 (1989), 343.

16. Cressy, *Literacy*, p. 73. See also, K. Wrightson, *English Society 1580–1680* (London, 1982), p. 194.

cent respectively compared to the national figure of 30 per cent.[17] Male literacy rates in Bristol in the 1660s were well over 60 per cent.[18] Evidence for the north of England shows that for the more literate middle sections of society signature literacy rates were considerably higher in cities than in small towns, and higher in these towns than in villages. The signature literacy rates for the crafts and trades in the seventeenth- and eighteenth-century north were 84 per cent for the cities, 71 per cent for towns, and 54 per cent for villages.[19] Though the difference between market towns and villages is more problematic, the superiority of the cities is clear. Female literacy rates in London in the 1640s were 45 per cent compared to a paltry 10 per cent in rural England; by the end of the seventeenth century they were over 60 per cent.[20] An analysis of Durham diocesan wills (predominantly seventeenth- and eighteenth-century) found that about 80 per cent of men in the cities of Newcastle and Durham could sign their own names, while for the villages the rate was not much over 50 per cent. The female rates were respectively 50 and 25 per cent.[21]

III

The most obvious objection to this methodology is that people may have learned to write just their names and that a signature is thus a meaningless gauge of literacy.[22] This is unlikely given the context of the learning of reading and writing in the early modern period. Writing, well into the nineteenth century, was treated as a technical skill acquired after a person had learned to read.[23] The two skills were taught separately. Today, with the two skills taught simultaneously, and with a cultural stigma attached to illiteracy, those who can neither read nor write may well be capable of signing. But in pre-industrial England there was little point in faking the ability to write, given the phasing of instruction just discussed, the lack of

17. Ibid.

18. J. Barry, 'Popular culture in seventeenth-century Bristol', in B. Reay (ed.), *Popular Culture in Seventeenth-century England* (London, 1985), p. 62.

19. Houston, *Scottish Literacy*, p. 50.

20. Earle, 'Female labour market', p. 335; Cressy, 'Literacy in context', p. 315.

21. Houston, *Scottish Literacy*, p. 275.

22. P. Collinson, 'The significance of signatures', *Times Literary Supplement*, 9 January 1991.

23. For the technicalities of writing and writing instruction, see J. Goldberg, *Writing Matter: From the Hands of the English Renaissance* (Stanford, Calif., 1990), ch. 2 (although Goldberg's agenda is much grander).

writing materials in the majority of homes, and the fact that most people rarely needed to use a signature. In short, it has been argued that although it will overestimate those with an ease of written expression, the presence of a signature gives a rough indication of the ability to write.[24] It will also – coming back to the phasing of instruction – provide a confident *minimum* estimate of those able to read. It is, in the words of Roger Chartier, 'a kind of rough, composite index'.[25] But while we can be confident that those who cannot sign their names were not able to write, we should not extend this logic to their reading ability. As Margaret Spufford has long argued, 'reading was a much more socially diffused skill than writing'.[26] Many of those who scratched a simple cross may well have been able to read but not write. Many children – for reasons that we do not need to go into now – left school before they had learned to write; but 'schooling to the level of reading was a commonplace'.[27] The major problem with the 'middle range' measurement, then, is its potential neglect of readers: what Keith Thomas has referred to as its 'spectacular underestimation'.[28] Obviously it is difficult to measure the extent of this group of hidden readers, but nineteenth-century studies, based on more detailed information, suggest that the proportion able to read was about one-and-a-half times the proportion able to sign.[29]

It is also likely that women are disproportionately underrepresented in the traditional measurement. The low proportions of female signatures doubtless mask a high percentage of women able to read but not write. A study of a group of women involved in a religious revival in an eighteenth-century Scottish village found that only one in ten could write but all could read.[30] In nineteenth-century Bottesford (in Leicestershire), the female signature literacy rate was only 50 per cent, but a much higher 90 per cent were able to read. Many of these Bottesford signature illiterate were readers.[31] Writing was not considered to be a cultural necessity for women. At

24. Schofield, 'Dimensions of illiteracy', pp. 440–1.
25. R. Chartier, 'The practical impact of writing', in R. Chartier (ed.), *A History of Private Life: Passions of the Renaissance* (Cambridge, Mass., 1989), p. 112.
26. M. Spufford, *Small Books and Pleasant Histories: Popular Fiction and its Readership in Seventeenth-century England* (London, 1981), p. 27.
27. Ibid., p. 29.
28. K. Thomas, 'The meaning of literacy in early modern England', in G. Baumann (ed.), *The Written Word: Literacy in Transition* (Oxford, 1986), p. 103.
29. B. Reay, *Microhistories: Demography, Society and Culture in Rural England, 1800–1930* (Cambridge, 1996), p. 235.
30. T.C. Smout, 'Born again at Cambuslang: new evidence on popular religion and literacy in eighteenth-century Scotland', *Past and Present* 97 (1982), 121–3.
31. Information from Roger Schofield.

all levels of society, well into the nineteenth century, high percentages of women used a cross instead of a signature.

Thus we should certainly not simply dismiss those who could not write their own names as illiterate. Those who made a mark included large numbers of readers, and to exclude them from the category 'literate' would be to fundamentally misunderstand the cultural context of early modern England, where, for the bulk of the population, reading was literacy. The best description of what precisely is being measured by the quantifiers, then, is 'signature literacy' and 'signature illiteracy' rather than the misleading 'literate' and 'illiterate' – although it is a mistake that highly respected scholars of the early modern period still make.[32] Neither Shakespeare's father nor his daughter could sign their own name. Yet we should not assume that they were unable to read and therefore describe them as 'illiterate'.[33]

Twentieth-century culture tends to draw neat distinctions between literate and non-literate, including various assumptions about 'mindsets'. Yet a case can be made for a more subtle approach, stressing complexity and interaction rather than hard-and-fast cultural division. Even using the quantifier's 'rough, composite index' there is little evidence for any great separation of the cultures. Detailed work on the profiles of literacy in individual rural households as late as the nineteenth century shows that in only a minority of families could both parents and all the children (if they had them) sign their names. Most of the totally literate families were to be found among the farmers and craftsmen, but even in these groups they were a minority. The most representative profile of literacy, then, was that in which signature literacy and illiteracy were present within one household. As David Levine has pointed out, 'the very haphazardness with which this skill was handed down from generation to generation seems to question the value which parents (and their children) placed on it . . . it does not seem that literacy was inordinately prized'.[34] As a fictional seventeenth-century countryman put it, 'We can learn to plow and harrow, sow and reape, and prune, thrash and fanne, winnow and grinde, brue and bake, and all without booke.'[35]

32. For example, C. Haigh, 'Conclusion', in C. Haigh (ed.), *The English Reformation Revised* (Cambridge, 1987), p. 213; A. Gurr, *Playgoing in Shakespeare's London* (Cambridge, 1996 edn), p. 56.

33. Thomas, 'Meaning of literacy', p. 103.

34. Reay, *Microhistories*, pp. 239–42, 252; D. Levine, 'Education and family life in early industrial England', *Journal of Family History* 4 (1979), 378.

35. Wrightson, *English Society*, p. 188.

Such people could manage well enough. Nineteenth- and twentieth-century sources provide evidence of small businesses run by those who could neither read nor write. Farmers, carriers, beershop-keepers, and dealers were able to transact business and keep orders and accounts in the mind rather than on paper. It is unlikely that the practice would have been any less widespread in the early modern period.[36] It was always possible to draw upon the skills of others in household or neighbourhood. Fully literate individuals in the community and adjoining parishes could write (and decipher) letters, draw up accounts, indentures and petitions, and make wills for the semi-literate. The yeomen Simon Rider and Adam Eyre and the shopkeeper Thomas Turner certainly fulfilled this function.[37] Nicholas Breton's fictional seventeenth-century countryman says: 'Now if we cannot write, we have the Clerke of the church, or the schoolmaster of the towne to help us, who for our plaine matters will serve our turnes well enough.'[38] The diary of the seventeenth-century Lancashire apprentice, Roger Lowe, also shows that he frequently read and wrote for neighbours, penning accounts, bonds, constables' presentments, wills, indentures, and love letters.[39] A street-seller of stationery in the nineteenth century told Henry Mayhew that he wrote letters for some of his customers; he estimated about forty a year. But the man said that he was never asked to write love letters: 'Women does that for one another, I think, when the young housemaid can't write as well as she can talk.' Mayhew was of the opinion that the letter writer was once a regular 'street-labourer' in London, but that now most of the letter writing for the 'uneducated' (and the reading and replying) was done 'by those who are rather vaguely but emphatically described as – "friends" '.[40]

We need to think of a diversity of literacies in the pre-modern rural world. As we have seen, there were people who could read but not write. Some could read black-letter type – found in primers, ballads, and chapbooks – but not the white-letter or roman with which we are more comfortable today.[41] Reading print did not mean

36. See Vincent, *Literacy*, pp. 125–6; Reay, *Microhistories*, pp. 250–1.

37. M. Campbell, *The English Yeoman in the Tudor and Early Stuart Age* (New York, 1968 edn), pp. 265–6; D. Vaisey (ed.), *The Diary of Thomas Turner 1754–1765* (Oxford, 1984), pp. xxii–xxiii.

38. Campbell, *English Yeoman*, p. 263.

39. W.L. Sachse (ed.), *The Diary of Roger Lowe* (New Haven, 1938).

40. H. Mayhew, *London Labour and the London Poor*, 4 vols (New York, 1968 edn), Vol. 1, pp. 268–9.

41. Thomas, 'Meaning of literacy' and Cressy, 'Literacy in context' provide the best accounts.

that the person could read handwriting, of which there were also multiple types, including secretary hand, gothic, and italic (which became the 'ordinary hand' of the early modern period).[42] Once again we know from later evidence, applicable to an earlier period, that many of those taught to read from the Bible could manage that but stumbled when faced with more secular material.[43] Spufford has used autobiographies to evoke the different worlds of literacy. Thomas Tyron, the son of a tiler, was taken from school at the age of 6 : 'I scarcely learnt to distinguish my Letters, before I was taken away to Work for my Living.' He later learned to read with the help of fellow shepherds, but his companions could not write so he had to seek out the paid help of a writing instructor. The autobiographies of Oliver Sansom and John Whiting, on the other hand, provide 'insight into the literate yeoman world of the seventeenth century' where reading and writing were simply taken for granted.[44] The astrological diary of the Sussex merchant Samuel Jeake – itself a product of his literacy – lists 124 books that he had 'read over' by the time he was 15 years old: from John Foxe's *Acts and Monuments* (1632 edn) to a 1591 history of Russia. By the time he was 19, he had 'somewhat acquainted' himself 'with the Latine, Greek & Hebrew, Rhetorick, Logick, Poetry, Natural Philosophy, Arithmetick, Geometry, Cosmography, Astronomy, Astrology, Geography, Theology, Physick, Dialling, Navigation, Calligraphy, Stenography, Drawing, Heraldry, and History'.[45] The potentials of middling-sort literacy reached an extraordinary extreme with the estimated 50 notebooks of letters, memoirs, reflections, rules for self-discipline, judgements on sinners, political comment, and sermon notes – some 20,000 pages – written by the London turner, Nehemiah Wallington, between 1618 and 1654.[46]

There was a world of difference between the literacy of someone like Wallington or Jeake and that of a labourer who made a mark and who could neither read nor write. But even those at the bottom of the social scale varied in their literacies and non-literacies. Some

---

42. Goldberg, *Writing Matter*, pp. 51–4.   43. Reay, *Microhistories*, p. 233.

44. M. Spufford, 'First steps in literacy: the reading and writing experiences of the humblest seventeenth-century spiritual autobiographers', *Social History* 4 (1979), 415–16, 430–3.

45. The editors of his diary say that he 'had read' the books, but his own term 'read over' is more in keeping with early modern reading practices: M. Hunter and A. Gregory (eds), *An Astrological Diary of the Seventeenth Century: Samuel Jeake of Rye 1652–1699* (Oxford, 1988), pp. 41, 92–7, 117.

46. See P.S. Seaver, *Wallington's World: a Puritan Artisan in Seventeenth-century London* (Stanford, Calif., 1985), esp. ch. 1.

could sign their names with confidence, and presumably could read. Others were unable to write but could read. Even the marks of the signature illiterate seem to indicate some hierarchy of facility, ranging from confident Xs to pained scratches. For some labouring men and women, holding a pen was a truly alien experience.[47]

IV

The potential number of hidden readers – combined with signature literacy's more certain measurement of the minimum number of those reasonably at ease with print hand – provides the context for the developing culture of early modern print.[48] England was simply awash in a sea of commercial printed literature. About 22,000 tracts and newsbooks survive from the English Revolution in a single London bookseller's collection.[49] The London waterman, John Taylor, wrote possibly 150 different pamphlets in the first half of the seventeenth century, about 500,000 individual copies of verse, travel accounts, political comment, and jest books.[50] Almanacs were selling at the rate of 400,000 a year in the seventeenth century: William Lilly's sales alone were estimated at 30,000 copies a year.[51] Chapbooks also sold in great quantities: one English publisher, Charles Tias, had a stock of 90,000 volumes in 1664. Ballads, printed on a single sheet of paper, were also particularly numerous – Tias had reams for about 37,500 ballad sheets.[52] Only about 3,000 ballad titles were registered with the Stationers' Company in the sixteenth and seventeenth centuries, but it is thought that 15,000 or so different ballads were in print during that period. Tessa Watt has estimated that several million ballad copies were circulating by the end of the sixteenth century.[53] Even more astonishingly, a recent estimate

47. For varieties of literacy, see D. Cressy, 'The environment for literacy: accomplishment and context in seventeenth-century England and New England', in D.P. Resnick (ed.), *Literacy in Historical Perspective* (Washington, 1983), pp. 23–42. See also, Reay, *Microhistories*, ch. 8: 'Literacies'.

48. R.A. Houston, *Literacy in Early Modern Europe* (London, 1988), esp. ch. 8: 'The world of the book'.

49. B. Reay, 'Radicalism and religion in the English Revolution: an introduction', in J.F. McGregor and B. Reay (eds), *Radical Religion in the English Revolution* (Oxford, 1986), p. 13.

50. B. Capp, *The World of John Taylor the Water-poet 1578–1653* (Oxford, 1994), pp. 66–7.

51. B. Capp, *Astrology and the Popular Press: English Almanacs 1500–1800* (London, 1979), pp. 23, 44.

52. Spufford, *Small Books*, pp. 98–9.

53. T. Watt, *Cheap Print and Popular Piety 1550–1640* (Cambridge, 1991), p. 11.

of the number of newsbooks distributed in the 1620s and 1630s has put the figure as high as 5 million.[54]

Such numbers are impressive. However, it is extremely difficult to get printed material into the hands (or onto the walls) of those at the popular level. Historians generally argue that the mere fact that printed items were produced commercially in such great numbers indicates demand, a mass market. Yet the problem with this logic is that it is not clear whether the product is being bought in small quantities by a wide cross-section of society or in large quantities by a more select group. Indeed, the social boundaries of cost and distribution continually modify crude first impressions about quantity.[55]

Cost is an obvious factor in relation to the accessibility of print. Quite simply, could people afford to purchase such items? Ballads sold for between a halfpenny and a penny. Chapbooks and almanacs cost from 2d. to 6d.[56] More substantial books – say 200 pages or more, depending on the binding and the century – sold for 1s. and upwards. So wealthier tradesmen and yeomen would certainly have had the income (if they had the inclination) to purchase such literature. But given the wage rates of the early modern period – 12d. a day for labourers – even a modest penny broadsheet does not seem as cheap as at first sight. And the 'income' of many craftsmen and small farmers at subsistence level would not have been disposable.[57]

Already, then, we have the likelihood of a hierarchy of print consumption reflecting the literacy rates discussed earlier. This is further supported by research on the ownership of more expensive and durable items of print. Although levels of book ownership of this kind were much higher than in the late medieval period, it is striking from the work on inventories – lists of a person's goods and possessions taken after their death, which by their very nature favour the middle and upper levels of society – just how *little* book ownership there was. Only about 20 per cent of a sample of Kentish townsmen owned such books in the sixteenth century and under

54. M. Spufford, 'The pedlar, the historian and the folklorist: seventeenth century communications', *Folklore* 105 (1994), 14. Spufford is communicating the findings of Michael Frearson.

55. See J. Barry, 'Literacy and literature in popular culture: reading and writing in historical perspective', in T. Harris (ed.), *Popular Culture in England, c. 1500–1850* (London, 1995), pp. 74–5.

56. Watt, *Cheap Print*, pp. 11–12; Capp, *Astrology*, p. 41; Spufford, *Small Books*, p. 48.

57. Watt, *Cheap Print*, pp. 261–2 discusses costs in terms of incomes, though reaches slightly different conclusions than I do.

50 per cent in the 1630s.[58] Only 20 per cent of a much larger national sample of households owned books during the period 1675–1725.[59] Unsurprisingly, ownership in the national survey follows the trends of signature literacy, with higher levels in London (31 per cent of household inventories) than in the villages (17 per cent), and with books more likely to appear in the inventories of tradesmen and yeomen (around 20 per cent) than those of husbandmen or labourers (only 4 per cent each).[60] The books in these inventories ranged from 6d. to 4s. in value, but they tended to be the more costly items: the Bible was ubiquitous in the Kent survey.[61] Almanacs, ballads, and chapbooks, probably treated by owner or appraiser as printed ephemera, were scarcely mentioned. This does not mean that they were not bought.

Other contours can be traced. Roger Chartier has emphasised an urban–rural divide in early modern France, with print ubiquitous in the city but scarce in the country.[62] In contrast, Spufford and her students have been at pains to stress the wide distribution networks of the early modern English print trade, and the ubiquity, in particular, of the chapbook and ballad.[63] Henry Chettle complained in 1592 of the influence of chapmen, of the 'singing and selling of ballads and pamphletes full of ribaudrie' in fairs, markets, and public gatherings 'in every corner of cities and market townes of the realme'.[64] Spufford has certainly assembled impressive documentary support for the widespread geographical impact of the chapmen, hawkers, and pedlars who travelled the nation on horseback or on foot during the late seventeenth century, selling books and a range of other consumer items door to door from packs or on stalls in markets and fairs.[65] But it has to be said that the evidence is rather fragmentary and illusive. Books are not often

58. P. Clark, 'The ownership of books in England, 1560–1640: the example of some Kentish townfolk', in L. Stone (ed.), *Schooling and Society* (Baltimore, 1976), p. 99.
59. L. Weatherill, *Consumer Behaviour and Material Culture in Britain 1660–1760* (London, 1988), Table 2.1. Less than 5 per cent of late medieval York wills mentioned books: P.J.P. Goldberg, 'Lay book ownership in late medieval York: the evidence of wills', *The Library* 16 (1994), 181–9.
60. Weatherill, *Consumer Behaviour*, pp. 76, 168.   61. Clark, 'Ownership of books'.
62. R. Chartier, *The Cultural Uses of Print in Early Modern France* (Princeton, 1987), esp. ch. 5: 'Publishing strategies and what the people read, 1530–1660'.
63. M. Spufford (ed.), *The World of Rural Dissenters, 1520–1725* (Cambridge, 1995), pp. 47–55, 236–40, 275–87.
64. K. Charlton, ' "False fonde bookes, ballades and rimes": an aspect of informal education in early modern England', *History of Education Quarterly* 27 (1987), 458.
65. Spufford, *Small Books*, ch. 5; M. Spufford, *The Great Reclothing of Rural England: Petty Chapmen and their Wares in the Seventeenth Century* (London, 1984).

listed in the inventories of chapmen, and the quantities in each pedlar's pack must have been very small. It would have been very tempting for the producers and distributors of cheap literature to have targeted the concentrations of potential consumers in the towns.

There is, then, at least a prima facie case for a hierarchy of print corresponding to a hierarchy of literacy, with a grid of consumption covering all social groups but weighted towards the middling and upper levels and favouring town over country. While small books undoubtedly reached the remoter rural areas of England, contact was probably in terms of individual items and small quantities rather than a mass of printed material. This would certainly correspond to the patterns of literacy, book ownership, and the reading practice of focusing on a limited number of texts rather than widespread consumption. The future writer and radical, Thomas Holcroft, who helped his parents peddle in rural Berkshire in the 1750s, acquired two chapbooks which he read again and again until they were as familiar to him as the catechism.[66] Clearly, if we want to think of popular literature in the sense of print with a wide appeal, we need to move away from the world of the more substantial book towards that of the small books and ballads. Holcroft, who traversed large areas of rural England, claimed that books – apart from 'those of daily religious use' – were 'scarcely to be seen' except among 'the opulent'. But he did note the prevalence of ballads.[67] A late-sixteenth-century observer said that examples of the cheapest forms of print were to be found in the cottages of husbandmen as well as the homes of the gentry.[68]

V

Henry Mayhew's account of the street sellers of print in London in the mid-nineteenth century provides clues to the readership of identical types of cheap literature and the way in which the vendors attempted to appeal to a mixed audience. One patterer explained the specific appeal of accounts of gruesome murders, one involving the seduction of a clergyman's daughter by a young naval officer and her subsequent murder of her illegitimate child, the other a mother's slaying of her own son. The seller said that stories of this

66. Vincent, *Literacy*, pp. 197–8.
67. *Memoirs of the Late Thomas Holcroft* (Oxford, 1926 edn), p. 55.
68. Watt, *Cheap Print*, p. 12.

sort held particular fascination for women, who were his main customers. The young liked the first murder best because of its seduction scene – 'they like to hear about the young woman being seduced
by the naval officer' – while mothers took more to the story about
the murder of the son. Stories such as this, often with accompanying verse, could sell lucratively for decades and would be hawked
all around the country: 'There's nothing beats a stunning good
murder.' Another killing was too disgusting for a genteel readership, but 'poor women' bought accounts of the crime in great
quantities, telling the vendor just exactly what they wanted to do
with the criminal. A ballad about General Haynau, the unpopular
Austrian military leader who, in a case widely publicised in London,
had ordered the public flogging of an upper-class Hungarian woman,
sold particularly well, to 'poor women mostly', at 1d. a sheet. '[I]t
ended, sir, with a beautiful moral as appeals to every female bosom:
"That man who would a female harm, / Is never fit to live." We
always likes something for the ladies, bless 'em. They're our best
customers.'[69] Those who sold the street literature varied their pat-
ter to suit the clientele. Standard pieces were adapted to appeal to
the occupational make-up of the neighbourhood or the village,
town or street in which the piece was being hawked. A good seller
knew the specific attraction of individual titles, what type of murder
would intrigue tradespeople, for example. 'Gentlefolks' heard about
horrible crimes from the newspapers and were therefore unlikely
to 'have anything to do with murders sold in the street'. Their
servants liked items such as the 'Rich Man and his Wife quarrelling
because they have no family', which did good trade among the
footmen, grooms, and maidservants of London's West End. Stories
about apprentices appealed to apprentices. Old women liked descriptions of Hell. Costermongers were fascinated by tales of the
antics of the 'harristocrats'. The dockers of Limehouse preferred
'anything comic'.[70]

   Although the world that Mayhew described was the tail end of
the early modern period, there is a compelling logic to his in-
formants' analysis which is applicable to other contexts. Purely in
terms of its vast range of subject matter, the early modern printed
literature must have appealed to a wide range of potential readers:
religious ballads, godly chapbooks, newsbooks, jests, fables, riddles,

---

69. Mayhew, *London Labour*, Vol. 1, pp. 223, 225, 228. For the reaction to Haynau,
see A.J. Hammerton, 'The targets of "rough music": respectability and domestic
violence in Victorian England', *Gender and History* 3 (1991), 23–44.
   70. Mayhew, *London Labour*, Vol. 1, pp. 26, 234–5.

plays, proverbs, courtship advice, palmistry, dream interpretation, legal advice, beauty tips, cookery hints, monsters, lower-class heroes, upper-class heroes, middle-class heroes, heroines, women who dressed as men, men who dressed as women, battles, famous criminals, terrible crimes, marvellous acts of manhood, silly foreigners (including the Welsh and Scots), wanton wives, and cuckolds. Almanacs gave astrological information about farming, the weather, and medical care; they provided political prognostication and social comment; and they set out brief histories of the world.[71]

Prospective purchasers could buy an *Excellent Ballad of Joseph the Carpenter and the sacred Virgin Mary* in which Joseph voices his suspicions of Mary's immaculate conception:

> Perceiving that Mary with Child was gone
> Said tell me Mary now and anon
> who hath done this my dear my dear.[72]

They could choose a tale of gender inversion in *The Famous Flower of Servingmen*, about a woman who cut her hair, wore male garb, changed her name from Elise to William, and disguised herself as a male servant. She became the king's chamberlain and then ended up marrying him when her true identity was discovered:

> He took sweet William for his Wife
> The like before was never seen,
> A Serving-man to be a Queen.[73]

71. Based on the more than 1,700 ballads and about 200 small books in the collection of Samuel Pepys at Magdalene College Library, Cambridge: the ballads are reproduced in W.G. Day (ed.), *The Pepys Ballads* (Cambridge, 1987), 5 vols; the chapbooks are on microfilm. See also, D. Valenze, 'Prophecy and popular literature in eighteenth-century England', *Journal of Ecclesiastical History* 29 (1978), 75–92; Capp, *Astrology*; Spufford, *Small Books*; B. Capp, 'Popular literature', in Reay (ed.), *Popular Culture*, ch. 6; J.A. Sharpe, 'Plebeian marriage in Stuart England: some evidence from popular literature', *Transactions of the Royal Historical Society* 36 (1986), 69–90; Watt, *Cheap Print*; J. Wiltenburg, *Disorderly Women and Female Power in the Street Literature of Early Modern England and Germany* (Charlottesville, Va., 1992); E. Foyster, 'A laughing matter? Marital discord and gender control in seventeenth-century England', *Rural History* 4 (1993), 5–21; P. Lake, 'Deeds against nature: cheap print, Protestantism and murder in early seventeenth-century England', in K. Sharpe and P. Lake (eds), *Culture and Politics in Early Modern England* (London, 1994), ch. 10. The historians of the early modern chapbook and almanac stress the widespread appeal of the small books: 'purchasers belonged to almost every social group' (Capp, *Astrology*, p. 60). Spufford's discussion of readership of chapbooks, based on content, argues for a potentially very wide appeal: Spufford, *Small Books*, ch. 3. See also, a recent account of the early modern jest book which refers to it as embracing high and low cultures: D. Brewer, 'Prose jest-books mainly in the sixteenth to eighteenth centuries in England', in J. Bremmer and H. Roodenburg (eds), *A Cultural History of Humour* (Cambridge, 1997), ch. 7.

72. Day (ed.), *Pepys Ballads*, Vol. 2, p. 27.   73. Ibid., Vol. 3, p. 142.

They could pick a moving song of aristocratic infanticide; of the twins which a lady gave birth to alone against a tree, and killed with a knife to 'hide her shame', and how the desperate young mother's dead infants came back to haunt her.[74] Or they could buy a more light-hearted ballad about a wine cooper's courtship of a merchant's widow:

> He told her in his Breec[h]es,
> There was the best of Riches,
> right pleasant to behold.[75]

Chapbook readers were told the story of Thomas Hickathrift, the fenland giant (eight feet tall by the age of 10!) who lived 'in the Reign before William the Conqueror', who could kick a football out of sight and many other 'manly acts', and who killed a giant, confiscating his land to provide a commons for the poor;[76] or of his female equivalent, Long Meg of Westminster, who demonstrated her 'manly courage' by boxing the ears of gentry and vicars and by donning male armour to fight the French.[77] They could purchase the mocking dialogue between Andrew and Joan: 'Oh Joan thou hast an eye like a Prune, but thou may look in thy A[rse] for beauty.' 'I love thee more far than a bear loves Honey, and I hope you'l affect me as much as a Sow does a bunch of Carrots.'[78] They were provided with the moral fable of the country mouse and the city mouse, 'enlarged out of Horace'; the story of Faustus in verse; and abridged versions of *Don Quixote* and *Jack of Newbury*.[79]

The way in which this literature was presented, the hybridity of the textual form, lent itself to multiple readings and varied appeal. Both chapbook and ballad combined different types, black-letter and roman or white-letter. In fact nearly all the ballads in the Pepys collection, including those which at first seem black-letter, contain a combination of types to provide different emphases.[80] Chapbooks

---

74. Ibid., Vol. 5, p. 4.   75. Ibid., p. 226.

76. *The Pleasant History of Thomas Hic-ka-thrift*: Pepys Chapbooks, Penny Merriments Collection, Vol. 1, no. 3.

77. *The Life of Long Meg of Westminster*: Pepys Chapbooks, Penny Merriments Collection, Vol. 2, no. 26.

78. *A Merry Dialogue Between Andrew and his Sweet heart Joan*: Pepys Chapbooks, Penny Merriments Collection, Vol. 1, no. 5.

79. See *The Country Mouse and the City Mouse* (1683); *The First Part of Dr. Faustus*; *The Famous History of Don Quixote De La Mancha* (1686); *A most Delightful History Of the famous Clothier of England, Called, Jack of Newbery* (1684): Pepys Chapbooks, Penny Merriments Collection, Vol. 1, nos 8, 54, Vol. 2, nos 29, 50.

80. H. Weinstein, *Catalogue of the Pepys Library at Magdalene College Cambridge, Volume 2, Ballads Part 1* (Cambridge, 1994), pp. xvii–xix.

also employed different forms, prose and verse. And both chapbook and ballad used classical and demotic themes and metaphors; it was not unusual to encounter Latin phrases or classical imagery and characters.[81] Stories from the elite *Arcadia* were used in chapbooks. The larger, more expensive, chivalric romances like *Valentine and Orson* (consisting originally of over 100 chapters) were shortened to about twenty pages and sold as chapbooks for 2d.[82] People from varied cultural backgrounds and different genders could read the same pamphlet and come away with different messages – not to mention the responses of those who were listeners rather than readers. Figures who were objects of mirth for one might be objects of identification for another. Classical allusions could add to a text or be skipped in the rush of the narrative or the beat of the verse. A woodcut illustration could be 'read' as a central indicator to the message of the sheet or book, as complementing the written word, or as the only guide to the broadsheet or book's contents (in the case of the illiterate), or might be ignored entirely as a standard image reproduced again and again to illustrate a variety of topics.[83]

It is almost certain, therefore, that printers had 'several reading publics' in mind.[84] One of the principal consumers was youth, of all classes and both sexes. The ballads and chapbooks are packed with the sort of courtship subject matter calculated to appeal to youth, and the title pages of the latter frequently recommend their contents to young men and maids.[85] John Milton, Richard Baxter, and John Bunyan all referred to the influences of cheap print upon their formative years; John Clare and Samuel Bamford said very similar things for the end of the eighteenth century.[86] A 'fictional' late seventeenth-century merchant's son described the early effects of sixpenny books like *Fortunatus*, *Doctor Faustus*, *Fryar Bacon*, *Ornatus and Artesia*, and *Parismus*, which he either bought or borrowed. He had fantasies about becoming a loyal retainer to a brave knight, or

81. Based on my observation of the ballads and chapbooks in the Pepys Collection.

82. J.L. Gaunt, 'A study of English popular fiction' (University of Maryland, Ph.D., 1972), pp. 60–3; P. Salzman, *English Prose Fiction 1558–1700: a Critical History* (Oxford, 1985), pp. 266–7.

83. Again based on the Pepys Collection. See also, the useful discussions in R. Chartier, 'General introduction: print culture', in Chartier (ed.), *The Culture of Print* (Cambridge, 1989), pp. 1–10; M.E. Fissell, 'Readers, texts, and contexts: vernacular medical works in early modern England', in R. Porter (ed.), *The Popularization of Medicine 1650–1850* (London, 1992), ch. 3.

84. Hall, *Culture of Print*, p. 49.

85. Pepys Chapbooks, Penny Merriments Collection, Vol. 1, nos 24, 25, 31, 32, 33, 47, 49, Vol. 2, nos 12, 13, 30, 37, 40, 42, 46, 47.

86. Spufford, 'First steps', pp. 418–20; Vincent, *Literacy*, pp. 61–2.

discovering, like the characters in his reading, that he was really of noble birth.[87] Complaints about the corrupting influences of 'false fond bookes, ballades and rimes' upon the young provide further evidence that the literature was having an impact on this age group.[88] Spufford has discussed the role of 'schoolboys' in the market for chapbooks, but we should expand her category to youth in general.[89]

Other attractions were more general. National heroes like Robin Hood and Guy of Warwick were popular in a variety of literary forms and seem to have had a genuinely wide appeal, over centuries.[90] The *Cobbler of Canterbury* (1590), based on Chaucer's *Canterbury Tales*, claimed that its stories would intrigue gentlemen, farmers, and old women.[91] The title pages of chapbooks often advertised their suitablity 'to the Humours of all Sorts, Sexes, and Conditions', and 'all Stations and Conditions'. They were ideal 'for the Recreation of all Gentlemen, Ladies, and others', and 'fitted to the Capacities both of the learned and ignorant'.[92] Hannah More's co-option of the genre to impart conservative moral values to the poor at the end of the eighteenth century indicates penny literature's continuing perceived power.[93]

Just as we need to consider a range of literacies, so we need to recognise the complexity of print cultures. The simple division between elite and popular literature does not do justice to the variety of the early modern reading diet. The historian and bookseller Nathaniel Crouch, although he used the techniques of cheap literature (pictures and sensationalism) to facilitate the weaning, deliberately offered an alternative to 'vain and idle Songs and Romances'. Robert Mayer argues that Crouch was bridging high and low culture, offering – in his life of Oliver Cromwell, and histories of the Stuarts, Scotland and Ireland, earthquakes, and witches and demons – digested, shortened versions of longer, more expensive

87. L.B. Wright, *Middle-class Culture in Elizabethan England* (New York, 1958 edn), pp. 86–7.

88. Wright, *Middle-class Culture*, pp. 103–18; Charlton, 'False fonde bookes'.

89. Spufford, *Small Books*, pp. 72–5.

90. J.C. Holt, *Robin Hood* (London, 1982); R.S. Crane, 'The vogue of *Guy of Warwick* from the close of the middle ages to the romantic revival', *Publications of the Modern Language Association of America* 30 (1915), 125–94; V.B. Richmond, *The Legend of Guy of Warwick* (New York, 1996).

91. *The Cobbler of Canterbury* (Cambridge, 1976 edn), p. 3.

92. Pepys Chapbooks, Penny Merriments Collection, Vol. 1, no. 34, Vol. 2, nos 15, 16, 18.

93. S. Pedersen, 'Hannah More meets Simple Simon: tracts, chapbooks, and popular culture in late eighteenth-century England', *Journal of British Studies* 25 (1986), 84–113.

books. This seems perfectly reasonable. But we need not also follow Mayer's suggestion that the targeted market for Crouch's work was that of the chapbook and almanac reader.[94] Crouch's works were 200 pages long and sold at 1s., substantially longer and costing more money than the purchasers of songs and cheap romances were used to paying. It seems more feasible that Crouch was appealing to the more literate, wealthier upper end of this (probably middling-sort) popular market.

Prices and the page lengths of books alone suggest potential hierarchies: at the bottom, the penny ballads, the two- or three-penny almanacs and chapbooks; in the middle, Crouch's histories, popular chivalric romances which cost one or two shillings, and the middling-sort fiction of Thomas Deloney, which was probably purchased by the clothiers to whom he dedicated *Jack of Newbury* rather than by humble artisans; towards the top, Sir Philip Sidney's *Arcadia*, which sold for 9s. bound, enough money to buy over 100 ballads; and finally what have been termed 'the more serious books', Holinshed's *Chronicles* (1577), for example, bought by the young earl of Essex for £1. 6s., enough money for over 300 ballads![95] It is likely, then, that there were upper limits to the purchasing power and therefore the literary diet of a lower-class readership.

This does not apply to diet from the top down. Peter Burke's notion of cultural amphibiousness – the participation of the elite in both high and low culture – is very helpful when considering early modern gentry culture.[96] The elite purchased chapbooks and ballads; one of the best surviving collections of such literature resides in the library of the seventeenth-century bureaucrat, Samuel Pepys. Pepys acquired the material as a collector, but there is evidence in his diary that ballads formed part of his commonplace social interaction: he bought them, learned them, had them written out for him, heard them, sang them himself, and alluded to them in conversation and correspondence.[97] Bernard Capp has suggested that the pamphlets of John Taylor, in roman type rather than black-letter,

94. R. Mayer, 'Nathaniel Crouch, bookseller and historian: popular historiography and cultural power in late seventeenth-century England', *Eighteenth-Century Studies* 27 (1994), 391–419.

95. Salzman, *English Prose Fiction*, pp. 110–11, 266–7; F.R. Johnson, 'Notes on English retail book-prices, 1550–1640', *The Library* 5 (1950), 92. For Deloney, see L.S. O'Connell, 'The Elizabethan bourgeois hero-tale: aspects of an adolescent social consciousness', in B.C. Malament (ed.), *After the Reformation* (Philadelphia, 1980), pp. 267–90.

96. P. Burke, *Popular Culture in Early Modern Europe* (London, 1978), p. 28.

97. R. Luckett, 'The collection: origins and history', in Weinstein, *Catalogue of the Pepys Library, Volume 2, Ballads Part 2*, pp. xi–xv.

and selling for from 3d. to 6d., were written principally for the gentry as well as for urban tradesmen.[98] Frances Wolfreston, member of the Staffordshire gentry, owned several of Taylor's books as well as other 'lighter and popular material', including jest books and a copy of *The Life and Death of the Famous Champion of England, S. George*.[99] Many of the ballads and chapbooks can be read as appealing to the elite: amusing the mature, instructing and entertaining the young. Ironically, it is very likely that this sector of society provided the purchasing power for the sales of large quantities of cheap literature. We may be sceptical of *Wanton Tom*'s claim to provide 'such pleasing Pastimes of Delight, That 'twould invite a Lady, Lord, or Knight To Read' – such advertisements may have been using a putative upper-class appeal to sell to other social groups – but the contents of some of the ballads and chapbooks certainly imply elite targeting.[100] They are crammed with gentry values, gentry heroes and heroines, woodcut representations of gentry demeanour and dress, and allusions to the classics which were the staple of a grammar-school and university education. This would help to explain the ballad and chapbook mockery of rural and lower-class characters, the mix of black-letter and roman, the references to classical characters, and the Latin phraseology.

VI

But the hierarchy of print is only part of the story. To understand early modern English culture we need to return to the importance of orality.[101] It is difficult for historians with their craft dependence on the written to grasp this other, unrecorded dimension. Of course we touch on this sphere when we ponder the rich, localised vocabulary which agricultural workers used to describe their natural environment, or when we read dialect dictionaries and collections of proverbs.[102]

98. Capp, *World of John Taylor*, p. 67.

99. P. Morgan, 'Frances Wolfreston and "Hor Bouks": A Seventeenth-Century Woman Book-Collector', *The Library* 11 (1989), 197–219.

100. *Wanton Tom: or the Merry History of Tom Stitch the Taylor* (1685): Pepys Chapbooks, Penny Merriments Collection, Vol. 1, no. 13.

101. For orality, see Houston, *Scottish Literacy*, ch. 6; A. Fox, 'Aspects of oral culture and its development in early modern England' (University of Cambridge, Ph.D., 1993).

102. K. Thomas, *Man and the Natural World* (London, 1983), pp. 70–87; J. Obelkevich, 'Proverbs and social history', in P. Burke and R. Porter (eds), *The Social History of Language* (Cambridge, 1987), ch. 3; D.R. Woolf, 'History, folklore and oral tradition in early modern England', *Past and Present* 120 (1988), 26–52; Fox, 'Aspects of oral culture', chs 2, 3.

But it is useful to remember that what we encounter is but a seg-
ment of long-vanished traditions. The political libels that survive in
manuscript, for example, are the mere shadow of this effective
discourse of political discontent.[103] We know of whole generations
of dialect verse never committed to writing and thus permanently
banished from the record.[104] Gone, too, are most of the early modern
work songs.[105]

Yet, as was suggested in the introduction to this chapter, this is
not to argue for some kind of pure, residual oral culture, entrenched
against a new literacy. In a dispute over tenant rights in Westmorland
in the 1620s, the protesting group's resolution – written by a vicar –
was read aloud publicly before several copies of the document were
distributed. A petition was drawn up and sent to London. Later, a
play, written this time by a schoolmaster, was performed, using the
protesting tenants as actors and depicting a Hell filled with landlords, puritans, and bailiffs, and the imagery of ravens (landlords)
feeding off sheep (poor people). In other words, this protest combined orality (reading the resolution out loud, dramatic performance) and literacy (writing the resolution, petition, and play), with
the vicar and schoolteacher acting as scribes or cultural brokers.[106]

It is the hybridity of print, orality, and literacy which is so important to this period. As Adam Fox has shown, the phenomenon of the
mocking rhyme – similar to the Westmorland incident – provides a
striking illustration of this interaction. Verses, rhymes, and ballads,
composed by a wide range of people, including those at the lower
level, were aimed at those who had offended the community in
some manner. They could be set to well-known tunes, recited and
thus learned orally, or written down on pieces of paper and posted
at a public venue where they would, in turn, be read aloud. The
composer did not need to be literate: Fox has found evidence of
people getting others to write out the rhymes for them. Pictorial
representations complemented the message, seizing the attention
of the viewer and conveying meaning to those unable to decipher

103. A. Bellany, ' "Raylinge rymes and vaunting verse": libellous politics in early
Stuart England, 1603–1628', in Sharpe and Lake (eds), *Culture and Politics*, ch. 11;
T. Cogswell, 'Underground verse and the transformation of early Stuart political
culture', in S.D. Amussen and M.A. Kishlansky (eds), *Political Culture and Cultural
Politics in Early Modern England* (Manchester, 1995), ch. 12.
    104. Vincent, *Literacy*, p. 199.
    105. G. Porter, ' "Work the old lady out of the ditch": singing at work by English
lacemakers', *Journal of Folklore Research* 31 (1994), 35–55; G. Porter, 'Cobblers all:
occupation as identity and cultural message', *Folk Music Journal* 7 (1995), 43–61.
    106. Campbell, *English Yeoman*, pp. 150–3.

handwriting. One sketch on the back of a ballad attached to a Sussex market cross in 1608 was said to have communicated 'even amongst the baser sort of people who doe the better remember and take greater apprehension . . . bye signes and pictures then by the bare report, seeing, reading or hearinge of the same'.[107] Some of these verses even managed to breach the local context by finding their way into print as ballads, setting off a potential new chain of interaction between orality and literacy.[108] Alastair Bellany's study of political libels likewise demonstrates a mix of orality and literacy: mocking verse, ballads, and rhyming couplets were written, copied, memorised, spoken and whispered, sung, and left in public places.[109]

VII

It is vital to be aware of what could be termed the orality of popular print. Watt has reminded us that the single-sheet ballad was not just a text to be read or an image to be stuck on the wall but also a song to be sung.[110] Singers varied from the minstrels whose repertoire was based principally on an oral tradition, though not unaffected by the printed ballad, to the pedlar who cried out the ballad along with other wares, and the amateur who learned such songs. They were sung at work, fairs, markets, in alehouses, and in, and outside, plays.[111] It is also important to be aware of the tunes – a thousand or more – which lay behind the printed word.[112] Many different ballads were sung to the same tune; the prompt would be in the words at the top of the ballad sheet: 'To the tune of . . .'. But the melodies themselves were transmitted orally. One nineteenth-century seller said that the tune was the most important ingredient in a fast-selling ballad.[113]

Many ballads exhorted potential purchasers to 'listen'; sale and performance went hand in hand.[114] Natascha Wurzbach has cleverly used the early modern ballad texts to sketch out the possibilities of

---

107. A. Fox, 'Popular verses and their readership in the early seventeenth century', in J. Raven, H. Small, and N. Tadmor (eds), *The Practice and Representation of Reading in England* (Cambridge, 1996), p. 131. See also, A. Fox, 'Ballads, libels and popular ridicule in Jacobean England', *Past and Present* 145 (1994), 47–83; and M. Ingram's earlier analysis of mocking verse in his 'Ridings, rough music, and mocking rhymes in early modern England', in Reay (ed.), *Popular Culture*, ch. 5.

108. Fox, 'Ballads, libels', p. 145. 109. Bellany, 'Raylinge rymes'.

110. Watt, *Cheap Print*, p. 6. 111. Ibid., ch. 1. 112. Ibid., p. 33.

113. Mayhew, *London Labour*, Vol. 1, p. 275.

114. N. Wurzbach, *The Rise of the English Street Ballad, 1550–1650* (Cambridge, 1990), pp. 13–17.

performance: the creation of sensation, sentimentality, or horror; the drawing in of the listener through personalised appeal; the claims to authenticity; the use of colloquialisms.[115] We can predict the performative potentials of the voyeuristic ballads in which the narrators recount watching lovers:

> I laid me down and I listen'd a while,
> To hear if the Man could the Maiden beguile.[116]

Sometimes it was requited love, sometimes it was an unrequited passion which ended in tragedy, but the eye-witness fiction was a common technique to engage the hearer.[117] A few authors recounted their own supposed experiences so that the reader or listener became a voyeur of rape or other predatory sexual behaviour.[118]

It is possible to picture the performance of *Comical News from Bloomsbury*, a ballad about a woman who assumed the identity of a man and who courted and married a gentlewoman, living with her for a month and 'using a strange Instrument for generation':

> But what he did with it, or whether 'twas put
> I'll leave you good Folks to consider:
> The innocent Bride no difference knew,
> and seem'd to be greatly delighted;
> But Lasses I'll warrant there's none among you
> that would be so cleverly cheated.[119]

We can assume the comic potential of *The Wanton Widows pleasant Mistake*, a song recounting the story of a widow who slept with a carved model of her dead husband, Simon. The ballad describes how a suitor managed to substitute himself for the carving one night, with predictable consequences:

> She thought she toucht somthing that did not feel wooden
> For something she felt which was all soft and warm,
> Nay, at last something stir'd too; but thinking no harm
> She hug'd him still closer, resolv'd to be try'd,
> What had alter'd the wooden old Sim by her side.

The song ends with the ravenous couple consuming vast quantities of food the following day, and burning the wooden Simon for fuel.[120]

It is likely that the printed ballads are sanitised versions of more earthy, oral renderings – though not as self-censored as those

---

115. Ibid., chs 1–3.   116. Day (ed.), *Pepys Ballads*, Vol. 3, p. 3.
117. E.g. ibid., Vol. 1, pp. 264–5, 354–5, 360–1, Vol. 3, pp. 3, 35, 139.
118. Ibid., Vol. 3, pp. 78, 132, Vol. 4, p. 20.   119. Ibid., Vol. 5, p. 424.
120. Ibid., Vol. 3, p. 306.

collected by the genteel folklorists of recent centuries. Francis Place remembered ballads from the 1780s, including one about a man whose wife's sexual demands reduced him to a skeleton. Place recalled the rousing finale:

> For which I'm sure she'll go to Hell
> For she makes me fuck her in churchtime.[121]

Such performative elements have disappeared for ever as far as the early modern material is concerned – the inflections of tone, the facial expressions, bodily gestures, and the rapport with the audience which is central to every oral rendition.[122] A nineteenth-century ballad seller, who could sing the songs he sold and was able to remember others from past repertoires, told Mayhew that he could flatter a servant girl into buying a ballad by pretending that he mistook her for her lady: that 'chloroforms her'.[123] 'Sandman Joe', another song in Place's remembered collection – note that he had committed oral memory to writing – had lines such as:

> Why blast you, Sall, I loves you!
> And for to prove what I have said,
> This night I'll soundly fuck you.

Place recalled that the female performers, who sang the song on Saturday nights outside an alehouse off the Strand, thrust their bodies backwards and forwards to simulate intercourse, and imitated orgasm. 'This used to produce great shouts of applause at the end.'[124] Nor can we enter what Peter Bailey has so aptly described as the 'conspiracies of meaning', the cultural collusion at the heart of popular performance and which lay behind the 'knowing looks' of Mayhew's street entertainers.[125]

Reading aloud was one of the main bridges between literacy and orality. Those who could not read had ballads pasted to their

121. Quoted by V.A.C. Gatrell, *The Hanging Tree: Execution and the English People 1770–1868* (Oxford, 1994), p. 137. Spufford remarks of the bawdy humour of the chapbooks, 'it is still practically unquotable, even by a woman writing now' (Spufford, *Small Books*, p. 62). Even so, it is relatively clean compared to the performances recorded by Place.

122. One has only to experience the modern-day performance of the southern Chinese narrative songs, *Pingtan*, to become aware of the blandness of mere words on a page.

123. Mayhew, *London Labour*, Vol. 1, p. 227.

124. Gatrell, *Hanging Tree*, pp. 138, 152–3.

125. P. Bailey, 'Conspiracies of meaning: music hall and the knowingness of popular culture', *Past and Present* 144 (1994), 138–70. See also the important contributions to J.S. Bratton (ed.), *Music Hall: Performance and Style* (Milton Keynes, 1986). For Mayhew's reference to 'knowing' looks, see Mayhew, *London Labour*, Vol. 1, p. 41.

cottage walls so that they could get literate visitors to convert print to the spoken word.[126] A potential purchaser of a ballad in William Cavendish's play, *The Triumphant Widow* (1677), asked the pedlar to tell him the contents because he could not read. However, his inability to read did not prevent him from learning the contents of the printed sheets; he later said to a companion,

> Oh Cicely, here's the brave Ballet you and I use to sing,
> I know it by the Picture.[127]

An eighteenth-century pedlar recalled having seen ballads pasted to the walls of the numerous rural cottages and alehouses which he visited: much as in the labourer's cottage in Clare's poem, 'Dobson and Judie', with its

> . . . Ballads, songs, and Cutts, that hide
> Both window-shutters, wall, and door,
> Which tell of many-a-murder'd bride
> And desperate Battles daubed oer.[128]

Mayhew said that the nineteenth-century costermongers of London, most of whom could neither read nor write, enjoyed having newspapers or periodicals read aloud to them. They would interact with the verbal text, commenting, reacting, or shouting out when they became particularly engaged by what the reader was saying. They would also purchase printed material with illustrations and ask readers to explain the content of the accompanying story. One seller of gallows literature told Mayhew that he had seen a group of Norfolk villagers sitting in a cottage while an old man read a broadsheet relating a recent execution. He said that in such villages it was not unknown for two poor families to club together to find the 1d. needed for an execution broadsheet.[129]

Although generations of literary scholars and historians were oblivious to the historical and cultural construction of reading, it is now clear that when people in the early modern world wrote (or talked) of reading they frequently meant reading aloud rather than silently. Reading could be a performative rather than a contemplative experience. In *Dobsons Drie Bobbes*, for example, a black-letter jest book published in 1607, the narrator actually says, 'Thus is George Dobson (as you have *heard*)', and another book of humorous stories, the *Cobbler of Canterbury*, opens by referring to it being read

126. Watt, *Cheap Print*, pp. 12–13.
127. Extract in Wurzbach, *Rise of the English Street Ballad*, Appendix, pp. 280–2.
128. Vincent, *Literacy*, pp. 197–8; *Early Poems of John Clare*, Vol. 1, p. 175.
129. Mayhew, *London Labour*, Vol. 1, pp. 25, 280–1.

aloud.[130] Naomi Tadmor has shown that much reading in the household of the eighteenth-century shopkeeper, Thomas Turner, was
done aloud, as a social activity, involving social interaction between
Turner and his wife, as well as with the couple's servants, neighbours, and kin.[131] The same was true of the household of Pepys.[132]

Historians have not been sufficiently alert to the myriad ways in
which orality suffused the world of print. Normally a distinction is
drawn between the chapbook and the ballad: the former prose, the
latter verse and hence more attuned to orality. In fact many of the
chapbooks are in verse, or are a mixture of prose and rhyme, lending themselves to memorisation and/or performance as compel-
lingly as any street ballad. The common technique of dialogue in
prose also suited the frames of orality. *John & his Mistris Or A Merry
Dialogue Betwixt the Wanton Wife, And her Handsome Prentice*, for
example, reads almost like a play.[133] The form of the chapbook
'pleasant histories' – broken into short chapters or sections with
introductory résumés, integral in themselves yet held together by
the continuity of the central character – was ideal for short periods
of reading.[134] *The Pinder of Wakefield* (1632) is an extremely interesting example of the mix. While it is itself printed, it has what its
editor has described as a 'colloquial breathlessness', an 'impromptu
quality'. The reader can easily imagine the work being read aloud
or even think of the piece as an oral 'text'. Furthermore, the story
is interspersed with jokes, stories, ballads, proverbs, and catches or
rounds. It resonates with orality, and actually concludes with a ballad, a later version of which appears in the Child Collection. There
were also sixteenth-century ballad and play versions of the story.[135]

Bridging did not need to occur through direct reading of a text.
Those able to read could have memorised written narratives or

130. E.A. Horsman (ed.), *Dobsons Drie Bobbes: a Story of Sixteenth-Century Durham*
(Oxford, 1955), p. 12; *Cobbler of Canterbury*, p. 3.

131. N. Tadmor, '"In the even my wife read to me": women, reading and household life in the eighteenth century', in Raven, Small, and Tadmor (eds), *Practice and
Representation*, ch. 9.

132. M.S. Dawson, 'Pepysian texts and the exploration of early modern English
culture' (University of Auckland, MA, 1997), p. 109.

133. Pepys Chapbooks, Penny Merriments Collection, Vol. 1, no. 35.

134. See discussions of the French equivalent to the chapbook: H.-J. Martin,
'The bibliotheque bleue', *Publishing History* 3 (1978), 70–102; R. Chartier, 'The
bibliotheque bleue and popular reading', in Chartier, *Cultural Uses of Print*, ch. 7.

135. E.A. Horsman (ed.), *The Pinder of Wakefield* (Liverpool, 1956), pp. viii, xii. It
has been described by Bernard Capp as a chapbook, but it is about 70 pages long
and therefore much more substantial than a chapbook, although it has many of the
characteristics of that type. For the Child ballad, see F.J. Child (ed.), *The English and
Scottish Popular Ballads*, 5 vols (New York, 1965 edn), Vol. 3, pp. 131–2.

texts and then recited them in relay – much in the way of the oral folklore – to non-reading hearers.[136] This is probably what happened in Clare's village when the gleaners paused to rest in the shade to listen to the songs and stories of the old women, including the story of the chapbook hero, Thomas Hickathrift:

> Here Lubin listn'd wi a struck supprise
> When hickerthrifts great strength has met his ear
> How he killd jiants as they were but flies
> & lifted trees as one would lift a spear
> & not much bigger then his fellows where
> He knew no troubles waggoners have known
> Of getting stalld & such dissasters drear
> Up hed chuck sacks as one woud hurl a stone
> & draw whole loads of grain unaided & alone.[137]

The narrator of the *Cobbler of Canterbury* refers to it providing old wives with the opportunity 'to learne a tale to tell amongst their gosseps'.[138] The white-letter chapbook, *Canterbury Tales* (1687), by 'Chaucer Junior', advertised itself as a source of stories for tradesmen and craftsmen and their wives to tell their customers at forge, bakehouse, mill, inn, and coffee-house. The jests, stories, and songs which it provided were to be read, learned, and passed on.[139]

The cultural loops between the printed and oral ballad are particularly intriguing. Oral ballads were recorded in print and then fed back to oral transmission; printed ballads were sung out, remembered, and then collected later as traditional or folk ballads.[140] Dianne Dugaw's work on Anglo-American folksong is critical of drawing distinctions between the written and oral in this genre. Commercial, printed transmission has been central to the history, survival, and development of the female warrior ballads which she has studied, and she describes them – and Anglo-American folksong in general – as 'simultaneously commercial, non-commercial, written, printed, and oral'.[141] A study of the folksongs collected early in the twentieth century has argued similarly that the vast majority

136. R. Chartier, 'Leisure and sociability: reading aloud in early modern Europe', in S. Zimmerman and R.F.E. Weissman (eds), *Urban Life in the Renaissance* (London, 1989), ch. 4.

137. Robinson and Powell (eds), *Early Poems of John Clare*, Vol. 2, p. 146.

138. *Cobbler of Canterbury*, p. 3.

139. Pepys Chapbooks, Penny Merriments Collection, Vol. 2, no. 12.

140. Houston, *Scottish Literacy*, p. 206.

141. D.M. Dugaw, 'Anglo-American folksong reconsidered: the interface of oral and written forms', *Western Folklore* 43 (1984), 102–3. See also, D. Dugaw, *Warrior Women and Popular Balladry, 1650–1850* (Cambridge, 1989).

derived from printed ballads, and that a substantial number come from ballads published before the beginning of the eighteenth century.[142]

While the preliminary quantitative evidence (based on titles rather than actual content) is somewhat inconclusive, there may well be a link between British folk stories and the subject matter of chapbooks and ballads.[143] Certain characters – the Blind Beggar of Bethnal Green, Dick Whittington, Fair Rosamond, Faustus, Fortunatus, Friar Bacon, Guy of Warwick, Jane Shore, Long Meg, Mother Shipton, Patient Griselda, the Pinder of Wakefield, Robin Hood, St George, Thomas Hickathrift, Tom Thumb – appear again and again, over centuries, in ballads, chapbook histories, plays, puppet shows, and folk stories, once again evidence of the intermingling of orality and print.[144]

Guy of Warwick provides a good example. Books about this chivalric hero were in print before 1500, and by the beginning of the seventeenth century *Guy* was one of the romances mentioned as having unhealthy influences on the young. Different versions of the story were published from the late sixteenth century, with ballads, borrowed from oral tradition, introducing new elements into the narrative. There was a play by John Day and Thomas Dekker, performed many times in the first half of the seventeenth century. Ballad, chapbook, and book (c. 150 pages) versions of *Guy*, published in the second half of the seventeenth century, ensured that he was a genuinely popular hero.[145] When Samuel Pepys wanted to demonstrate the ubiquity of ballads dealing with the Duke of Albermarle, he referred to the popularity of Guy: 'there are so many, that hereafter will sound like *Guy of Warwicke*'.[146] Although the order or hierarchy of influences is obscure, the story of Guy of Warwick clearly represented a synthesis between folklore and print. During her visit to Warwick in 1697, Celia Fiennes was regaled with

142. Spufford, 'Pedlar', p. 20.   143. Ibid., pp. 20–1.

144. For chapbooks, see Pepys collection; Spufford, *Small Books*; Watt, *Cheap Print*, ch. 7; and J. Ashton (ed.), *Chap-books of the Eighteenth Century* (London, n.d.). For plays, see the list in A. Gurr, *The Shakespearean Stage, 1574–1642* (Cambridge, 1980 edn), pp. 216–28; R.A. Foakes and R.T. Rickert (eds), *Henslowe's Diary* (Cambridge, 1961); and M. Summers, *The Playhouse of Pepys* (New York, 1964). For puppets, see G. Speaight, *The History of the English Puppet Theatre* (London, 1990 edn), pp. 324–43. And for folktales, see K.M. Briggs, *A Dictionary of British Folk-tales in the English Language, Part A and Part B* (London, 1991 edn), indexes to story titles.

145. See Crane, 'Vogue of *Guy of Warwick*', and also Richmond's fascinating tracing of the legend through from the fourteenth to the late twentieth centuries: Richmond, *Legend of Guy of Warwick*.

146. R. Latham and W. Matthews (eds), *The Diary of Samuel Pepys*, 11 vols (London, 1970–83), Vol. 8, p. 99.

a history of Guy Earle of Warwick, there is his walking staff 9 foote long and the staff of a Gyant which he kill'd thats 12 foote long, his sword helmet and shield and breast and back all of a prodigious size, as is his wives iron slippers and also his horses armour and the pottage-pott for his supper, it was a yard over the top; there is also the bones of severall Beasts he kill'd, the rib of the Dun-Cow [actually a whale bone] as bigg as halfe a great cart wheele; 2 miles from the town is his Cave dugg out by his own hands just the dimention of his body as the common people say, there is also his will cut out on stone but the letters are much defaced; these are the storyes and meer fiction for the true history of Guy was that he was but a little man in stature, tho' great in mind and valour, which tradition describes to posterity by being a Gyant; such will the account be of our Hero King William the Third tho' little in stature yet great in achievements and valour.[147]

There may also have been interaction between the printed ballads and chapbooks and the English folk-plays, but this subject is somewhat more contentious.[148]

VIII

Theatre was very much a part of the cultural world which we have been traversing.[149] Plays were themselves products of literacy: playwrights *wrote* plays. Some were also printed; only a fraction of the actual number performed in the period before the 1640s, and the vast majority of those performed for the first time after 1660. However, the essence of drama was (is) performative; plays were written to be seen and heard rather than to be read. Literacy, as Andrew Gurr has put it, was not a necessary qualification to participate in the culture of the playhouse.[150] And participate many did. Gurr has estimated over 50 million visits to playhouses from 1560 to 1642. Alan Botica has calculated annual attendances of up to 200,000 a year in the 1660s and 1670s. In the first three decades of the eighteenth century, Augustan audiences in London saw nearly 12,000 performances of almost 900 different plays.[151]

147. C. Morris (ed.), *The Illustrated Journeys of Celia Fiennes 1685–c. 1712* (London, 1982), pp. 115–16.

148. Compare Spufford, *Small Books*, pp. 11–12, 227–31; and R. Hutton, *The Stations of the Sun: a History of the Ritual Year in Britain* (Oxford, 1996), ch. 7.

149. See D.M. Bergeron (ed.), *Reading and Writing in Shakespeare* (London, 1996).

150. A. Gurr, 'Theatre and society', in J. Morrill (ed.), *The Oxford Illustrated History of Tudor and Stuart Britain* (Oxford, 1996), p. 168.

151. Gurr, *Playgoing*, p. 4; A.R. Botica, 'Audience, playhouse and play in Restoration theatre, 1660–1710' (University of Oxford, D.Phil., 1985), p. 133; G.W. Stone,

Even so, mixed literacies brought mixed readings. The gentry, with their classical education, would pick up on references which would have been meaningless to the less educated. Some playwrights were adept at providing allusions for 'learned ears'.[152] If the play was printed, the discerning reader would have had even greater opportunity to search for learned citations. Wit, missed in the noise of performance, could be savoured at leisure. John Dryden thought that performance 'cast a mist', and that 'the propriety of thoughts and words' needed to be seen in print.[153] Pepys said that Ben Jonson's *Catiline* was 'only to be read' – 'a play of much good sense and words to read, but that doth appear the worst upon the stage'.[154] Plots could be summarised or commented on in commonplace books or journals: Pepys's diary is an important source for Restoration theatre history.

Playgoing had remarkable similarities to the consumption of literature discussed earlier. Just as print was consumed by a wide social profile who read and heard differently, early modern plays were attended by a mix of people who derived a variety of messages. Some dipped into performance much as they would a book, returning again and again to the playhouse to see the same play and deriving something different from each 'reading'. Pepys learned a dance from *The Tempest*; he liked the costumes and the fighting in *Catiline*. He treated a play like a 'collection of fragmented entertainments: a diversity of pleasures, each weighted independently from the others'.[155] Just as the printed literature offered varied fare, the sheer range of drama had something for the gentry, those engaged in trades and crafts, and their apprentices and servants, women as well as men: the choice of traditional romance, classical allusion, wit, spectacle, and blood and gore. As with books, variety of taste was also catered for within individual plays. By the early decades of the seventeenth century, observers in London were making a basic distinction between the theatre-going of gentlemen and that of those whom (in their more polite moments) they termed 'citizens' – the one, as James Shirley intimated in 1640, preferring cool wit, the other ballads, clowns, devils, and fighting.[156]

'The making of the repertory', in R.D. Hume (ed.), *The London Theatre World, 1660–1800* (Carbondale, Ill., 1980), p. 194.

152. Gurr, *Playgoing*, ch. 4, esp. pp. 98–105: 'Learned ears'.

153. Quoted in Botica, 'Audience', pp. 162–3.

154. Latham and Matthews (eds), *Diary of Samuel Pepys*, Vol. 9, p. 395.

155. Botica, 'Audience', p. 142.

156. Gurr, *Playgoing*, p. 259. For women in the audience, see R. Levin, 'Women in the Renaissance theatre audience', *Shakespeare Quarterly* 40 (1989), 165–74.

The civil wars and English Revolution mark a dividing point in early modern theatre history. In the period up to 1642, audiences at the private playhouses or halls, Blackfriars, Whitefriars, Salisbury Court, the Cockpit, with their admission prices of between 6d. and 2s. 6d., were equivalent to the readers of the more expensive books. These halls held up to 700 people and attracted the gentry and more wealthy middling sort. The public playhouses or amphitheatres, the Fortune, Globe, Red Bull, Rose, Swan, the Theatre, with admission prices from 1d. to 1s., drew audiences which were the theatrical equivalent of the ballad and small-book reader.[157] Accommodating several thousand in comparison to the halls' hundreds, the bulk of the amphitheatres' clientele was the middling and poorer sort: 'Citizens, and the meaner sort of People', as a late-seventeenth-century observer noted.[158] Thus Thomas Dekker's *The Shoemaker's Holiday* (1599) and Thomas Heywood's *The Four Prentices of London* (1600), with their apprentice and journeyman heroes, played at the 'citizen playhouses'; while Francis Beaumont's *The Knight of the Burning Pestle* (1607), which satirises grocers and their tastes (including the citizen character's fondness for the *Four Prentices*), was written for the more exclusive audience at the private playhouse.[159] Plays with the same subject matter as the ballads and chapbooks, Henry Chettle and John Day's *The Blind Beggar of Bednal Green* (1600), and Chettle, Dekker, and William Haughton's *Patient Grissil* (1600), were performed at the penny theatres.[160] We should recall that ballads were sung as endpieces after plays. After 1660, playhouses were exclusively of the private playhouse or hall variety: small and sumptuous, catering mainly for an elite clientele. Seating prices began at the upper range of the old public playhouse rates, at 1s. for the upper gallery, 1s. 6d. for the middle gallery, 2s. 6d. for the pit, and 4s. for boxes.[161]

Although public/private theatres set a basic division between gentry and citizen, both types recognised social divisions in their seating and pricing arrangements (in one, the gentry sitting closest to the stage, in the other the poor standing in the pit), so while the overall tone of the production could be set by the nature of the venue, plays were performed to mixed audiences at either theatre. The situation in the period before the 1640s was very similar to the gentry amphibiousness noted earlier. 'The rich and the poor audiences were not mutually exclusive; rather the rich went to public

157. Gurr, *Shakespearean Stage*, pp. 11–12, 115; Gurr, *Playgoing*, chs 2, 3.
158. Gurr, *Shakespearean Stage*, p. 199.   159. Ibid., pp. 14–18.
160. Ibid., pp. 216–28.   161. Botica, 'Audience', pp. 15, 129.

and private playhouse alike, the poor more exclusively to the public.'[162] The public option did not exist during the Restoration,
however. Although a range of social groups attended the Carolean
playhouses, and citizens provided up to a third of the takings and a
half of the audiences in some performances (as they sat in the galleries, often to hear and see their social type mocked), it is likely that
prices deterred the vast majority from regular playgoing during
this period.[163] Pepys limited himself to the 12d. and 18d. seats for
many years, and if he was constrained by the cost of the cheapest
seats, the majority of the middle sort of people must have thought
even more about such expenditure.[164] There is no need to deny
the presence of what has been termed the 'invisible audience' of
the darkened galleries (literally hidden in contrast to the well-lit
elite and aspiring elite on display in the boxes and pit below), but
the 'ordinary people', 'prentices', and 'citizens', though often complained of, are hardly likely to have represented the bulk of London's population. Despite the impressive attendance figures quoted
earlier, only 5 to 11 per cent of the city's population attended the
theatre each year.[165] Attendance figures – like book sales – are
skewed by individual multiple consumers.

IX

It is difficult to find a simple description for the cultural terrain that
we have been mapping. David Hall considers what he has termed
the 'traditional literacy' of early modern Europe and European
America to be characterised by reading being valued over writing as
a cultural skill, the importance of reading aloud and memorising,
the limited impact of books because of cost and distribution, and
people's contact with a narrow range of printed items which were
read slowly and with intensity.[166] Although this description captures
important elements of the borderland region between literacy and
orality, 'traditional literacy' will hardly do for the complex mix of
literacy and orality that we have encountered. V.A.C. Gatrell comes
closer with his vivid portrayal of the culture of the early modern

162. Gurr, *Shakespearean Stage*, p. 199.
163. For takings and audience numbers at two performances in 1677, see Botica,
'Audience', p. 112.
164. Latham and Matthews (eds), *Diary of Samuel Pepys*, Vol. 9, p. 2.
165. Botica, 'Audience', pp. 25–6, 157.
166. Hall, *Culture of Print*, pp. 36–78, esp. 57.

public execution, where woodcut pictures, ballads, both printed and sung, stories, gossip, graffiti, street drama, and remembered and recounted experience 'wove a collective idea of the scaffold in the space between print and orality'.[167] But 'spaces', 'margins', and 'borderlands' do not adequately describe the sheer cultural range of a world which encompassed the rural orality of the young John Clare and the urban literacy of Nehemiah Wallington. The important work of Laura Gowing on litigation in early modern London suggests that popular culture contained a series of family stories of violent husbands and unruly wives, gendered narratives of sex and marriage, romance, conflict, and fantasy, found not only in the repertoire of chapbook, ballad, and folktale, but in the stories told by those who appeared in court. She writes of 'a stock of stories in both oral and printed form whose contexts, events, and results could be rifled for the tales told in everyday life, in the moments of dispute, and at court'.[168] And these stories, in turn, would become part of the store or repertoire. It is the overlaps and hybridity that are so important in the cultural history of early modern England – in particular, the omnipresent, though often ignored, orality of print.

167. Gatrell, *Hanging Tree*, chs 4–5 (the quote comes from p. 119).
168. L. Gowing, *Domestic Dangers: Women, Words, and Sex in Early Modern London* (Oxford, 1996), pp. 42–4, 52–8, 232–62. The quote comes from p. 58.

CHAPTER THREE

Religions

I

Arthur Dent's *Plaine Mans Path-way to Heaven* (1601) was written in dialogue form 'for the better understanding of the simple'. Over 400 pages in length, it is essentially a lesson in enthusiastic Protestantism. The characters are Theologus, a divine; Philagathus, one of the godly; Asunetus, an ignorant man; and Antilegon, a sceptic. The dialogue between the godly character and the divine allows for a display of Protestant doctrine, including an exposition of predestinarian theology, and guidance to godly living. The other two characters represent (respectively) the benign ignorance of the multitude and the more wilful hostility of a small group of sceptics. It is interesting that the ignorant man is brought to God but that the conversion of the sceptic is never on the agenda. It is also significant that – in 1601 – Catholicism is barely represented. Catholics appear as Papists, invoked as a kind of archetypal evil, either as examples of 'the most wicked men', those who will not be saved, or as the true personae of 'carnall Protestants' who make an outward show of religion but whose 'heart is with Poperie: they have a Pope in their belly'.[1]

The book culminates in the conversion of the ignorant man. Hence the author of *Plaine Mans Path-way*, an Essex preacher, describes it as a comedy rather than a tragedy, that is beginning with sorrow and ending in joy rather than starting with joy and finishing in sorrow. The expositions of the divine are in black-letter type and those of the other characters in white-letter, presumably because it

---

1. A. Dent, *The Plaine Mans Path-way to Heaven* (London, 1601; repr. Theatrum Orbis Terrarum, Amsterdam, 1974), pp. 17, 18, 140.

is important for his message to get across to the simple, those thought to be more at ease with the older form of print. The tract is interesting too for its internal tensions, the very real danger that its readers would not necessarily find the argument of the divine the most convincing, even though the form and structure of the book – authorial intent – leans in that direction. Readers may well have read (or heard) selectively, being more convinced by the arguments of the sceptic or the common sense of the ignorant character. It is also possible that the statements of the theologian were interpreted with discrimination, with more attention being given to his denunciations of oppression, say, than his condemnation of idleness. However, the main reason for beginning with Dent's book is that it is a good summary of religious cultures at the start of the seventeenth century, an ideal entry into the religious world of early modern England.

The different types of religion are set out cumulatively. The sceptic is a foil to the godliness of Theologus and Philagathus. He represents a different social ideal, one where going to the alehouse and playing for ale is but 'good fellowship, and a good meanes to increase love amongst neighbours'. When Asunetus becomes depressed about his spiritual state, Antilegon recommends that he turn to a chapbook or jest book, 'pleasant and merry bookes' sure to cure his 'dumpishness'. Antilegon's hostility to the godly is obvious: 'a company of . . . controllers', 'these scripture men: you are all of the spirit: you are so full of it, that it runneth out at your nostrils'. Although, significantly, he never doubts the existence of God, the sceptic does believe that the scriptures are but 'mens inventions', that there is no hell except for the hell of a person's conscience, and that God can be served well enough without preaching. In contrast to the divine's division of humankind into the elect and the reprobate, Antilegon is 'of the minde that all men shalbe saved: for Gods mercy is above all his works. Say you what you will, and what you can, God did not make us, to condemne us.' 'I can hardly be perswaded that God made so many thousands to cast them away, when he hath done. Do you thinke that God hath made us, to condemne us?' The sceptic was not troubled about his salvation: 'if I may have space and grace, and time to repent before death, and to ask God forgivenesse, and say my prayers, and cry God mercy, I hope I shall do well inough'.[2]

2. Ibid., pp. 186, 293, 295, 299, 300, 302, 303, 305, 307, 408.

Theologus and Philagathus represent the author's preferred reading of the text. They are archetypal Puritans. The divine is responsible for the rather dark tone of the book, for if its structure is comedic, much of the tone is tragic. Arthur Dent's age is an 'age of iron'; his world is 'this theatre of misery'. Nearly a half of the text's pages deal with the signs of damnation or condemnation, nine in all: pride, whoredom, covetousness, contempt of the gospel, swearing, lying, drunkenness, idleness, and oppression. Infection with three of these is enough to 'poyson the soule, and sting it to death'. This focus upon damnation provides denunciations of pride in apparel, particularly of women, with their painted faces, 'laying open of naked breasts, dying of haire, wearing of Periwigges'. There are eloquent descriptions of the temptations of the flesh: 'men are so violently carried after their lusts, and so desperately bent, that they wil have the present sweet, and pleasure of sinne, come of it what will'. The 'great strength' of the world

> lieth in her two brests, the one of pleasure, the other of profit: for she like a notable strumpet by laying out these her breasts, doth bewitch the sonnes of men, and allureth thousands to her lust; for if shee cannot winne them with the one breast, yet she gaineth them with the other: if not with pleasure, then with profit: if not with profit, then with pleasure. He is an odde man of a thousand, that sucketh not on the one breast, or the other. But sure it is, which soever he sucketh, he shall be poysoned: for she giveth none other milke but ranke poyson. The world therefore is like to an alluring Jaell, which sitteth at her doore to entise us to come in, and eate of the milke of her pleasures: but when she hath once got us in, she is readie (even while we are eating) with her hammer, and her naile, to pierce through our braines.[3]

Unsurprisingly, Theologus was of the opinion that few would be saved. 'I thinke they would be very fewe in every Village, Towne, and Citie. I doubt they would walke very thinly in the streets, so as a man might easily tel them as they goe.' The 'number of the Elect is very small, and when all comes to all, fewe shall be saved'.[4]

However, the divine was also keen to convey the more positive side of predestinarian doctrine. In reply to the sceptic's observation that 'the preaching and publishing of this doctrine of predestination hath done much hurt', he stressed its 'great and comfortable use':

---

3. Ibid., pp. 35, 45, 49, 64–5, 82, 90–1, 93.   4. Ibid., pp. 287, 289.

> when once the Lords people perceive by their sanctification, and
> newe birth, both that the Lord hath rejected and reprobated so
> many thousande thousandes, and made choise of them to bee heires
> of his most glorious kingdome: being in themselves of the same
> moulde and making that others are: and that he hath done al this of
> his free grace, and undeserved mercy towardes them. Oh how doth
> it ravish their hearts with the love of him: Againe: how frankly, and
> chearfully, doo they serve him . . .[5]

This brand of Christianity left no room for individual behaviour
determining or influencing a person's salvation: 'Gods eternall
predestination excludeth all merites of man, and all power of his
will, thereby to attaine unto eternall life: and that his free mercy,
and undeserved favour, is both the beginning, the middest, and
the ende of our salvation. That is to say, all is of him, and nothing
of our selves.'[6] However, there was a clear focus on human action as
a reflection of an individual's spiritual state. The eight 'signes of
salvation' or 'infallible notes and tokens of a regenerate minde'
were love to the children of God, delight in the word of God, often
and fervent prayer, zeal of God's glory, self denial, patience, faith-
fulness in calling, and honest dealing. When asked again for some
of the signs of election – 'whether the state of a mans soule before
God, may not by certaine signes and tokens, bee certainly discerned
even in this life' – the divine mentioned reverence of God's name,
keeping of the sabbath, truth, sobriety, industry, compassion, humil-
ity, chastity, and contentment. Indeed, the dialogues keep returning
to the signs of election, how a person might know that he or she was
one of the elect. When Theologus rejects Antilegon's assumption
that he will be saved, he resorts again to behaviour as a mark of
salvation:

> there is nothing in you of those things, which the scriptures do
> affirme, must be in al those that shall be saved. There be none of the
> forenamed signes and tokens in you. You are ignorant, prophane,
> and carelesse. God is not worshipped under your roofe. There is no
> true feare of God in your selfe, nor in your houshold. You seldome
> heare the word preached. You content your selfe with an ignorant
> Minister. You have no praiers in your family: No reading, no singing
> of Psalmes, no instructions, exhortations, or admonitions, or any
> other Christian exercises. You make no conscience of the observa-
> tion of the Sabbath . . .[7]

Hence the potential for a godly culture, to which we will return later.

5. Ibid., pp. 320–3.   6. Ibid., p. 318.   7. Ibid., pp. 257, 259, 274–5, 277–8.

The final character, the target of the book's Protestant message, is the ignorant Asunetus, representative of a widespread parish Christianity, the 'common opinion, that if a man that holde the trueth in judgement, be no Papist, or hereticke, but leadeth an honest civill life, then he must of necessitie be saved'. Here the emphasis is unambiguously on human actions as a determiner of salvation, in what has been termed a type of pelagianism. In the words of the divine, the common people think that 'all Religion consisteth in the outward service of God, though their hearts be far from him'. The scriptures and preaching, so central to enthusiastic Protestantism, play little part in Asunetus's religious framework: 'I cannot read, and therefore I cannot tell what Christ or Saint Paul may say: but this I am sure of, that God is a good man, he is mercifull, and that we must be saved by our good prayers, and good serving of God.' Until the divine casts doubt, the ignorant character is confident that if he lives well he will be saved: 'For so long as I doo, as I woulde bee done too, and say no bodie no harme, nor doo no bodie no harme, GOD will have mercie on my soule. And I doubt not but my good deedes shall weigh against my evill deedes: and that I shall make even with God at my latter ende.' 'I knowe, that so long as I keepe his Commaundements, and live as my neighbours doo, and as a Christian man ought to doo, he will not damne my soule.'[8]

'How does one discover what "the people" believed over 400 years ago?' Geoffrey Elton asked in 1977.[9] This field of research has been transformed in the twenty years since Elton's rhetorical musing. There are detailed studies of the grass-roots implementation of the various legislative measures impacting on religious practice. We have both an intricate picture at parish level, based on churchwardens' accounts, and a more general (and controversial) view of regional changes derived from the religious preambles of wills.[10] By counting the numbers of communion tokens distributed to parishioners, historians have provided parish estimates for the percentage

8. Ibid., pp. 18, 29, 142, 342.
9. G.R. Elton, *Reform and Reformation: England 1509–1558* (London, 1977), p. 369. For two successful recent attempts, see P. Collinson, 'Popular and unpopular religion', in his *The Religion of Protestants: the Church in English Society 1559–1625* (Oxford, 1982), ch. 5; and M. Ingram, 'From reformation to toleration: popular religious cultures in England, 1540–1690', in T. Harris (ed.), *Popular Culture in England, c. 1500–1850* (London, 1995), ch. 5. For an important, and relevant, survey of religion in New England, see D.D. Hall, *Worlds of Wonder, Days of Judgment: Popular Religious Belief in Early New England* (New York, 1989).
10. See the works mentioned in notes 15 and 16 below.

of the eligible population attending church at Easter to receive communion.[11] David Cressy has explored the religious significance of the early modern life-cycle rituals of birth, marriage, and death, and the multiple impact of Protestantism upon their observances.[12]

Yet there is a niggling sense in which Elton was right. It is possible to gauge in great detail what the churches looked like at a particular time, what their official teachings were, and whether or not this or that legislation was enforced. There are even amusing stories of the sort of behaviour that went on in some churches during the service: fighting, urinating, letting off guns, playing cards, singing (not religious songs), talking, sleeping (ministers complained that parishioners only seemed to come to church to sleep), practical joking, and groping.[13] But it is very difficult indeed to get inside the heads of those who sat, or stood, or slept, or felt one another up in these churches. Dent's *Plaine Mans Path-way* reflects our state of knowledge. We know most about committed minorities: the godly (Theologus and Philagathus), and the radicals of the English Revolution (anticipated, in part, by Antilegon). We know least about what we assume were the silent majority, characterised by Asunetus.

II

The first point to make about early modern popular religion is that it was dynamic. Not only was there a variety of popular religions, but the nature of these religions was constantly shifting, undergoing change in what can usefully be seen as a series of English reformations.[14] For the parishioners of early modern England were subjected to a succession of legislative changes forced from above by monarchs and powerful elites. A person who was in his or her sixties in 1558 would have lived through Catholicism, healthy and vibrant until Henry VIII's reforms from 1529 onwards.[15] They would have experienced rapid changes in the single decade before

11. J.P. Boulton, 'The limits of formal religion: the administration of holy communion in late Elizabethan and early Stuart London', *London Journal* 10 (1984), 135–54; M. Spufford, 'Can we count the "godly" and the "conformable" in the seventeenth century?', *Journal of Ecclesiastical History* 36 (1985), 428–38.

12. D. Cressy, *Birth, Marriage, and Death: Ritual, Religion, and the Life-cycle in Tudor and Stuart England* (Oxford, 1997).

13. B. Reay, 'Popular religion', in B. Reay (ed.), *Popular Culture in Seventeenth-century England* (London, 1985), pp. 92–3.

14. C. Haigh, *English Reformations* (Oxford, 1993).

15. J.J. Scarisbrick, *The Reformation and the English People* (Oxford, 1984); C. Haigh, 'Introduction', in C. Haigh (ed.), *The English Reformation Revised* (Cambridge, 1987), pp. 1–17; R. Whiting, *The Blind Devotion of the People: Popular Religion and the English*

Elizabeth came to the throne: the radical Edwardine assault upon the rituals and ceremonies and images of the Catholic faith (1547–53); the swing back to Catholicism with the Marian restoration of the ritual and imagery of Catholicism (1553–8); a return to Protestantism under Elizabeth.[16] Indeed, this book begins almost schizophrenically in 1550. Its starting date is bordered on one side by the orders of the royal visitation of 1547 for the people of England to 'take away, utterly extinct and destroy all shrines, covering of shrines, all tables, candlesticks, trindles or rolls of wax, pictures, paintings and all other monuments of feigned miracles, pilgrimages, idolatry, and superstition; so that there remain no memory of the same'[17] and on the other by the Marian visitation of Kent in 1557 which showed the rapid restoration of Catholicism in a county acknowledged to be strongly Protestant.[18]

Our hypothetical 60-year-old would next witness Elizabeth's programme to suppress superstition and (in the words of the Injunctions of 1559) 'plant true religion'. He or she may have smelled the bonfires of images and Catholic liturgical books or personally observed the removal of altars, broken up for use in building material.[19]

If we were to take another 60-year-old in the 1630s, they would have lived the whole of their life under a Protestant church, and a good part of it under Elizabeth. They would have experienced the decades which saw the Protestantisation of England. By the 1630s our hypothetical witness would have been seeing changes which, if he or she was one of the godly, may well have been interpreted as a move back to Popery, a counter-reformation lead by monarch and archbishop: including greater use of ritual in church services, what Laudians called 'the beauty of holiness'; and the return of the altar, railed in at the east end of the church as a sacred, separate and central feature of the church, replacing the Elizabethan portable

---

Church (Cambridge, 1989); E. Duffy, *The Stripping of the Altars: Traditional Religion in England c. 1400–c. 1580* (New Haven, 1992), part 1; Haigh, *English Reformations*; R. Hutton, *The Rise and Fall of Merry England: the Ritual Year 1400–1700* (Oxford, 1994), chs 1–2; A.D. Brown, *Popular Piety in Late Medieval England: the Diocese of Salisbury 1250–1550* (Oxford, 1995).

16. For this process, see Scarisbrick, *Reformation*; R. Hutton, 'The local impact of the Tudor reformations', in Haigh (ed.), *English Reformation Revised*, ch. 6; Whiting, *Blind Devotion*; S. Doran and C. Durston, *Princes, Pastors and People: the Church and Religion in England 1529–1689* (London, 1991); Duffy, *Stripping of the Altars*, part 2; Haigh, *English Reformations*; Hutton, *Rise and Fall of Merry England*, chs 3–4; Brown, *Popular Piety*, ch. 10 and Conclusion.

17. Duffy, *Stripping of the Altars*, p. 480.   18. Ibid., pp. 527, 555–64.

19. Ibid., pp. 568, 569, 573.

communion table. The altar, for Archbishop Laud, was 'the greatest place of God's residence upon earth, greater than the pulpit';
for Charles I it was a symbol of his divine kingship.[20]

By the 1640s and 1650s, if our witness managed to live that long,
he or she would have lived through iconoclasm reminiscent of the
sixteenth century. Once again, 'monuments and images of idolatry
and superstition' were broken and burned, and wash reappeared to
paint the walls white. Down came the altar rails, crosses, crucifixes,
and religious statues and images. Bishops and church courts were
temporarily removed. The Church of England Book of Common
Prayer was replaced by the Presbyterian Directory, and the festivals
of Chrismas, Easter, and Whitsuntide were abolished. This change
did not happen everywhere. John Morrill has used local sources
from Cheshire, the west, and East Anglia to show that in the 150
parishes he studied more churches possessed the officially banned
Anglican prayer book than the Presbyterian alternative. Easter communion was still celebrated in over 40 per cent of parishes. The
outlawed Rogationtide perambulation of parish boundaries continued in over a third of parishes. In other words, earlier church
rituals survived. However, Morrill's map of Anglican survival also
demonstrates religious division: nearly 60 per cent of churches did
not celebrate communion at Easter; the rituals of Rogationtide
ceased in over 60 per cent of parishes.[21] Ronald Hutton's much
larger sample of 367 parishes for the 1650s, covering a wider area
of England, reinforces this negative emphasis. The old religious
calendar fell into disuse in the majority of churches and may well
have vanished had the republic continued. Only 14 per cent of
parishes in Hutton's group persisted with Easter communion
throughout the 1650s. As Hutton rather kindly glosses, this does
not undermine Morrill's general point about Anglican survivalism;
indeed, almost half of the churches anticipated the restoration of
the old ceremonies by observing Easter in 1660.[22] But it does seriously modify our picture of the strength of that survival: Morrill's
west- and east-county churches were not typical of the nation as a

20. P. Lake, 'The Laudian style: order, uniformity and the pursuit of the beauty of
holiness in the 1630s', in K. Fincham (ed.), *The Early Stuart Church, 1603–1642* (London,
1993), ch. 7; J. Davies, *The Caroline Captivity of the Church: Charles I and the Remoulding
of Anglicanism* (Oxford, 1992), stresses the role of Charles I, Carolinism, to describe the
innovations of the 1630s rather than the historiographically preferred Arminianism.
He also charts the complexities of the enforcement of the altar policy (ch. 6).
21. J. Morrill, 'The church in England', in J. Morrill (ed.), *Reactions to the English
Civil War 1642–1649* (London, 1982), ch. 4.
22. Hutton, *Rise and Fall of Merry England*, pp. 213–14.

whole. As Christopher Haigh once observed, England's reformations – of which the civil wars and Revolution are an integral part – produced a divided nation rather than a Protestant one.[23]

Although Anglican continuities are important, the era of the 1640s and 1650s saw great religious change, including the emergence of a variety of radical religious groups. People during the early modern period were rarely able to exercise freedom of belief and worship; they were governed by rules and regulations on religious opinions and behaviour, just as they were on political and sexual matters. They seldom had the opportunity to form their own congregations or to fashion their own beliefs. However, one such moment occurred during the civil wars and revolution when a *de facto* religious freedom permitted the emergence of hundreds of congregations, sects, religious prophets, and radical groups and movements: Baptists, Seekers, Levellers, Diggers, Ranters, and Quakers. They were minority movements, it is true, comprised mainly of the 'middle sort of people'; they were probably no more than 10 per cent of the population at their height. But these groups terrified conservatives and had an impact that far outweighed their numerical importance.[24]

If we were to take one final 60-year-old witness in 1720, this person's life would have spanned the period from the restoration of monarchy, the bishops, and the Church of England in the early 1660s, when the world was turned right side up again. He or she would have witnessed, perhaps experienced, the waves of persecution of nonconformity at the start of the 1660s, 1670–1, and the 1680s, and then toleration in 1689, when the dissent which had established itself in the Revolution was finally recognised as a permanent fixture of English religious life.[25]

---

23. Haigh, 'Conclusion', in Haigh (ed.), *English Reformation Revised*, p. 215.

24. C. Hill, *The World Turned Upside Down* (Harmondsworth, 1972); J.F. McGregor and B. Reay (eds), *Radical Religion in the English Revolution* (Oxford, 1986); N. Smith, 'The charge of atheism and the language of radical speculation, 1640–1660', in M. Hunter and D. Wootton (eds), *Atheism from the Reformation to the Enlightenment* (Oxford, 1992), ch. 5.

25. M.R. Watts, *The Dissenters* (Oxford, 1978); N.H. Keeble, *The Literary Culture of Nonconformity in Later Seventeenth-century England* (Leicester, 1987); J. Spurr, *The Restoration Church of England, 1646–1689* (London, 1991); B. Stevenson, 'The social integration of post-restoration dissenters, 1660–1725', in M. Spufford (ed.), *The World of Rural Dissenters, 1520–1725* (Cambridge, 1995), ch. 9; J. Spurr, 'From Puritanism to dissent, 1660–1700', in C. Durston and J. Eales (eds), *The Culture of English Puritanism, 1560–1700* (London, 1996), ch. 8; M. Goldie, 'The search for religious liberty 1640–1690', in J. Morrill (ed.), *The Oxford Illustrated History of Tudor and Stuart Britain* (Oxford, 1996), ch. 14.

When we generalise about early modern religion, then, we need to remember that we are dealing with cohorts of historical experience. Many of the Quakers of the 1650s were from the generation of the 1640s, reacting to the pressures of that decade rather than, as had the radicals of the early 1640s, the Laudianism or Carolinism of the 1630s. It was possible for some individuals to experience a range of commitments in the space of a mere decade. The radical Lawrence Clarkson notoriously moved from faith to faith. He began as a Puritan within the Laudian Church in Lancashire in the 1630s, 'fasting all the day', travelling ten miles to hear a godly minister, refusing to kneel at the altar when he received the sacrament. He was a Presbyterian in London in the early 1640s; he recalled the Presbyterian ministers at the onset of civil war, pressing 'the people to send out their husbands and servants to help the Lord against the Mighty . . . taking the Bible in their Pockets, and the Covenant in their Hats'. He became an Independent, an itinerant preacher, a Baptist, a Seeker, a Ranter, and a Muggletonian. He even went through a period of religious scepticism: the Bible was full of contradiction, 'no more than a history'. 'I really believed no Moses, Prophets, Christ, or Apostles, nor no resurrection at all: for I understood that which was life in man, went into that infinite Bulk and Bigness, so called God, as a drop into the Ocean, and the body rotted in the grave, and for ever so to remain.'[26]

III

Protestantism replaced Catholicism as the dominant religion in England. The current orthodoxy is that this ascent was slower and less inevitable than historians once thought; that England's reformations were forced on a predominantly reluctant people. Yet the proponents of this view sometimes ignore their own evidence. They point in their conclusions to the lack of local anticipation of official reform, and mention evasion, when their own research reveals instances of the extension of reforms, and of an iconoclasm and abandonment of ceremonies which went beyond that officially ordered. Presumably, one explanation for this would be Protestant zeal at a grass-roots level.[27]

26. B. Reay, 'Laurence Clarkson: an artisan and the English Revolution', in C. Hill, B. Reay, and W. Lamont, *The World of the Muggletonians* (London, 1983), ch. 6 (pp. 164, 171 for the quotes); Smith, 'Charge of atheism', pp. 134–43.

27. Compare the conclusions of Haigh on p. 12 and Hutton on p. 137 of *English Reformation Revised* with Hutton's actual findings on pp. 122–4.

It would be a mistake to underestimate the Protestant impact on popular culture. The Protestant drama of the sixteenth century, with its anti-Catholic messages; the Protestant gallows literature; the anti-popish crowd action in Jacobean London; and the Pope-burning processions of the late seventeenth century: all represented an engagement with culture at a level wider than that of a narrow elite.[28]

However, it is Puritanism that has dominated the historiography of early modern English religious history. There is a certain irony in the fact that what was essentially a minority movement should become the object of so much attention.[29] But Puritanism is important because it represents the zealous potential of a reformation with an impulse to cultural revolution. It is inconceivable that this enthusiastic Protestant tendency would not have an impact on popular religion, for its impetus was to reform and reshape. The ignorant character in the Puritan George Gifford's *A Briefe discourse of certaine points of the religion, which is among the common sort of Christians* (1581) describes the godly as 'busie Controllers', and the book sets up a polarity between the 'precise fellowes' who 'allowe no recreations' and who would have people 'sitte mooping always at their bookes', and the 'good fellowshippe' and 'good neighbour-hoode' of the ordinary villager.[30] Those whom their enemies called 'controllers' waged a war against traditional sports and pastimes, a cultural struggle in the streets and villages of England which would link the conflict of the late sixteenth and early seventeenth centuries with its wars of religion in the 1640s, an attempt at godly rule in the 1650s, and the return of tradition in 1660.[31]

28. For the drama, see R. Pineas, *Tudor and Early Stuart Anti-Catholic Drama* (The Hague, 1972); P. Collinson, *The Birthpangs of Protestant England* (London, 1988), ch. 4. For gallows literature, see P. Lake, 'Deeds against nature: cheap print, Protestantism and murder in early seventeenth-century England', in K. Sharpe and P. Lake (eds), *Culture and Politics in Early Modern England* (London, 1994), ch. 10. For anti-popery, see A. Walsham, ' "The fatall vesper": providentialism and anti-popery in late Jacobean London', *Past and Present* 144 (1994), 36–87; S. Williams, 'The Pope-burning processions of 1679, 1680 and 1681', *Journal of the Warburg and Courtauld Institutes* 21 (1958), 104–18.

29. The literature is extensive. It is best to start with Collinson, *Religion of Protestants*; P. Collinson, *English Puritanism* (Historical Association pamphlet, London, 1983); G.E. Aylmer, 'Collective mentalities in mid seventeenth-century England: I. The Puritan outlook', *Transactions of the Royal Historical Society* 36 (1986), 1–25; P. Lake, 'Defining Puritanism – again?', in F.J. Bremer (ed.), *Puritanism: Transatlantic Perspectives on a Seventeenth-century Anglo-American Faith* (Boston, Mass., 1993), pp. 3–29; and the essays in the best recent survey, Durston and Eales (eds), *Culture of English Puritanism*, especially pp. 1–31: the editors' introduction, 'The Puritan Ethos, 1560–1700'.

30. D.D. Wallace, 'George Gifford, Puritan propaganda and popular religion in Elizabethan England', *Sixteenth Century Journal* 9 (1978), 27–49.

31. This is the argument of D. Underdown, *Revel, Riot and Rebellion: Popular Politics and Culture in England 1603–1660* (Oxford, 1985). See also, J. Goring, *Godly Exercises*

As Patrick Collinson has explained, Puritanism is best seen as
a tendency. Puritans believed what Protestants believed, but with
more intensity.[32] They were iconophobes, whose hostility to images
extended way beyond antipathy towards the ritual, liturgy, architecture, and iconography of the English Church.[33] They were fervently
anti-popish, and redefined 'Popery' to include an ever-widening
range of moderate and radical Protestantism.[34] They were biblicists.[35]
The word and will of God was central. God's word was revealed in
the Bible, and communicated by preaching and bible-study. God's
divine intervention was detected in every aspect of human behaviour and natural phenomena (from bee stings to the hoped-for fall
of the restored monarchy).[36] Divine wrath was assuaged by collective acts of prayer and fasting.[37] The godly man in *Plaine Mans Path-
way* recommended attending sermons, reading the scriptures, and
perusing catechisms and 'other good bookes' – in that order – as
the path from ignorance to 'true knowledge of God'.[38] But the
scriptures were the linchpin of this whole mentality. William Dowsing, a Suffolk yeoman best known for his iconoclastic activity in the
churches of Cambridgeshire and Suffolk in the 1640s, collected
scores of printed sermons and annotated them with copious
biblical references; John Morrill counted nearly 200 references
to twenty-six books of the Bible in just ten sermons.[39] Puritans

---

or the Devil's Dance? Puritanism and Popular Culture in Pre-civil War England (London,
1983); Collinson, *Birthpangs of Protestant England*, ch. 5: 'Wars of religion'; Hutton,
Rise and Fall of Merry England, chs 4–7; C. Durston, 'Puritan rule and the failure of
cultural revolution, 1645–1660', in Durston and Eales (eds), *Culture of English Puritanism*, ch. 6. For a recent attempt to set the 'reformation of manners' impulse in a
much wider context, see M. Ingram, 'Reformation of manners in early modern
England', in P. Griffiths, A. Fox, and S. Hindle (eds), *The Experience of Authority in
Early Modern England* (London, 1996), ch. 2.

32. P. Collinson, 'The Jacobean religious settlement', in H. Tomlinson (ed.),
Before the English Civil War (London, 1983), pp. 29–30.

33. Collinson, *Birthpangs of Protestant England*, ch. 4: 'Protestant culture and the
cultural revolution'; M. Aston, 'Puritans and iconoclasm, 1560–1660', in Durston
and Eales (eds), *Culture of English Puritanism*, ch. 2.

34. P. Lake, 'Anti-popery: the structure of a prejudice', in R. Cust and A. Hughes
(eds), *Conflict in Early Stuart England* (London, 1989), ch. 3.

35. For the Bible in English history and culture, see C. Hill, *The English Bible and
the Seventeenth-century Revolution* (London, 1993).

36. Reay, 'Popular religion', p. 107.

37. For fasting, see P. Collinson, 'Elizabethan and Jacobean Puritanism as forms
of popular religious culture', in Durston and Eales (eds), *Culture of English Puritanism*, ch. 1.

38. Dent, *Plaine Mans Path-way to Heaven*, p. 356.

39. J. Morrill, 'William Dowsing, the bureaucratic Puritan', in J. Morrill, P. Slack,
and D. Woolf (eds), *Public Duty and Private Conscience in Seventeenth-century England*
(Oxford, 1993), p. 182.

were predestinarians who, as we have seen, believed in the doctrine of double predestination: that God had divided humankind into the elect, destined for heaven, and the reprobate, predestined for hell. This, they believed, was preordained or predetermined by God. Behaviour could not earn or win a place in heaven, but godly behaviour was a sign or indication of election. They were what have been termed experimental predestinarians.[40] As a godly artisan expressed it, 'I may look to my graces as evidence of my part in Christ and salvation but not as causes; I may make use of duties as a means to bring me to Christ and salvation but not to be saved by them.'[41] Thus there was a preoccupation with morals, manners, and discipline among the more fervent Protestants.

There was therefore a culture of Puritanism, a distinct lifestyle archetypically reflected in the case of the London turner, Nehemiah Wallington, who read, and was much influenced by, Dent's *Plaine Mans Path-way*. In one of his fifty notebooks, Wallington wrote that it was not an easy thing to be a Christian: 'it is not reading of the Scripture, or boasting of faith or Christ, though these be good; they cannot prove one to be an absolute Christian; there must be a conformity of life.'[42] Wallington bound himself to a series of articles or orders for future behaviour – nearly eighty in all – and fined himself by placing money in the poor box every time there was an infraction.[43] He was an avid sermon-goer (nineteen in one unusual week), taking notes, rereading them, repeating their message to his household in the evenings, and buying printed versions when they were available. As he observed, 'the hearing of God's Word it is a part of God's worship; it is a tendering of the creature's homage to God'. He would rise before dawn to pray, or to write in his notebooks: 'my sweet Savior did arise early for my redemption, and shall I not arise early to write of his mercies?'[44] Much of his writing was a record of providential acts, God's mercy towards himself and his family, and of judgements against sinners, including one memorable story he had heard about a Hertfordshire minister who had set his altar up according to the Laudian fashion and who bowed before it 'so low that he could not rise up again, but was crooked, and as he was going to the Bath for help, he died by the way'.[45]

40. R.T. Kendall, *Calvin and English Calvinism to 1649* (Oxford, 1979), pp. 8–9.

41. P.S. Seaver, *Wallington's World: a Puritan Artisan in Seventeenth-century London* (Stanford, Calif., 1985), p. 17.

42. Ibid., pp. 17–18.   43. Ibid., pp. 31–2.   44. Ibid., pp. 10, 37, 40.

45. Ibid., ch. 3 (p. 61 for the quoted example of God's punishment of Popish idolatry of the altar).

The godly impulse reached its apogee with the Quaker movement. Quaker culture was serious culture: 'How many plays did Jesus Christ and his apostles recreate themselves at? What poets, romances, comedies, and the like did the apostles and saints make or use to pass away their time withal?' Quakers rejected the ritual and imagery of the old religion for the powerful symbolism of the new. They wanted the complete elimination of the 'smell of popery' from England: the erasure of crosses on churches, ships, taverns, weights and measures, and coats of arms; the removal of the 'St' in English place names (as in St Ives and Bury St Edmunds). The woodcut prints found in chapbooks and on ballads were held to be in violation of the second of the ten commandments. Quaker marriages consisted of simple declarations. Their religious 'services' were plain meetings. Quaker burials were shorn of ritualism too. When the Leveller leader, John Lilburne, was given a Quaker funeral in 1657, not even a cloth covered his coffin, which was carried, unadorned, through the streets of London.[46]

Although Puritanism made some inroads at the popular level, it was always a minority movement. Those who rejected what they considered to be Popish first names in favour of godly alternatives for their children – Be-thankful, Comfort, Constant, Fear-not, God-ward, Goodgift, Hope-still, Mercy, More-gift, No-strength, Obedience, Refrain, Repent, Sin-deny, Sorry-for-sin, Standwell, Sure-trust, Thankful (active male and passive female) – tended to be confined to a few parishes at one historical moment in the 1580s and 1590s. These archival remnants of cultural Puritanism are relatively rare.[47] Indeed, Puritan identities were fashioned by the conviction of minority exclusivity and forged in a dialectical relationship with the ungodly – what Peter Lake has described as the godly watching the ungodly hating the godly.[48] The rigid doctrine, literacy bias, and demanding ethos of Puritanism were unlikely to appeal to the majority of the population. It was a religion of towns in a predominantly rural society. As one of the creators of godly Dorchester put it, 'bodies nearly compacted are more easily and better governed . . . than a people scattered and dispersed abroad'.[49] Puritanism appealed

46. B. Reay, *The Quakers and the English Revolution* (London, 1985), p. 119.
47. N. Tyacke, 'Popular mentality in late Elizabethan England', in P. Clark, A.G.R. Smith, and N. Tyacke (eds), *The English Commonwealth, 1547–1640* (Leicester, 1979), ch. 4.
48. P. Lake, ' "A charitable Christian hatred": the godly and their enemies in the 1630s', in Durston and Eales (eds), *Culture of English Puritanism*, ch. 5.
49. Collinson, 'The Protestant town', in his *Birthpangs of Protestant England*, ch. 2. For Dorchester, see D. Underdown, *Fire from Heaven: the Life of an English Town in the Seventeenth Century* (London, 1992), ch. 4 (the quote comes from p. 91).

across social divisions and its theology was not socially specific, but it was, as Keith Wrightson has rightly stated, 'disproportionately successful among the upper and middling ranks of parish society'.[50]

IV

I wrote earlier of the dynamics of religious change. Yet there were those who lived through such changes relatively unaffected. In 1644, the preacher John Shaw came across an old man from Cartmel (Cumbria) who could not tell him how many gods there were. He asked him how '"he tho't to be saved?" he answered, he could not tell, yet tho't that was a harder question than the other'. Shaw told him that the way to salvation was by Jesus Christ, 'God-Man', who shed his blood for us on the cross. '"Oh sir," said he, "I think I heard of that man you spake of, once in a play at Kendall, called Corpus Christi play, where there was a man on a tree, and blood ran down".' Here was someone who had lived his whole life in a Protestant nation, 'was a good churchman, that is, he constantly went to Common-Prayer', yet had never 'heard of salvation by Jesus Christ' except in his childhood in the 1580s in a play being suppressed by Protestant reformers.[51]

Historians used to assume that what happened at the centre of power was reflected in the local communities: they have now become more aware of gaps between centre and locality. The official church might change from Catholic to Protestant, yet this did not mean that the whole nation transformed its religious complexion. We cannot assume that because the Church of England was Protestant in name from 1559, the English people were Protestant as well, or even that their ministers were reformed. Haigh has argued that it took until the end of the sixteenth century, allowing time for an old generation of priests and committed laity to die out and for a new Protestant generation to take hold, before England was

50. K. Wrightson, 'Postscript: Terling revisited', in K. Wrightson and D. Levine, *Poverty and Piety in an English Village: Terling, 1525–1700* (Oxford, 1995), p. 207. This postscript to the second edition of *Poverty and Piety* contains an excellent summary and critique of the debate over the social appeal of Puritanism.

51. 'The Life of Master John Shaw', in *Yorkshire Diaries and Autobiographies* (Surtees Society, 65, 1875), pp. 138–9. This encounter is often used as an example of rural ignorance; however, Eamon Duffy interprets it as evidence of the effectiveness of the religious plays and the 'disastrous effect' of their suppression: Duffy, *Stripping of the Altars*, p. 68.

a Protestant nation. Even then, its people were not thoroughly Protestant.[52] Although they never make for neat explications, such continuities are as important as the dynamics of historical change in mapping out a picture of early modern religion.

When discussing early modern Catholicism it is necessary to distinguish between 'a body of opinion' and 'membership of a community'.[53] Historians have concentrated almost exclusively on the latter. By the early seventeenth century, it has been argued, Catholicism (as behaviour rather than belief) was essentially a 'non-conformism of the gentry', Catholics were an 'upper-class sect'.[54] Indeed it was Catholic policy to concentrate efforts on the elite sections of society: those who were potentially in a position to influence future politics.[55] The only areas of what could be termed popular Catholicism were on the Welsh borders, and the north, particularly in Lancashire. Although there were independent plebeian Catholic communities in Lancashire in 1641, the most common pattern was for isolated Catholic gentry households, or for seigneurial Catholicism where a gentry family protected a population of co-religionists of the middling or lower sort.[56] John Bossy, who has argued that the early modern Catholic community (a brand of nonconformity) is best considered as a small, consolidating religious group rather than a decimated majority movement, has calculated the Catholic population at around 40,000 to 60,000 in the seventeenth century and at about 70,000 in the eighteenth century – approximately the same numbers as the early Quakers. The counties where Catholics consistently comprised more than 1 per cent of the population in the mid-seventeenth and later eighteenth centuries were the northern counties of Lancashire, Yorkshire, Durham, and Northumberland, Monmouth on the south Wales border, and Warwickshire and Staffordshire in the midlands.[57] Such statistics give no indication of the influence of the Catholic beliefs and rituals which lingered on in folk religion and magical healing.

One of the most interesting problems of early modern English religious and cultural history is the fate of popular Catholicism. If the centuries-old Catholic faith was so vibrant on the eve of the nation's first reformation – and the evidence for its health is

52. Haigh, *English Reformations*, chs 15–16.

53. J. Bossy, *The English Catholic Community 1570–1850* (London, 1976), p. 183.

54. Ibid., pp. 60, 100.   55. Haigh, *English Reformations*, ch. 15.

56. A. Dures, *English Catholicism 1558–1642: Continuity and Change* (London, 1983); B.G. Blackwood, 'Plebeian Catholics in the 1640s and 1650s', *Recusant History* 18 (1986), 42–58.

57. Bossy, *English Catholic Community*, ch. 8, and maps on pp. 404, 408.

compelling – what happened to this mentality in the succeeding years? What was the fate of the 'arithmetical piety', the masses, votive lights, prayers, and vigils for departed souls, this purgatorial faith, so aptly described as a cult of the living in service of the dead?[58] Puritanism and its nonconformist offshoots provided the ideological zeal to challenge and replace, but we know that their impact was fragmented, limited to a few pockets. Although Puritanism made inroads at a grass-roots level, it never offered the prospect of a genuine popular Protestant alternative. If there was no such conversion to godliness, what happened to English Catholicism? For it is inconceivable that an organic faith, etched deeply into the communal and mental framework of a nation, could merely disappear over decades, or even centuries.

One answer lies with the realm of folk or folklorised Christianity, the mix of Christian and non-Christian which informed many people's beliefs, and which included a lingering Catholicism that did not simply vanish with England's reformations. We can see this most clearly in the popular healing rituals of the time, part magic, part religion, though it is inappropriate to distinguish between the two: the use of Catholic prayers; the invocation of the names of the Father, Son, and the Holy Ghost, or of St Peter and St Paul. An early seventeenth-century healer reputedly cured worms by saying three times: 'In the name of God I begin and in the name of God I do end. Thou tetter-worm [or thou canker-worm] begone from hence in the name of the Father, of the Son, of the Holy Ghost.' A cure for toothache was to write on three pieces of paper,

> Mars, hur, abursa, aburse
> *Jesu Christ for Marys sake*
> Take away this Tooth-ach.

The charm was repeated aloud, and the paper burned each time the words were spoken; the ache vanished as the last paper smouldered. An early modern charm against the ague involved writing a magical formula, binding it around the arm of the afflicted for nine days, every day reciting three Our Fathers 'in worship of St Peter and St Paul', then removing the writing and burning it – 'and the sick shall be whole'.[59]

58. A.N. Galpern, *The Religion of the People in Sixteenth-century Champagne* (Cambridge, Mass., 1976).

59. K. Thomas, *Religion and the Decline of Magic* (Harmondsworth, 1973), pp. 211–13; J. Aubrey, *Three Prose Works*, ed. J. Buchanan-Brown (Carbondale, Ill., 1972), p. 86.

Such charms – written and spoken, or worn as talismans – were handed down through generations and collected by folklorists in the nineteenth and early twentieth centuries. There were charms to staunch blood, and for toothache, fever, scalds and burns, aches, swellings, blistering, gout, worms, and sprains. Christian imagery was suffused with sympathetic magic, as in a charm 'to stop blud' recorded in a Shropshire blacksmith's book dating from the early nineteenth century:

> Our Saviour Jesus Crist was borne in Bethalem was basptsed of Jon in the river of Jordan. God commanded the water to stop & it stoped So in his name do I command the blood to Stop that run from this orrafas vain or vaines as the water Stoped in the River of Jordan wen our Saviour Jesus Crist was baptized in the name of the Father. Stop blud in the name of the sun stop blood in the name of the Holeygst not a drop more of blud proceduth Amen Amen Amen – to be sed 3 times but if the case be bad 9 times and the Lords praier before & after holding your rithand on the place and marck the place thus + with your midel finger.

Some of these charms were derived from the Bible, others were apocryphal. We know that the charms against toothache, for example, are part of a tradition of medieval medical magic. It is ironic that the scriptures, so central to reformed Protestantism, were put to magical uses. There was a christology about magical healing – a Devon charm against ague ended with the words 'So Lord help they servants that put their trust in thee through Jesus Christ. Amen' – but it was far from the christology of the godly.[60]

It is important to be aware that these forms of thaumaturgy were not mere cultural marginalia. The principal means of healing in the early modern medical marketplace were self-medication and resort to the cunning folk (discussed in Chapter 4), and both used the rituals just described. The connection between religion and healing may have been further reinforced by the central role that the early modern clergy played in popular healing.[61] The astrologer-healer Richard Napier, who treated up to 2,000 people a year, was

60. For the above, see O. Davies, 'Healing charms in use in England and Wales 1700–1950', *Folklore* 107 (1996), 19–32. See also, P. Rushton, 'A note on the survival of popular magic', *Folklore* 91 (1980), 115–18; D. Cressy, 'Books as totems in seventeenth-century England and New England', *Journal of Library History* 21 (1986), 92–106. For medieval magic, see R. Kieckhefer, *Magic in the Middle Ages* (Cambridge, 1989), ch. 4.
61. R. Sawyer, 'Patients, healers and disease in the southeast midlands, 1597–1634' (University of Wisconsin-Madison, Ph.D., 1986), pp. 126–46.

also rector of Great Linford in Buckinghamshire until his death in 1634. The healing techniques of this minister of the early Stuart church included contact with the angels through the use of Catholic prayers, as well as providing amulets, charms, and magical remedies. In the words of Ronald Sawyer, 'neither this rector nor his many patients seemed to feel constrained to keep their explanations of disease and its treatment within the limits of Protestant doctrine'.[62]

Among the most significant work on the survival and adaptation of pre-reformation rites and beliefs is that of Ronald Hutton. He has discovered examples of the Catholic celebration of Candlemas, the feast of the Purification of the Virgin Mary, being transferred from the church to the household; of Palm Sunday hallowings moving into the realm of popular custom; of Easter rites transformed into magical and medical folklore; and of the feast of All Saints or All Souls, with its purgatorial function abolished under Protestantism, surviving in popular doling rituals into the nineteenth century (albeit with its original function forgotten).[63]

Sin-eating – the practice of paying a poor person to eat food over the coffins of the dead to ritually assume their sins – surviving in the fens in the nineteenth century, is almost certainly a folk version of the Catholic doctrine of purgatory. The late seventeenth century antiquary John Aubrey met a Herefordshire sin-eater, 'a long leane, lamentable, poor raskal'.

> The manner was that when the Corps was brought-out of the house and layd on the Biere; a Loafe of bread was brought out, and delivered to the Sinne-eater over the corps, as also a Mazar-bowle [of Maple] full of beer, which he was to drinke up, and sixpence in money, in consideration whereof he tooke upon him (*ipso facto*) all the Sinnes of the Defunct, and freed him [or her] from Walking after they were dead.

Aubrey thought that the distribution of doles at funerals, still used in the seventeenth century, had some resemblance to sin-eating.[64] Even more directly related to purgatorial belief was the Yorkshire

62. Ibid., pp. 228–43 (p. 237 for the quote). For Napier, see also M. MacDonald, *Mystical Bedlam: Madness, Anxiety, and Healing in Seventeenth-century England* (Cambridge, 1981), esp. ch. 2.

63. R. Hutton, 'The English Reformation and the evidence of folklore', *Past and Present* 148 (1995), 89–116. See also, his remarkable book, *The Stations of the Sun: a History of the Ritual Year in Britain* (Oxford, 1996).

64. Aubrey, *Three Prose Works*, pp. 179–80; E. Porter, *Cambridgeshire Customs and Folklore* (London, 1969), pp. 26–7. See also, C. Gittings, *Death, Burial and the Individual in Early Modern England* (London, 1984), pp. 45–6, 162–3.

superstition that the souls of the dead lingered over the moors, where those who had been uncharitable towards their neighbours would be punished by the harshness of the environment. A song sung at 'country vulgar Funeralls' in the seventeenth century referred to this passage of souls:

> From Whinny-moor that thou mayst pass
> every night and awle
> To Brig o'Dread thou comest at last
> and Christ receive thy Sawle
>
> From Brig of Dread that thou mayest pass
> every night and awle
> To Purgatory fire thou com'st at last
> and Christ receive thy Sawle.[65]

At least some of the rituals of Catholicism were re-formed in the shape of folk practices. David Cressy has referred to a persistence of traditional Catholic burial practices in the face of a slowly victorious Protestantism: of a 'hybrid religious culture, in which reformed and unreformed elements intermingled while being pressured towards conformity'.[66]

V

It is becoming increasingly clear that cheap print in the form of the chapbook and ballad is a vital source for the interaction between pre- and post-reformation religious discourses. Although religious ballads declined from about one in every two titles printed in the sixteenth century to about one in ten in the late seventeenth century, the penny ballad was an important way of getting a godly message across in song and print, at first using lively popular song and dance tunes to impart a Protestant theme, later using more sombre godly melodies.[67] But if the godly ballads are an indication of popular religious taste, it is, in the words of Tessa Watt, 'a religious culture which is far from monolithic, showing a fragmentary reception of Protestant doctrine'.[68]

---

65. Aubrey, *Three Prose Works*, pp. 176–8.
66. Cressy, *Birth, Marriage, and Death*, pp. 401–2.
67. T. Watt, *Cheap Print and Popular Piety 1550–1640* (Cambridge, 1991), ch. 2.
68. Ibid., pp. 83, 85.

There is little that is reformed Protestant about the ballad, *Death Triumphant*. It deals with the age-old theme of death as a great leveller:

> Death cares no more for Rich than Poor,
> for he doth smite down all.

Even Guy of Warwick, chivalric hero of ballad and chapbook, the verse continues, 'did dye by this same potent foe'. Fear of death is used as an encouragement to pelagianism rather than predestinarianism:

> Then happy those that hath done well
> for they to Heaven shall go;
> And wicked ones be turn'd to Hell,
> where nothing is but woe.[69]

The Dead Mans Song (sung to the tune of 'Flying Fame') provided medieval visions of death, judgement, and hellfire, reinforced visually with woodcuts depicting the tortures of the damned. After a brief description of heaven, with its walls of precious stones and houses of beaten gold, the ballad concentrates on the horrors of hell, where sinners were inflicted with punishments to fit their crimes: a proud man had his face slashed with knives; the covetous had molten gold poured down their throats; the gluttonous were fed dishes of crawling toads; the lecherous were fried on burning beds; and liars were hung up by their tongues. Like the ballad, *St. Bernard's Vision*, it 'is a powerful argument for the continuity of a medieval religious outlook well into the early modern period'.[70]

There were definitively Protestant ballads. *The Godly Maid of Leicester* recounted the story of Elizabeth Stretton, whose assurance of her own election enabled her to face Satan: 'my sweet Christ redeem'd my Soul'.

> For I have fought a happy Fight
> and overcome by Gods good Grace,
> The Devil in his power and might,
> and run with Comfort now my race,
> For henceforth is laid up for me,
> a Crown of immortality,
> Where I shall very shortly be,
> with Heavenly Saints that never die.

The ballad was sung to the tune of 'In Summer time'.[71]

69. W.G. Day (ed.), *The Pepys Ballads*, 5 vols (Cambridge, 1987), Vol. 2, p. 3.
70. Watt, *Cheap Print*, p. 111.   71. Day (ed.), *Pepys Ballads*, Vol. 2, p. 40.

But more often there was a mix between the traditional and varieties of reformed religion, as in the case of the ballad known as the *Clerk of Bodnam. A very godly Song . . . the Earnest Petition of the Faithful Christian, being Clerk of Bodnam, made upon his Deathbed*, printed in the 1620s as well as the 1680s, was 'thoroughly Protestant' in its message.[72] One version has a woodcut of the dying man peacefully praying, comforted by a Bible-reading minister and friends or family kneeling in prayer by his bed – a scene of household godliness. But another version, though the verse is the same, has woodcuts dominated by images of death and bodily decay, including a blazing skeleton. The dying man is all alone in bed, threatened by the arrow-wielding and bell-ringing bony figure of death. The iconography of a comforting Protestantism has vanished.[73] Watt has argued persuasively that a visual Catholicism (the words are mine, not hers) lingered in post-reformation cheap print through the re-use of traditional woodcuts.[74]

The small religious chapbooks which sold for 2d. or 3d., replacing the religious ballad as the main item of cheap religious print from the 1620s onwards, made up about a third of the output of the publishers of such material by the end of the seventeenth century.[75] As discussed in Chapter 2, chapbooks were aimed at a wide audience and contained a mix of types and forms, including songs, verse, prayers, shortened sermons, and the question-and-answer formula of the catechism. They also made use of woodcut prints, with the icon of death as the most common image. Although many were aimed at sinners in general, both young and old – 'all people, and useful for Families' – the title pages repeatedly refer to youth, apprentices, and young men and women, 'the sins that daily attend youth', 'the behaviour of children'. They were written for 'the benefit of youth', as 'an example for youth to amend their lives', and were 'very fit for all children and servants'.[76] *The School of Godliness* contained catechising, prayers, graces, and rules of civility, a strange jumble, possibly linked to the trance which its author had supposedly lain in for 'several days'! Its aim was 'to instruct Youth in the knowledge of the Scripture', but it also contained advice on godly behaviour such as not handling parts of the body 'not ordinarily

72. Watt, *Cheap Print*, p. 106.
73. Compare Day (ed.), *Pepys Ballads*, Vol. 2, p. 41 with Watt, *Cheap Print*, p. 107.
74. Watt, *Cheap Print*, pp. 168–72.
75. M. Spufford, *Small Books and Pleasant Histories: Popular Fiction and its Readership in Seventeenth-century England* (London, 1981), p. 197; Watt, *Cheap Print*, ch. 8.
76. Pepys Chapbooks, Penny Godlinesses Collection, nos 3, 4, 9, 11, 15, 16, 23, 25, 37, 43.

discovered', blowing the nose too loudly and looking into the hand-kerchief afterwards, spitting in the fire, gnawing on one's fingernails, or delousing in public. Before they were questioned on creation and the fall, readers were given lesson eleven – 'If thou see any filth on the ground as thick Spittle, or the like, put thy foot thereon dextrously' – and lesson thirteen – 'Let the gestures of thy body be agreeable to the matter of thy Discourse'.[77] *The Youngman's Guide in his way to Heaven* provided separate morning prayers for young men and maids. The latter recognised that God 'hast ordained Women to be the weaker Vessels, both in labours of the Body and endeav-ours of the mind'.[78]

There is a difference of opinion among historians of the reli-gious chapbooks. Margaret Spufford has emphasised the gloomy and fearsome nature of the penny books in Pepys's collection. Their predominant message was one of repentance, death, and judgement, with limited sense of divine mercy and love. However, Eamon Duffy has argued that this literature, often written by nonconformist ministers, contained a more positive core, 'above all the gospel of penitence, forgiveness and grace which was the centre and best of English Puritanism'.[79]

Although the religious chapbooks of the 1680s were undoubtedly more recognisably Protestant than the ballads of the 1620s, Duffy's emphasis is somewhat misleading. His Puritan chapbooks formed only 30 per cent of Pepys's penny religious collection.[80] Far more of the religious chapbooks related a traditional – and, as Spufford noted, highly negative – message of death and damnation, and implicitly or explicitly stressed works rather than faith and grace in a way that would have reinforced the beliefs of Dent's Asunetus. A more accurate characterisation of the religious message of these books would be its variety, the 'patchwork' described by Watt, clearly '"post-Reformation", but not always thoroughly "protestant"'.[81] The picture is further complicated by the publishers' practice of mar-keting old titles. Elizabethan religious ballads were being sold fifty years later, in the mid-seventeenth century, and almost 25 per cent of such consistent sellers survived for a century or more.[82]

77. Ibid., no. 16.   78. Ibid., no. 4.

79. E. Duffy, 'The godly and the multitude in Stuart England', *Seventeenth Century* 1 (1986), 31–55 (quote at pp. 48–9).

80. Duffy lists fourteen awakening chapbooks out of forty-six in Samuel Pepys's Penny Godlinesses Collection: Duffy, 'Godly and the multitude', p. 54, notes 78–9.

81. T. Watt, 'Piety in the pedlar's pack: continuity and change, 1578–1630', in Spufford (ed.), *World of Rural Dissenters*, pp. 245, 270.

82. Ibid., pp. 244–5.

It is true that a group of the small books offered assurances to believers and persuasions for poor sinners to 'leave their sins, and to come to Christ by Repentance', holding out glimpses of 'the heavenly Joys of the Soul, in the Blessed kingdom of Glory', the 'Rivers of Joys, that shall feed the Soul':

> Make sure of saving grace,
> which will thy soul defend,
> Sin will thy soul deface,
> except Christ be thy friend.[83]

The Poor Doubting Christian Drawn unto Christ (1683) offered 'comfortable Directions how to live by Faith, and so attain unto Grace and Salvation'.[84] Despite its chilling woodcut of the skeleton death casting his arrow at a family group, with the caption 'I kill you all', Andrew Jones's *Death Triumphant* offers visions of a 'happy Death' for the godly:

> O Death at thy pleasure, for it is a pleasure to me to die. To me to live is Christ, and to die is gain. Come thou O my joy, for it is a joy to me to enjoy thee. Welcome Death, the beginning of joy that first fruit of pleasure, when thou comest, farewel sorrows; and farewel miseries, my winter is past, thou art to me a messenger of joy, O life thou art my death, O death thou art life.[85]

Yet Spufford is surely correct in her detection of an overwhelming focus on death, judgement and hell. At best, readers of this popular literature were given the choice of 'Salvation if you open to Christ; Damnation if you refuse': 'the Necessity of opening your hearts to Christ, or else he will open Hells mouth to devour you'.[86] Many of the small books merely invoked fear in the form of horrible visitations upon sinners or the threat of impending judgement. *An Almanack For Two Days* calendared but two days: the day of death and the day of judgement. There are stories of a lying woman whose tongue swells too big for her mouth; and of a young Bible stealer whose hands and legs rotted off and who, while dying in agony attended by ministers praying 'for and with him', was put on public display to the 'thousands' who, holding herbs to their noses to counter the smell of putrefying flesh, came to see the barely living 'Monument of Divine Severity'. This small book, like the *auto-de-fe* it describes, was a warning to others.[87] *An Almanack But for one Day* describes the terrors of judgement day, the 'Great Assizes', with its

83. Pepys Chapbooks, Penny Godlinesses Collection, nos 2, 3.   84. Ibid., no. 30.
85. Ibid., no. 19.   86. Ibid., no. 8.   87. Ibid., nos 6, 44, 46.

imagery of a darkening sun and moon, the conflagration and dissolution of the world, the opening of graves and the marching of bodies out of fire, sea, and river as the elements relinquish their dead for the final reckoning.[88]

It is also easy to see how the religious chapbooks would have done little to undermine pelagianism. The majority have a fixation with behaviour and duties, warning against vanity, debauchery, and swearing, which, by the very focus on such activities, implies the centrality of human morality and behaviour in the quest for salvation. Even the 'awakening' godlies dwelt on behaviour. *Death Triumphant* provides directions on how to lead a godly life 'so we may Die a happy death, and not fear him when he Comes'.[89] The horrifying story of the murderer Thomas Savage, who partially recovered after he was hanged only to be taken back to the gallows to complete the execution, was a warning against the temptations of youth rather than an example of the workings of grace on the worst of sinners.[90] Others are more openly Pelagian in their implications: at the final judgement in *An Almanack But for one Day* those who 'have done well' will have bodies 'fair, beautiful, and brightly shining as the Sun', those who have 'done ill' will become deformed 'Devils'. The song in the *Dying Christians Pious Exhortations and Godly Counsel* gave clear advice:

> What thou dost give, give with a good will
> rejoyce not at thy brothers fall,
> make neighbours freinds pray use your skill
> a day will come will pay thee all.[91]

VI

Margaret Spufford has long argued for the importance of Christianity at a popular level, 'a deep interest in religious matters in the sixteenth and seventeenth centuries, which crossed all social divides, and which involved some of the very poor'.[92] Basic religious concepts were imparted along with a rudimentary literacy: that is, religion permeated educational instruction in the dame schools and the household, primarily through the instructional primers

88. Ibid., no. 14.   89. Ibid., no. 19.

90. Ibid., no. 37. It was, as Duffy points out, a shorter version of a longer pamphlet which it stripped of its 'Christological content': Duffy, 'Godly and the multitude', p. 47.

91. Pepys Chapbooks, Penny Godlinesses Collection, nos 7, 14.

92. M. Spufford, 'The importance of religion in the sixteenth and seventeenth centuries', in Spufford (ed.), *World of Rural Dissenters*, p. 3.

and hornbooks which sold for a few pence and combined the ABC
with religious instruction. Catechisms, summaries of religious belief
in question and answer form, were combined with instruction in
reading in the popular *ABC with the catechisme*. 'If you could read,
you were also religiously indoctrinated.'[93] Spufford's argument is
that if the widespread dissemination of basic reading skills is considered alongside the impact of cheap print in the form of godly
chapbooks and ballads, primers, and catechisms, there is a logical
argument for a popular familiarity with 'basic religious concepts',
'a kind of general familiarity . . . with religious discussion and argument, which no longer exists in contemporary society'.[94] But what
sort of religious familiarity?

Ian Green has found nearly 700 English catechisms surviving from the period 1530–1740, circulating in their estimated mil-
lions during the early modern period. The *ABC with the catechisme*,
alone, had a possible 500,000 to 750,000 copies in print by the mid-
seventeenth century.[95] Catechising was a hybrid of orality and literacy. Catechisms were printed and written but much learning and
testing was by rote, with an emphasis on oral instruction; both the
literate and illiterate could be catechised. Catechisms were read and
heard. Printed versions were used as prompts to what was primarily
verbal instruction, but the literate could also employ the printed
text as a quiet reinforcement of doctrinal learning. Catechising was
therefore a 'mixed mode' in terms of literacy and orality.[96] We also
see techniques encountered in Chapter 2: the use of verse and
black-letter to appeal to 'children in years and understanding'.[97]

Because catechising was closely linked to the aquisition of reading literacy and employed in church, school, and household, it was
'an established – if sometimes short-lived – feature of the religious
life of the young'. In other words, Green is making much the same
point as Spufford. However, he is more pessimistic in his conclusions about the implications for popular religiosity. He refers to
the sometimes fleeting exposure of the young to religious instruction, and is sceptical about the impact on adolescents and 'ignorant adults'.[98] The basic structure of the catechism was to set forth
the creed, ten commandments, Lord's prayer, and sacraments.
Green has found that the statements of faith set out for elementary
catechumens said little about predestination and justification by

93. Ibid., pp. 64–85 (quote at p. 74).   94. Ibid., p. 85.
95. I. Green, *The Christian's ABC: Catechisms and Catechizing in England c. 1530–
1740* (Oxford, 1996), ch. 2, esp. pp. 51, 65.
96. Ibid., ch. 5, esp. p. 243.   97. Ibid., pp. 254–6.
98. Ibid., chs 3–4 (quote at p. 94).

faith (even during the pre-1640s period of supposed Calvinist hegemony) and would not have challenged popular Pelagianism.[99]

It is very difficult to work out the religious beliefs of the majority
of the population in early modern England. Protestant bishops
and ministers complained of popular ignorance, comparing their
parishioners to Africans or the 'savages of America'. Many were so
ignorant, said one bishop, that 'they know not what the Scriptures
are; they know not that there *are* any Scriptures'.[100] We should not
put too much weight on such complaints. They tell us more about
the exacting theological standards of those complaining (usually
the hotter sort of Protestants) than they do about those being
complained about. Ironically, there is a suggestion of this attitude
in Haigh's description of the majority group of English Christians
in the early seventeenth century. These 'parish anglicans' were
attached to the rituals of the Church of England; but Haigh re-
fuses to describe them as Protestant. They were neither Protestant
or Catholic: 'These churchgoers were de-catholicized but un-
protestantized.'[101] It seems something of a distortion to refuse these
people the description 'Protestant' because they did not conform
to the stricter requirements of the godly reformer. Indeed, it would
make more sense to redefine English Protestantism in terms of the
belief systems of these un-Catholic un-Protestants. However, Haigh's
general identification of this group is a useful one, for observers in
the early modern period continually came across men and women
who would attend communion each year at Easter, resorted to
church for baptisms, marriages, burials, and churching after childbirth, liked its ritual and ceremony, and saw it as an integral part of
the community, but who did not want the constant interference of
the minister, long sermons, and scriptural exegesis. They were
not conversant with the finer points of double predestination, but
merely believed that if people did well in life, in the sense of living
honestly and doing good rather than harm, they would be saved.[102]
There must have been many English men and women like the
character in *Plaine Man's Path-way*:

> Tush, tush: what needs all this adoo? If a man say his Lords prayer,
> his tenne Commaundements, and his beleefe, and keepe them, and
> say no body no harme, nor doo no bodie no harme, and doo as he

---

99. Ibid., pp. 346, 384.
100. Thomas, *Religion and the Decline of Magic*, pp. 195–6.
101. C. Haigh, 'The Church of England, the Catholics, and the people', in
C. Haigh (ed.), *The Reign of Elizabeth I* (London, 1984), ch. 8; Haigh, *English Reformations*, pp. 290–1.
102. Ibid., pp. 280–4, 291.

would bee done too, have a good faith to Godward, and be a man of Gods beliefe, no doubt he shall be saved, without all this running to Sermons, and pratling of the scriptures . . . As long as I serve God, and say my prayers duly, and truly, morning and evening, and have a good faith in God, and put my whole trust in him, and do my true intent, and have a good mind to Godward, and a good meaning: although I am not learned yet I hope it will serve the turn for my soules health: for that God which made me, must save me. It is not you that can save me for all your learning, and all your Scriptures.[103]

This is what George Gifford described as the religion of 'the common sort of Christians', 'countrie divinitie', the faith of 'the most in number, who having Popery taken from them, and not taught thoroughly and sufficiently in the Gospell, doe stand as men indifferent, so that they may quietlie injoy the worlde, they care not what religion come':

If a man labour all the weeke truely and honestly, and upon the Saboth day come to the Church and make his praiers, shall wee say God regardeth not his prayer, because hee doth not understande what hee prayeth: his intent is good, hee doth his good will: he hath a wife and children to provide for, hee muste followe the worlde, and let preaching goe, or els hee shall begge: and so long as hee doth hurt no man, but dealeth uprightly: I think God doth require no more at his hands.[104]

As we have seen, this Pelagianism would have found ample reinforcement in the discourses of catechism, chapbook, and ballad.

VII

Robert Scribner has used overlapping circles to provide a structural sense of the popular religions of early modern Germany.[105] It is difficult to reduce the complexity of popular religion to this kind of visual representation, but the most appropriate image would be a bricolage, indicating variety and cultural interaction. We need to consider a range of popular religions rather than a single entity.[106] Protestantism consisted of a series of fractions, including a range of nonconformities. The Church of England contained a variety of faiths; what Duffy has termed the impulses of Catholicism attached to Anglican ritual existed alongside a more actively Protestant prayer-book Anglicanism and the popular Pelagianism described

103. Dent, *Plaine Man's Path-way*, pp. 27–8.
104. Wallace, 'George Gifford', pp. 27–49.
105. R. Scribner, 'Ritual and popular religion in Catholic Germany at the time of the Reformation', *Journal of Ecclesiastical History* 35 (1984), 75.
106. Reay, 'Popular religion'; Ingram, 'From reformation to toleration'.

earlier.[107] One way of viewing the period from 1550 to 1750 is as one of momentous religious change. A Protestant calendar replaced the 125 holy days of Catholic England with the Elizabethan prayer book's 27 holy days and the new Protestant national festivals of Gunpowder Treason Day (5 November) and Queen Elizabeth's Day (17 November).[108] The Protestantisation of church and community, what Hutton has termed the 'fall of merry England', entailed an almost continuous war on religious ritual and festivity, with only limited respite and reversal until a compromise of sorts was reached in the 1660s, but with a separation being drawn finally between church and civic or communal festivities.[109] C.J. Sommerville has described this history as 'the secularization' of early modern England: secularisation of space with the seizure of monastic lands; secularisation of time with the Protestant calendar; secularisation of language through the impact of literacy and print; secularisation of art with Puritan iconoclasm and the suppression of religious drama; and secularisation of power with a shift in the influence of the church and the institution of legal toleration.[110] This is indeed a grid of a change in early modern mentalities from a world where religion was culture to one where religion is a cultural choice.

It is therefore possible to highlight such examples of cultural transformation: a new godly culture, taken to its logical conclusion in the purity of Quaker culture as opposed to the visual, oral, ritualistic culture of Catholicism. Such contrasts, as we have seen, indicate

107. Duffy, *Stripping of the Altars*, p. 589; J. Walsh and S. Taylor, 'Introduction: the church and Anglicanism in the "long" eighteenth century', in J. Walsh, C. Haydon, and S. Taylor (eds), *The Church of England, c. 1689–c. 1833* (Cambridge, 1993), ch. 1; W.M. Jacob, *Lay People and Religion in the Early Eighteenth Century* (Cambridge, 1996). Donald Spaeth has argued for the strength of village Anglicanism in Restoration England. In his study of Wiltshire he found parishioners who refused to take communion from their rector because they considered him unfit to administer the sacrament. He argues that although these Anglicans defined their religious practice on their own terms – they were active rather than passive in their religiosity – they were attached to the Book of Common Prayer: D.A. Spaeth, 'Common prayer? Popular observance of the Anglican liturgy in Restoration Wiltshire', in S. Wright (ed.), *Parish, Church and People: Local Studies in Lay Religion 1350–1750* (London, 1988), ch. 5. It is possible, however, that some of Spaeth's 'conforming Anglicans' were in fact nonconformists! See also, J. Maltby, ' "By this book": parishioners, the prayer book and the established church', in Fincham (ed.), *Early Stuart Church*, ch. 5.

108. See D. Cressy, *Bonfires and Bells: National Memory and the Protestant Calendar in Elizabethan and Stuart England* (London, 1989); D. Cressy, 'The Protestant calendar and the vocabulary of celebration in early modern England', *Journal of British Studies* 29 (1990), 31–52.

109. Hutton, *Rise and Fall of Merry England*; Cressy, *Birth, Marriage, and Death*.

110. C.J. Sommerville, *The Secularization of Early Modern England: From Religious Culture to Religious Faith* (Oxford, 1992); C.J. Sommerville, 'The secularization puzzle', *History Today* 44 (October 1994), 14–19. Whether what is in effect the Protestantisation of a nation is meaningfully described as secularisation is another issue.

an important characteristic of the religions of the people in early modern England, the sheer range of belief and practice. Yet such an approach also misses something important: it does not deal with continuities. Although the reformations did not recognise the Lent prohibition of marriage, English couples were reluctant to marry in March; the troughs in the demographers' graphs of seasonality only slowly disappear in the eighteenth century.[111] The rites of passage, purification after childbirth, baptism, marriage, and burial, were strongly associated with the established church and even people with little other attachment to the church would seek out its services at these important moments. For centuries the Church of England would accommodate the folk beliefs enmeshed in its rituals.[112]

Certainly, a simple polarity between Protestant and Catholic will not do. The great value of Tessa Watt's work on the ballad and chapbook literature is that it challenges any sharp demarcation between reformed Protestantism and traditional culture. Cheap print suggests an overlap between the two, the ability 'to absorb new beliefs while retaining old ones, to forge hybrid forms, to accommodate contradictions and ambiguities'.[113] This chapter has attempted to demonstrate this cultural interaction and compromise. We have seen it in the traditional visions of death replicated in Protestant ballads; in the way in which Catholic doctrine and ritual was transmuted into folk practice; and in the important affinity between popular Pelagianism and residual Catholicism. Popular religions were re-forming as well as reformed.

---

111. E.A. Wrigley and R.S. Schofield, *The Population History of England 1541–1871* (London, 1981), pp. 298–301. This is in contrast to the Quakers and to New England populations who married readily in March: D. Cressy, 'The seasonality of marriage in old and new England', *Journal of Interdisciplinary History* 16 (1985), 1–21; R.T. Vann and D. Eversley, *Friends in Life and Death: the British and Irish Quakers in the Demographic Transition* (Cambridge, 1992), pp. 84–6.

112. A. Wilson, 'The ceremony of childbirth and its interpretation', in V. Fildes (ed.), *Women as Mothers in Pre-industrial England* (London, 1990), ch. 3; D. Cressy, 'Purification, thanksgiving and the churching of women in post-reformation England', *Past and Present* 141 (1993), pp. 106–46; Durston, 'Failure of cultural revolution', pp. 226–9; and Cressy's important new book, *Birth, Marriage, and Death*. For the later period, see J. Obelkevich, *Religion and Rural Society: South Lindsey 1825–1875* (Oxford, 1976), pp. 271–4; D. Clark, *Between Pulpit and Pew: Folk Religion in a North Yorkshire Fishing Village* (Cambridge, 1982), ch. 7; S. Williams, 'Urban popular religion and the rites of passage', in H. McLeod (ed.), *European Religion in the Age of Great Cities, 1830–1930* (London, 1995), ch. 8.

113. Watt, *Cheap Print*, p. 126.

CHAPTER FOUR

Witchcraft

I

The assize records for the north-east circuit for the 1660s contain details about the fractured relationship between two Newcastle women, Dorothy Stranger and Jane Milburne. Stranger, a cooper's wife, was examined by the mayor of Newcastle to establish whether she had used witchcraft against Milburne in a series of incidents spanning many months. Potentially more damaging was the further allegation that Stranger's malice and power had led to the death of another woman, also called Jane Milburne, 'six or seven' years before. The task of the mayor was to establish whether Stranger 'did the said Jane Milburne any bodyly harme: or ever appeared to her in ye likenesse of catt or any other creature: or did ever use or exercise any sorcery or witchcraft: or any such diabolical act to wast or consume ye body of ye said Jane'.[1]

The events outlined in the depositions will seem bizarre to the twentieth-century observer. Of the first encounter, Milburne claimed that when she was alone in her house at night something 'in ye pfect similitude and shape of a catt' appeared before her and leapt at her face, saying 'wth a very audible voyce . . . yt it had gotten ye life of one in this house: and came for this informer['s] life and would have itt before Saturday night'. Milburne said that she retorted with the words 'I defye the devill & all his works', and that upon hearing this, the cat vanished. On another occasion she was sitting upstairs when a grey cat came through her window and then transformed itself into the person of Dorothy Stranger. Stranger was alleged to have appeared again and again in either human or

---

1. Public Record Office, ASSI 45/7/1/185-189: North-East Circuit Assize Depositions.

feline form to commit malefic acts: there was a purported attempted hanging, verbal threats upon Milburne's life ('thy life I seek: thy life I will have'), mysterious visitations behind locked doors in the middle of the night, and various nippings, pinchings, bitings, and scratchings. The encounters punctuated the everyday activities of the brewer's wife. When Milburne went to her cellar to draw some beer, her enemy was leaning against a hogshead. When she was getting dressed for church one Sunday, the cat leapt at her throat. While Milburne and her husband were sleeping in the middle of the night, Stranger materialised and wrestled with the bedclothes. In one dramatic episode the cat leapt upon its victim's shoulders as she was coming down the stairs, and its weight (Stranger's weight!) brought Milburne crashing to the floor. 'The power of body and tongue were taken from her.'

It is significant that recourse to law was accompanied by a popular remedy for witchcraft: the victim scratched the alleged witch's face. Milburne said that she had felt better after drawing Stranger's blood and had not been bothered for a couple of months. When the witchcraft resumed, she returned to the magistrates. Stranger had reluctantly submitted to the scratching on the very point of prosecution, presumably in an effort to clear her name, settle the dispute, and stave off legal action. Milburne also used words to counteract the witchcraft; her verbal defiance of the Devil, she claimed, led to the disappearance of the cat. She told Stranger that she defied her and her disciples; the 'witch' replied, 'although thou be strong in faith I'll overcome it at ye last'. Although there are allusions to a more cosmic battle between good and evil (and Stranger proclaimed her innocence of 'any such devellish art'), references to the demonic do not dominate the depositions. The women concerned alleged and denied the practice of maleficium, the infliction of harm upon neighbours and kin. The predominant focus is on power: the power of words, the power to change form, the power to do bodily harm. In the incident that had happened six or seven years earlier, a chance meeting on the sandhills, a few words, and perhaps a glance, had led to the death of the other Jane Milburne. Dorothy Stranger had said to her 'thou shall never see the sandhill again'; the young woman had returned home, fallen sick, languished for six months, and died. As Milburne's mother – Stranger's own sister – put it, she never did see the sandhills again. The victim had fits and cried out, 'do you not see her: doe not you [see] her my a[u]nt Dorthy that witch'. She felt that her aunt was pulling out her heart.

The incident which supposedly sparked the dispute was, as historical anthropologists of English witchcraft have been stressing for

some time now, a breach in neighbourly interaction.[2] Stranger
had reputedly told Milburne's servant that she was offended that
her dame had not invited her to a wedding supper. Although the
accused witch denied ever having met her accuser until confronted
by her, it is likely that this incident had a longer community history. One women was married to a brewer, the other to a cooper
– indeed the brewer's servant had been sent to Stranger's house
to organise some casks. Also there were kinship links. The Jane
Milburne who had died several years earlier was married to another
man named Milburne – a brewer – and she was Stranger's niece.
(The 'witch' did not deny knowing her: as she pointed out in her
defence, she had often cared for that Jane when she was a child.)

Modern minds are most comfortable with such accounts: witchcraft can be explained by social tensions. They are attuned to material explanations. If a woman describes being set upon by a witch
who has assumed the form of a cat, perhaps she was attacked by a
real cat and got confused! Animal metamorphosis is beyond modern western intellectual comprehension. Thus the nineteenth-
century editor of the Milburne case could not refrain from editorial
intervention: 'The deposition of a weak deluded woman in Newcastle, who imagined that she had been bewitched. It is strange that
any magistrate should write down such ridiculous evidence.'[3] The
point is that the mayor, Sir James Clavering, did write the allegations down. It is the belief systems revealed in the depositions which
are most important for the purposes of this chapter. As Robert
Darnton has argued in his famous book *The Great Cat Massacre* (the
cat coincidence can be ignored), it is precisely these moments of
cultural incomprehension that are so important to historians of
past cultures. 'When we cannot get a proverb, or a joke, or a ritual,
or a poem, we know we are on to something. By picking at the
document where it is most opaque, we may be able to unravel an
alien system of meaning. The thread might even lead into a strange
and wonderful world view.'[4] We need to focus on scratched hands
and faces, women who think that other women can transform themselves into cats, and baronets who write such things down. The
witch-hunts of the early modern period cannot be explained without grasping the mental framework which made them possible.[5]

2. See A. Macfarlane, *Witchcraft in Tudor and Stuart England* (London, 1970); and
K. Thomas, *Religion and the Decline of Magic* (Harmondsworth, 1973).
3. J. Raine (ed.), *Depositions from the Castle of York* (London, 1861), p. 112. See also
B. Rosen (ed.), *Witchcraft* (London, 1969), pp. 43–9: 'What really happened?'
4. R. Darnton, *The Great Cat Massacre* (New York, 1984), p. 5.
5. B.P. Levack, *The Witch-hunt in Early Modern Europe* (London, 1987), ch. 2.

Stuart Clark's recent work has situated learned, demonological witchcraft theories firmly in the context of the broader intellectual continents of early modern European science, religion, and politics, arguing that a body of ideas which has survived for several hundred years must have 'made some kind of sense and that this probably lay in its coherence with ideas about other things'. Belief in witchcraft was rational in its own context; and demonology was a means by which the learned developed arguments about other issues. Hence the title of his book: 'thinking with demons'.[6] The aim of this chapter is to make sense of witchcraft at a more popular (and national) level of mentality and behaviour. For Clark's analysis of the witch as the inverted 'other' – animalistic, antichristian, deviant, evil, female, unruly – is so compelling, the unwary reader could be forgiven for imagining that there was nothing beyond the powerfully represented anti-figure of the learned text, that 'real' witches did not exist.[7]

II

We should first draw a distinction between witch trials – claiming the lives of from 500 to 1,000 English witches in the early modern period – and underlying beliefs in witchcraft, magic, and sorcery.[8] The underlying beliefs could convert into trials or hunting, but there was nothing inexorable about the process. In fact recourse to formal prosecution was the last rather than the first resort for those worried about witchcraft. The initial strategy was one of caution: avoiding a reputed witch; warding her off; or at least ensuring that she was not offended. An account of late-nineteenth- and early-twentieth-century Cambridgeshire witchcraft outlined the precautions (sometimes contradictory) which could be taken: making sure that the suspect did not get hold of one's possessions in order to work her magic through them; providing presents for the witch ('Girls in service, who return to Horseheath for their holidays,

6. S. Clark, *Thinking with Demons: the Idea of Witchcraft in Early Modern Europe* (Oxford, 1997), p. viii.

7. Clark, *Thinking with Demons*, esp. Part 1. Of course this is not the intent of his most impressive intellectual history.

8. The figures vary. Thomas's estimated 1,000 includes those hanged and those who died in gaol: Thomas, *Religion and the Decline of Magic*, pp. 535–6. James Sharpe, who has provided the most recent figure, estimates about 500 executions in England between 1542 and 1736: J. Sharpe, *Instruments of Darkness: Witchcraft in England 1550–1750* (London, 1996), ch. 4, esp. p. 125.

sometimes think it advisable to give the witch a few pence before leaving the village, in order to avoid bad luck'); placing metal under the doormat to prevent the witch crossing the threshold, or putting a knife under a chair to prevent her from sitting down.[9] We should not assume rituals unchanged from the early modern period, but the principles of avoidance would have been much the same. Richard Bernard's *Guide to Grand-Jury Men* (1629) referred to amulets about the neck, fragments of scripture, a needle or bodkin placed under a stool.[10] Herbs were hung over the door to ward off witchcraft.[11] People were wary of creating offence: as a character in George Gifford's *A Dialogue Concerning Witches* (1593) said, he was as careful to please the town witch 'as ever I was to please mine own mother'.[12]

If precaution failed, victims could attempt to placate the aggrieved witch. This is what a parish constable's wife did in 1651 when her child fell sick. She confronted the witch at her door, fell down on her knees, and 'asked her forgivenesse', and 'the child did soone after recover'.[13]

Failing this, the afflicted could either try counter-magic of their own or secure the services of a specialist who dealt with cases of witchcraft. A London cure for witchcraft in 1622 was the charm: 'Three biters have bit him – heart, tongue and eye; three better shall help him presently – God the Father, God the Son, and God the Holy Spirit.' This was a common formula indicating the three main sources of witchcraft: malevolence (heart), bad words (tongue), and evil looking (eye), as well as the power of Christianity to heal.[14] A St Osyth woman outlined a different remedy. She said that when she had been troubled with lameness she had gone to a woman who had taught her how to 'unwitche' herself:

> take hogge's dunge, and [chervil], and . . . hold them in her left hand, and to take in the other hande a knife, and to pricke the medicine three times, & then to cast the same into the fire, and to take the said knife & to make three pricks under a table, and to let the knife stick there: & after that to take three leves of sage, and as much of herbe John (alias herbe grace) and put them into ale, and drinke it last at night and first in the morning . . .[15]

9. C.E. Parsons, 'Notes on Cambridgeshire witchcraft', *Proceedings of the Cambridgeshire Antiquarian Society* 19 (1915), 31–49.
10. R. Bernard, *A Guide to Grand-Jury Men* (London, 1629), p. 132.
11. Thomas, *Religion and the Decline of Magic*, p. 648.
12. G. Gifford, *A Dialogue concerning Witches and Witchcraftes* (London, 1593), sig. B1.
13. Raine (ed.), *Depositions from the Castle of York*, p. 58.
14. Thomas, *Religion and the Decline of Magic*, p. 220.
15. *A true and just Recorde* (London, 1582), sigs A7–A7v.

The woman, Ursula Kemp, claimed that the ritual had eased her lameness and that she had subsequently employed the same technique to unwitch other women. The records of early modern healers serve to highlight the gap between an underlying belief in the reality of witchcraft and actual judicial prosecution. Keith Thomas has observed that not one of the hundreds of cases of suspected witchcraft recorded in the case books of the astrologer-healers Richard Napier and William Lilly actually made it into the courts.[16]

As we saw in the case of Dorothy Stranger, scratching the witch's face was also believed to be a palliative, though the remedy was usually temporary.[17] A victim of the Windsor witches went to a wizard or a wiseman who told him to seek out the witch and scratch her 'so that you drawe blood of her, you shall presently mende'.[18] A target of witchcraft in the Humberside marshes in the late 1640s or early 1650s

> said that he was cruelly handled at the heart with one Elizabeth Lambe, and that she drew his heart's blood from him, and did desire this informant to send for her to come to his house, for he desired to scratch her, saying that she had drowne [*sic*] blood of him, and, if he could draw blood of her, he hoped he should amend. And she, being brought by a wile, the said Browne said, 'Bes, thou hast wronged me. Why dost thoe soe? If thou wilt doe soe no more I will forgive thee.' And she answered nothing. He then scratched her till the blood came, but within a weeke after he died . . .[19]

Bewitched brewing was combated by plunging a red-hot iron or horseshoe into the vat. The same ritual was used in butter-making when witchcraft was suspected.[20] A common means of counteracting the witchcraft of animals was the live incineration of the afflicted beast or the cutting off and burning of its ears.[21] A Huntingdonshire farmer said in 1605 that he had burned a sick horse alive to successfully prevent the death of the rest of his bewitched stock and knew of another who had burned a live sheep: 'non after died'.[22] A further means of fighting witchcraft was to

16. Thomas, *Religion and the Decline of Magic*, p. 534.

17. It was, as Bernard put it, 'no certaine remedy': Bernard, *Guide to Grand-Jury Men*, p. 187.

18. *A Rehearsall both straung and true* (London, 1579), sig. B2.

19. Raine (ed.), *Depositions from the Castle of York*, p. 58.

20. Rosen (ed.), *Witchcraft*, p. 149; Gifford, *Dialogue*, sig. B2v; Macfarlane, *Witchcraft*, p. 108.

21. Rosen (ed.), *Witchcraft*, p. 149; W. Grainge (ed.), *Daemonologia: A Discourse on Witchcraft* (Harrogate, 1882), p. 35; G. Gifford, *A Discourse of the subtill Practises of Devilles by Witches* (London, 1587), sig. H3.

22. G.L. Kittredge, *Witchcraft in Old and New England* (Cambridge, Mass., 1929), pp. 95–6.

burn the thatch of the suspected witch's roof.[23] The country characters in the Jacobean play *The Witch of Edmonton* (c. 1621) used this
method against the witch Elizabeth Sawyer: 'A handful of thatch
plucked off a hovel of hers; and they say, when 'tis burning, if she
be a witch she'll come running in.'[24] Action against a thing touched
or bewitched, it was believed, would impact upon the bewitcher or
toucher.[25] The early seventeenth-century narrative of the witchcrafts
of Margaret and Phillip Flower mentioned that when a mother
had burned the hair and nail-parings of her bewitched child, the
witch had come into the house in agony.[26] The boiling of the
victim's urine was likewise believed to cause discomfort to the witch;
archaeological evidence of this practice has survived in the form of
witch-bottles.[27]

Finally, although godly experts were sceptical, swimming helped
a community decide on the guilt or innocence of a suspected witch:
Bernard included swimming in his section on 'great presumptions
of a Witch for which he or shee may bee brought before authority
to be examined'.[28] The suspect was cross-bound, thumb to toe, and
cast into a pond or stream; if she sank she was innocent, and if she
floated – rejected by the water – guilt was presumed.[29] Clive Holmes
has argued that the swimming of witches, legitimised by sporadic
official sanction in the seventeenth century, became an important
'public test' at the popular level. There are numerous examples for
the eighteenth century when official legal sanctions faded.[30]

In short, the inhabitants of early modern England tried a range
of methods for coping with suspected witchcraft. Violence and
recourse to law (with the implied ultimate sanction of death) came
at the end of a long process of negotiation. 'Some runne unto the
Witch when any friend of theirs is bewitched', wrote George Gifford

23. [R. Filmer], *An Advertisement to the Jury Men of England Touching Witches* (London, 1653), p. 11.

24. W. Rowley, T. Dekker, and J. Ford, *The Witch of Edmonton* (1658 edn), in P. Corbin and D. Sedge (eds), *Three Jacobean Witchcraft Plays* (Manchester, 1986), p. 185.

25. Bernard, *Guide to Grand-Jury Men*, p. 209.

26. *The Wonderful Discoverie of the Witchcrafts of Margaret and Phillip Flower* (London, 1619), sig. E.

27. Kittredge, *Witchcraft*, pp. 49, 102; Thomas, *Religion and the Decline of Magic*, pp. 648–9.

28. Bernard, *Guide to Grand-Jury Men*, pp. 200, 209–11.

29. For some examples, see *Witches Apprehended, Examined and Executed* (London, 1613); and *Great News from the West of England* (London, 1689).

30. C. Holmes, 'Popular culture? Witches, magistrates, and divines in early modern England', in S.L. Kaplan (ed.), *Understanding Popular Culture* (Berlin, 1984), pp. 104–5; Kittredge, *Witchcraft*, p. 236.

in 1587, 'and threaten her, that if she doe not take home her spirite, and if that he come any more they will cause her to bee hanged.'[31] Cases from Yorkshire and Humberside in the 1640s and 1650s include victims avoiding a suspected witch, consulting a minister for advice, negotiating with suspects in an effort to placate them, as well as more violent direct action in the form of drawing blood and beatings. We know about these cases because they were finally taken to court.[32]

III

Anthropologists draw a distinction between witchcraft and sorcery. Witchcraft is seen as an inherited power, in the blood so to speak, passed on from generation to generation. Sorcery, on the other hand, is an acquired technique rather than an internal power: the casting of a spell, the performance of a ritual. It too can be handed down from one generation to another, but in this case the art is learned. We do not know to what extent the people of the early modern period observed such anthropological distinctions – there is evidence for both magical technique and inherited power – but we do know of a commonplace belief that there were those in society who had the power to do harm and good to others. We will deal later with those who had the power to do good, the white witches. At the moment we are concerned with what Christina Larner has termed 'primary witchcraft', the belief that there were those in the community capable of doing harm by occult or magical means: that is, maleficium.[33] Maleficia included the sickness or death of family or neighbours, or their animals, and damage to their property or produce. In other words, black witches were bringers of misfortune, evil-doers. G.L. Kittredge wrote long ago that the essence of witchcraft was maleficium. The witch was 'hunted down like a wolf because she is an enemy to mankind. Her heart is full of malignity. For a harsh word, or the refusal of a bit of bread, she becomes your mortal foe.'[34] This spirit is manifest in the witch of Edmonton, for whom vengeance was 'sweeter far than life':

---

31. Gifford, *Discourse*, sig. H3.
32. Raine (ed.), *Depositions from the Castle of York*, pp. 6–9, 58. See also, the discussions of counter-magic in Macfarlane, *Witchcraft*, ch. 7; J.A. Sharpe, *Witchcraft in Seventeenth-century Yorkshire: Accusations and Counter Measures* (York, 1992), pp. 11–17; Sharpe, *Instruments of Darkness*, ch. 6.
33. C. Larner, *Enemies of God* (London, 1981), p. 7.
34. Kittredge, *Witchcraft*, p. 4.

Thou art my raven on whose coal-black wings
Revenge comes flying to me. O my best love!
I am on fire, even in the midst of ice . . .[35]

It is difficult for the modern observer to enter this world of the witches. We know that in England people believed that there were those in the community who had fearsome powers to do harm. These black witches, bad witches, or binding witches could hurt or kill, induce damage or sickness, by a spell, curse, comment, or a glance. The witch Margaret Landish responded to a child's taunts by clapping her hands in a 'Threatening manner, telling her she should Smart for it, and that very Night the said Child fell Sick in a Raving manner, and dyed within three Weeks after'.[36] The essence of these early modern witches, the 'hurting witch', was not unlike that of the (modern-day) French witches who 'hunger after other people's misfortunes, and whose words, look and touch have supernatural power'.[37] In a case of early seventeenth-century Devonshire witchcraft a man and woman had been sitting talking by a door. The woman observed that she wished that her child could run as well as the children they were watching in the street; the man, who had 'a general bad report' about him, replied 'It shall never run'. The words were spoken with 'great vehemency'. The very same week, the child fell sick, 'consumed away', and eventually died.[38] When the Hertfordshire witch, Joan Harrison, was abused by a yeoman, she retorted 'I will say little to thee, but thou shalt feel more from me hereafter' – and the yeoman did.[39] Words, to quote Jeanne Favret-Saada, killed 'as surely as a bullet'.[40] The Yorkshire witches of 1621 were believed to work their malice through touch: a clap on the back, a brush against the hem of a garment.[41] Elizabeth Bennet effected her witchcraft by touch, looks, and words. She clasped her quarry in her arms and kissed her, presumably looking her in the eye as she said 'a good woman how thou art loden'; 'Whereupon presently after [the victim's] upper Lippe swelled & was very bigge, & her eyes much sunked into her head.'[42]

Richard Bernard summarised the rest of the witches' repertoire. They used charms and spells. They praised excessively with reversed

---

35. Corbin and Sedge (eds), *Three Jacobean Witchcraft Plays*, p. 199.
36. *The Full Tryals, Examination and Condemnation of Four Notorious Witches* (London, n.d.), pp. 3–4.
37. J. Favret-Saada, *Deadly Words: Witchcraft in the Bocage* (Cambridge, 1980), p. 6.
38. Kittredge, *Witchcraft*, p. 8.   39. Rosen (ed.), *Witchcraft*, p. 325.
40. Favret-Saada, *Deadly Words*, p. 13.
41. Grainge (ed.), *Daemonologia*, pp. 50, 52, 60.
42. *True and just Recorde*, sigs B5v–B6.

malevolence. They constructed and manipulated images of their prey with a brand of voodoo magic. A Lancashire white witch accused of black witchcraft said that 'the speediest way to take a mans life away by Witch-craft' was to

> make a Picture of Clay, like unto the shape of the person whom they meane to kill, & dry it thorowly . . . then take a Thorne or Pinne, and pricke it in that part of the Picture you would so have to be ill: and when you would have any part of the Body to consume away, then take that part of the Picture, and burne it.[43]

Or they obtained a possession of the victim to work out their witchery, as we will see the Flowers did to wreak their vengeance upon the Earl of Rutland.[44] Bernard said that witches used enchanted food or drink. They might even breathe upon their victim (though this example comes from a Continental case). They employed animalistic spirits, their familiars, to carry out this evil work.[45]

The symptoms of witchcraft were akin to those experienced by the victims of Dorothy Stranger, discussed earlier. Physical or psychological distress without any natural explanation, 'violent and sudden torture in a healthy body', loss of speech or sight, paralysis of the limbs, heaving of the belly, supernatural and uncontrolled strength, vomiting of foreign objects (pins, coal, hair, straw), unusual perspicacity, visions: all were indications that an individual had been bewitched.[46]

It was believed that the powers of witchcraft were mainly to be found in women. In an interesting gender polarity, it was sometimes observed that the good or white witches were mostly (though not exclusively) male, while the bad or hurting witches were chiefly female.[47] Demonologists provided traditional misogynistic reasons: women were more credulous, impatient, superstitious, 'the weaker Vessels', and for this reason Satan worked on them as he had with Eve.[48] Such associations were, as Clark has pointed out, 'the merest of cliches'.[49] Yet there are other suggestions that contemporaries' empirical observations about the prevalence of women were explained by a recognition of the wider social and cultural role of

43. T. Potts, *The Wonderfull Discoverie of Witches in the Countie of Lancaster* (London, 1613) (Chetham Society edn, 1745), sig. B3v.
44. See p. 123 below.   45. Bernard, *Guide to Grand-Jury Men*, pp. 171–7.
46. Ibid., pp. 163–70.
47. Ibid., pp. 87–9; J. Stearne, *A Confirmation and Discovery of Witchcraft* (London, 1648), p. 10.
48. Bernard, *Guide to Grand-Jury Men*, pp. 88–9; *Full Tryals*, p. 8.
49. Clark, *Thinking with Demons*, p. 114.

women in the early modern period. Women were more prone to use words as a weapon, more 'tongue-ripe'.[50] A witch was 'She on whose tongue a whirlwind sits to blow'.[51] Susan Amussen has usefully described witching as 'invisible violence': men employed physical force, whereas women were thought more likely to resort to witchcraft.[52] There was, then, what James Sharpe has termed a 'complex zone of female power'.[53] But it is also crucial that most allegations of witchcraft emerged from a context of household and neighbourhood interaction, and from the inevitable frictions of community life. Women were pivotal to neighbourhood and family life, to making do (including begging), healing, and child-care. It was women's importance in this social world, rather than a simple equation between witch- and woman-hunting, which ensured their centrality to witchcraft.[54]

We know also that the power of witches was handed down in the family, either in the blood or by the imparting of the art by the witch to those around her, family and servants.[55] One of the sixteenth-century Chelmsford witches 'learned this art of witchcraft at the age of 12 years, of her grandmother'; another's mother had been executed as a witch.[56] Sisters and daughters of 'notorious' witches were suspected. Joan Harrison and her daughter were executed in Hertford in 1606.[57] The Suttons – mother and daughter – were executed in Bedford in 1612.[58] The Lincolnshire witches, the Flowers, put to death in 1619, were sisters, and also daughters of a known witch.[59] An accused Suffolk witch told his interrogator in the 1640s that 'He could not help it, for that all his generation was naught . . . his mother and aunt were hanged, his grandmother burnt for Witchcraft, and so others of them questioned and hanged.'[60] And Jennit Dibble, an elderly seventeenth-century northern witch, had a mother, two aunts, two sisters, a husband, and children 'all . . . long esteemed witches, for that it seemeth hereditary to her

50. Bernard, *Guide to Grand-Jury Men*, p. 89.

51. Corbin and Sedge (eds), *Three Jacobean Witchcraft Plays*, p. 188.

52. S.D. Amussen, 'Punishment, discipline, and power: the social meanings of violence in early modern England', *Journal of British Studies* 34 (1995), 27.

53. J.A. Sharpe, 'Witchcraft and women in seventeenth-century England: some northern evidence', *Continuity and Change* 6 (1991), 186.

54. Sharpe, 'Witchcraft and women', provides a useful discussion of the complexities of the subject. See also, C. Holmes, 'Women: witnesses and witches', *Past and Present* 140 (1993), 45–78.

55. Bernard, *Guide to Grand-Jury Men*, pp. 88–9.

56. Rosen (ed.), *Witchcraft*, pp. 73, 94.   57. Ibid., p. 323.

58. *Witches Apprehended.*   59. *Wonderful Discoverie.*

60. Stearne, *Confirmation*, p. 36.

family'.[61] This strong kinship characteristic of witchcraft may help
to explain the dramatic denunciations of witches by their children:
it may have been the only way for offspring to sever the curse of
their blood.[62]

The witch was thought to have a strong link with the forces of
nature, particularly the animal world. English witches had 'familiars',
animals kept by the witch and sent out to perform maleficia.[63] When
the neighbours of Joan Flower characterised her as a witch, they
said that she 'dealt with familiar spirits, and terrified them all with
curses and threatning of revenge'.[64] These strange spirits are there
in the earliest printed accounts of English witchcraft. The confessions of the Windsor witches, published in 1579, refer to spirits in
the likenesses of toads, cats, and rats, wicked spirits, fed by the
witch with her own blood.[65] Joan Cunny, an old Essex witch, was
alleged to have had four familiars which she kept in a box and fed
with bread and milk. 'Jack killed mankind. Jill womenkind. Nicholas
killed horses. Ned killed cattle.'[66] Significantly, the witchcraft stat-
ute of 1604 made it a felony to 'consult covenant with entertaine
employ feede or rewarde any evill and wicked Spirit'.[67] These harm-
ful spirits were so central to English witchcraft that by 1629 grand
juries were being told that all bad witches have 'familiar spirits'.[68]
They were pictured in the woodcut prints of the pamphlet literature.[69] They dominate the narratives of witchcraft which emerge
from the hunts of the 1640s. The 'imps', either visible or invisible,
appeared in insect- or animal-like form to effect the witch's and the
Devil's work. The witch-hunters of the 1640s searched the witches'
bodies for evidence that they suckled these malevolent offspring,
and 'watched' them for days and nights on end in the hope that the
imps would return to their 'mother'.[70] Very probably the popular

61. Grainge (ed.), *Daemonologia*, p. 33.
62. See the case of the St Osyth witches in *True and just Recorde*. The pamphlet is
reprinted in Rosen (ed.), *Witchcraft*, pp. 103–57.
63. Holmes, 'Popular culture', pp. 97–9; Sharpe, *Instruments of Darkness*, pp. 71–4.
64. *Wonderful Discoverie*, sig. C3v.   65. *Rehearsall both straung and true.*
66. Rosen (ed.), *Witchcraft*, p. 184.   67. Macfarlane, *Witchcraft*, p. 15.
68. Bernard, *Guide to Grand-Jury Men*, pp. 152–3.
69. E.g. *Wonderful Discoverie*; M. Hopkins, *The Discovery of Witches* (London, 1647);
and the illustrations in Rosen (ed.), *Witchcraft*, pp. 78, 83, 93, 105, 110, 113, 120,
136, 183, 370.
70. Stearne, *Confirmation*; J. Sharpe, 'The devil in East Anglia: the Matthew Hopkins
trials reconsidered', in J. Barry, M. Hester, and G. Roberts (eds), *Witchcraft in Early
Modern Europe: Studies in Culture and Belief* (Cambridge, 1996), ch. 9; Sharpe, *Instruments of Darkness*, ch. 5. *A true and exact Relation Of the severall Informations, Examinations, and Confessions of the late Witches . . . in the County of Essex* (London, 1645) contains
statements by watchers and searchers.

remedy of drawing the blood of a suspected witch (the scratching discussed earlier) represented a severing of the link between the witch and the familiar which fed on her blood. As Gifford put it, 'some fall upon the Witch and beate her, or clawe her, to fetch blood: that so her spirite may have no power'.[71] It is difficult to follow Keith Thomas in his claim that familiars were 'very far from being an indispensable feature' of the English witch trials.[72]

IV

The community also believed in another type of witch, a good witch, the unbinding witch; the white witches, cunning folk, blessers, or wise men and women.[73] They were, as far as we know, numerous in early modern England. Alan Macfarlane has calculated that in Elizabethan Essex no village was more than ten miles from a known white witch.[74] They performed good by occult means: they were healers, fortune tellers, prescribers of charms for a variety of problems, and, as we have seen, combatants of black witchcraft.

There was a certain ambivalence about their powers, shared by customer and witch. Bernard was of the opinion that although most white witches were 'healing Witches', some had 'the double facultie, both to blesse, and to curse, to hurt, and to heale'.[75] The witch-hunter John Stearne claimed that many cunning folk were 'hurting Witches, as well as curing'.[76] The witches themselves may have thought that because they had the power to do good they could harness or direct their supernatural powers to do harm if the need arose. A seventeenth-century Carmarthenshire witch, skilled in curing sheep, offered to retaliate against her client's abusive husband: 'given a band-string or a point from his cod-piece, she could make an end of him'.[77] Patients and neighbours certainly had an unease about the powers of these cunning folk and if an unwitching went wrong, or neighbours fell out, the parties could become convinced that the witch had worked evil instead of good.[78] Annabel Gregory has unravelled the faction and neighbourhood conflict surrounding the accused Rye witch, Anne Bennett, in Sussex

---

71. Gifford, *Discourse*, sig. H3.
72. Thomas, *Religion and the Decline of Magic*, p. 531.
73. Sharpe, *Instruments of Darkness*, pp. 66–70.
74. Macfarlane, *Witchcraft*, p. 120.   75. Bernard, *Guide to Grand-Jury Men*, p. 127.
76. Stearne, *Confirmation*, p. 57.
77. C.L. Ewen, *Witchcraft and Demonianism* (London, 1933), p. 331.
78. Raine (ed.), *Depositions from the Castle of York*, pp. 64–5, 82.

in the early seventeenth century, but it is surely also significant that Bennett and her mother were known white witches.[79] Joan Peterson, the witch of Wapping hanged in 1652, was said to be both a bad and good witch.[80] When she was accused of maleficium, the white witch Kemp replied that 'though shee coulde unwitche shee coulde not witche'.[81] But John Walsh, another sixteenth-century witch, claimed that those who were able to unwitch had the ability to hurt – although once they had done harm they could never do good again.[82]

Some of the white witches had spirits or angels which they claimed to consult, and this must have contributed to the confusion with black witchcraft.[83] Stearne thought that most witches, good and bad, worked 'by Familiars'.[84] Two Leicestershire white witches, examined for black witchcraft in 1618, said that they had good spirits to assist them in their work. Joan Willimott, one of the healers, said that she had been given the spirit by an employer:

> and that her Master when hee gave it unto her, willed her to open her mouth, and hee would blow into her a Fairy which should do her good ... and that presently after his blowing, there came out of her mouth a Spirit, which stood upon the ground in the shape and forme of a Woman, which spirit did aske of her her Soule, which shee then promised unto it, being willed thereunto by her Master. Shee further confesseth, that shee never did hurt any body, but did helpe divers that sent for her, which were stricken or forespoken: and that her Spirit came weekely to her, and would tell her of divers persons that were stricken and forespoken. And shee saith, that the use which shee had of the Spirit, was to know how those did which shee had undertaken to amend; and that shee did helpe them by certaine prayers which she used, and not by her owne Spirit ...[85]

It would have been difficult for clients to distinguish between good spirit and bad familiar, and demonologists helped to blur the distinction with their claims that all such spirits were evidence of league with the Devil.[86] But despite learned condemnation of all witchcraft as black witchcraft, the white witch maintained an autonomy in popular culture. People said that the cunning folk had a gift from

---

79. A. Gregory, 'Witchcraft, politics and "good neighbourhood" in early seventeenth-century Rye', *Past and Present* 133 (1991), 31–66.

80. *The Witch of Wapping* (London, 1652), p. 3.

81. *True and just Recorde*, sig. A2.   82. Rosen (ed.), *Witchcraft*, p. 70.

83. British Library, Sloane MS 1954/161–93: E. Poeton, 'The Winnowing of White Witchcraft'; Bernard, *Guide to Grand-Jury Men*, p. 126.

84. Stearne, *Confirmation*, p. 43.   85. *Wonderful Discoverie*, sigs E3v–E4.

86. E.g. W. Perkins, *A Discourse of the Damned Art of Witchcraft* (Cambridge, 1618).

God to do good, that they 'surely worke by God, because they use good prayers and good words, and often name God'.[87] It was, wrote one critic, 'The sottish conceit of many country people who think that white witches are illumined from above.'[88] One 'good woman' did 'more good in one yeare than all these scripture men will doe so long as they live'.[89]

Although they are agreed on the white witch's importance as a counter to black witchcraft, historians have disagreed over the extent to which white witches ended up as defendants in witchcraft trials.[90] It is true that statistically there is little support for the thesis that white witches were the targets of early modern witch-hunting.[91] Yet the brevity of the indictments which comprise the bulk of trial documents makes it impossible to identify a white witch in many cases, rendering quantitative analysis somewhat besides the point. Surely it is significant that when more detailed accounts of context and background are provided in the qualitative evidence of deposition and pamphlet, white witchcraft emerges as a stronger factor. This blurring of categories would have increased as demonological theories took hold, for Satan used both black and white. A revealing entry in the Kent quarter sessions papers for 1653 refers to an accusation of witchcraft against one Elizabeth Wood, '(among the neighbourhood about her) reputed a white witch'. But the word 'white' has been crossed out, leaving the simple ascription: witch.[92]

V

It should be noted that so far there has been little mention of the Devil, Satan, or demons. There is something of a historiographical orthodoxy, only recently challenged, which draws a distinction between learned and popular beliefs in witchcraft. The type of belief that we have been focusing on was merely that some individuals had the power to do harm; there was not an obsession with the diabolical.

---

87. Bernard, *Guide to Grand-Jury Men*, pp. 144, 146.   88. Sloane MS 1954/166.

89. Gifford, *Dialogue*, sig. M3v.

90. Compare Thomas, *Religion and the Decline of Magic*, p. 677; S. Clark, 'Protestant demonology: sin, superstition, and society (c. 1520–c. 1630)', in B. Ankarloo and G. Henningsen (eds), *Early Modern European Witchcraft: Centres and Peripheries* (Oxford, 1993), pp. 77–8; and W. de Blecourt, 'Witch doctors, soothsayers and priests . . . cunning folk in European historiography and tradition', *Social History* 19 (1994), 285–303, esp. p. 291.

91. Macfarlane, *Witchcraft*, pp. 127–8.

92. Centre for Kentish Studies, Maidstone, Q/SB 4/52: Kent Quarter Sessions Papers, 1653.

But the learned or elite view of witchcraft was that witches were the agents of the Devil, waging the war of evil against good.

Continental learned belief, although it varied over time and from place to place, has been well summarised by Brian Levack. The centrepiece of the learned stereotype was the pact that the witch made with the Devil, giving himself or herself to evil in return for the demonic help which made witchcraft possible. Witches, therefore, were the agents or dupes of Satan. The second cornerstone of the stereotype was the witches' sabbath, blasphemous and orgiastic meetings of the anti-society. And finally there were allied beliefs in night-flying and metamorphosis: witches, assisted by the Devil or demons, transported over long distances on the backs of animals or even transformed into animal shape.[93] Historians have therefore argued that it is possible to isolate two discourses of witchcraft – demonology and primary witchcraft – which could be characterised, sociologically, as Weberian ideal types. The French expert, Robert Muchembled, has described the witch-hunts as 'the point of intersection' of these two discourses 'completely foreign to one another'.[94]

However, the discourses and their intersections were by no means as pure, uncomplicated, and foreign to one another as this binary division implies. It is becoming evident that the characterisation of English witchcraft as non-demonological has been overdrawn.[95] From an early stage, the figure of the Devil was present in the discourses of witchcraft found in the pamphlet literature. English demonology may not have been identical to Continental demonology – the pact is stronger and the sabbath is weaker – but it was important nevertheless. Many early seventeenth-century patients of Richard Napier believed that they were at the mercy of an internal war between good and bad spirits, one associated with the angels, the other with demons, and they attributed a wide range of urges to the 'temptations of Satan'.[96] The belief in familiars meshed comfortably with theories of satanic influence through the agency of demons and, whatever the origins of this popular superstition, we have seen that the figure of the familiar remained central to English witch beliefs. Holmes has claimed that the notion of witches' familiars suckling

93. Levack, *Witch-hunt*, ch. 2.

94. R. Muchembled, *Popular Culture and Elite Culture in France 1400–1750* (Baton Rouge, La., 1985), p. 244.

95. Sharpe, 'Devil in East Anglia'; Sharpe, *Instruments of Darkness*, pp. 74–5, 82–5, 134–40.

96. M. MacDonald, *Mystical Bedlam: Madness, Anxiety, and Healing in Seventeenth-century England* (Cambridge, 1981), pp. 134, 144, 167, 175, 202, 203.

blood from witches' marks – sores or teats on the witch's body – was a perdurable popular belief incorporated by demonologists as evidence of a demonic pact: a sort of satanic stigmata.[97] Yet it would be difficult to prove this case. The images are so intermingled in the literature of pamphlet and deposition that separation of a traditional popular strand appears impossible. What is significant about the demonological discourses of early modern English witchcraft is their sheer variety rather than any consistency of representation. The work of Stuart Clark suggests that the interaction was not a case of simple acculturation of the powerless by the powerful, for the learned demonologist was forced to accommodate popular culture. Protestant demonology was thus stretched to 'include a very wide range of proscribed behaviour, most of it far removed from the classic stereotype of devil-worship'.[98]

The picture that is emerging in more recent work is one of cultural dynamism and malleability. Ministers published pamphlets, preached sermons, and personally confronted the accused to exhort them to confess the error of their ways. 'The pulpits . . . rang of nothing but divels and witches', an observer noted of a scare in Nottingham in the late sixteenth century.[99] Trials received publicity; spectators visited the accused in prison, flocked to the court, and attended hangings.[100] In 1712 testimonies against Jane Wenham, the Hertfordshire witch, were taken 'before a great Multitude of Spectators'; and when she was later tried at the assizes, the courtroom was full.[101] There were organised public confrontations between accuser and witch.[102] The case of the Warboys witches in Huntingdonshire in the late 1580s and 1590s was a highly public drama involving sustained gentry attempts to get the suspected witches, the Samuel family, to confess, as well as continual visiting of suspects and victims by ministers, Cambridge scholars, relatives, friends, and other interested parties. The public drama continued into the trial process itself. The assize judge witnessed the fits of one of the victims, and bewitched and bewitcher were forced to face one another in open court.[103] In like manner, at a trial in Northampton

97. Holmes, 'Popular culture', pp. 98–9.

98. Clark, 'Protestant demonology', p. 62.

99. Sharpe, *Instruments of Darkness*, p. 164.

100. Holmes, 'Popular Culture', pp. 89, 92–3.

101. P.J. Guskin, 'The context of witchcraft: the case of Jane Wenham (1712)', *Eighteenth-Century Studies* 15 (1981–2), 51, 53.

102. *Great News from the West of England*, p. 2.

103. *The most strange and admirable discoverie of the three Witches of Warboys* (London, 1593).

in 1612, victims of alleged witchcraft went to the prison to scratch a suspect, confronted their tormentors in the castle yard 'amongst the people', and fell into fits outside the court. One witness appeared before the bench in a state of convulsion, and the judge allowed the accused witches to be brought in to touch their alleged victim.[104] Well-publicised cases of demonic possession provided dramatic evidence of the powers of Satan.[105] There was even an exhibition of a demonic artefact (a sinewy and scorched piece of flesh allegedly given to a witch by the Devil) at the Swan Inn in Maidstone in the 1650s.[106]

Cheap witchcraft pamphlets and ballads bridged educated and partially literate cultures.[107] Although there are few surviving ballads about witches – the collection of Samuel Pepys contains only one: about the Lincolnshire witches[108] – we know that ballads were sung and hawked at the time of the execution of Elizabeth Sawyer, the witch of Edmonton. Henry Goodcole complained that he 'was ashamed to see and heare such ridiculous fictions of her bewitching Corne on the ground, of a Ferret and an Owle dayly sporting before her, of the bewitched woman brayning her selfe, of the Spirits attending in the Prison'. There was a pamphlet and a play about Sawyer's trial and execution.[109] Similarly, a play about the Lancashire witches – with its stories of metamorphosis, familiars, sexual impotence, and demonic intercourse – was performed at the Globe in London in 1634 to 'great concourse of people', including large numbers of 'fine folk'. It had particular resonance because the accused witches were, as one observer noted, 'still visible and in prison here'.[110] There was also a puppet show of the same name performed that year in Oxford.[111] By such means, the discourses of demonology could make mental inroads at a popular level and village beliefs influence learned doctrines.

104. Ewen, *Witchcraft*, p. 211.

105. Holmes, 'Women', pp. 59–65; Sharpe, *Instruments of Darkness*, ch. 8.

106. *A Prodigious & Tragicall History of the Arraignment, Tryall, Confession, and Condemnation of six Witches at Maidstone* (London, 1652), p. 4.

107. Holmes, 'Women', 58.

108. *Damnable Practices Of three Lincoln-shire Witches* (London, 1619), in W.G. Day (ed.), *The Pepys Ballads*, 5 vols (Cambridge, 1987), Vol. 1, pp. 132–3.

109. H. Goodcole, *The wonderfull discoverie of Elizabeth Sawyer* (London, 1621), sig. A3v.; Rowley, Dekker, and Ford, *Witch of Edmonton*; F.E. Dolan, '"Ridiculous Fictions": making distinctions in the discourses of witchcraft', *Differences* 7 (1995), 85–6.

110. The play was a version of Thomas Heywood and Richard Brome's *The late Lancashire Witches* (London, 1634). See H. Berry, 'The Globe bewitched and *El Hombre Fiel*', *Medieval and Renaissance Drama in England* 1 (1984), 211–30 (quotes on pp. 212–13); L.H. Barber (ed.), *An Edition of The Late Lancashire Witches by Thomas Heywood and Richard Brome* (New York, 1979).

111. S.C. Shershow, *Puppets and 'Popular' Culture* (Ithaca, NY, 1995), p. 37.

Bernard's book, for example, drew on the Bible, the classics, English theology, and Continental demonology, as well as a thriving indigenous popular literature. Intellectual traditions intermingled in his guide.[112] Moreover, the trial pamphlets which he drew on were the product of interactions between accuser, inquisitor, witch, judge, and community, filtered through an authorial lens, and which became, in turn, narratives informing written and oral discourses of witchcraft.[113] John Gaule, a Huntingdonshire minister, was concerned that his book on witchcraft would help to spread the very beliefs he was trying to counteract.[114] Bernard's own work also functioned in this way, but it had a more direct influence upon those whose task it was to deal judicially with witchcraft. It was, after all, a guide for juries and justices, and we know that it was heavily plagiarised by the witch-hunter Stearne and others.[115] Thus the cycle of interaction continued.

VI

One of the most influential theories of the causes of English witchcraft allegations – what is often termed the Thomas or Macfarlane theory – focuses on the social context of witchcraft. Witchcraft accusations arose out of a breach in neighbourly charity and the guilt associated with that rupture.[116] This connection between unexplained misfortune and the denial of charity was a link that early modern observers themselves made. Thomas Ady wrote in 1656:

> people are now so infected with this damnable Heresie, of ascribing to the power of Witches, that seldom hath a man the hand of God against him in his estate, or health of body, or any way, but presently he cryeth out of some poor innocent Neighbour, that he, or she hath bewitched him; for saith he, such an old man or woman came lately to my door, and desired some relief, and I denied it, and God forgive me, my heart did rise against her at that time, my mind gave me she looked like a Witch, and presently my Child, my Wife, my Self,

112. He drew on both Continental authorities (e.g. Martin del Rio, Jean Bodin) and English pamphlets (e.g. George Gifford, William Perkins, John Cotta, Thomas Cooper, and the accounts of the Lancashire, Leicestershire, Bedfordshire, and Northamptonshire witches). See also, Sharpe, *Instruments of Darkness*, pp. 100–1.

113. Dolan makes a similar point: 'Ridiculous Fictions', pp. 84–5.

114. J. Gaule, *Select Cases of Conscience Touching Witches and Witchcraft* (London, 1646), p. 76.

115. Kittredge, *Witchcraft*, p. 273.

116. Thomas, *Religion and the Decline of Magic*, pp. 660–80; Macfarlane, *Witchcraft*, pp. 173–6.

my Horse, my Cow, my Sheep, my Sow, my Hogge, my Dogge, my Cat, or somewhat was thus and thus handled, in such a strange manner, as I dare swear she is a Witch, or else how should those things be, or come to pass?[117]

Yet the problem with this explanation is that neighbourly conflict and breaches in community obligations were commonplace in early modern society. We still need to explain why particular instances became accusations of witchcraft while thousands of others did not.[118] Indeed, this was a point made by Ady himself, who observed that there would have been few in England who had not had a poor person at the door.[119]

What made a particular request for neighbourly help potentially risky for the refuser was the character or reputation of the requester. The poor person at the door was not just any poor person. Although it was a dangerous game to play, it is clear that some members of the community survived through the acquisition of a malevolent reputation. A Yorkshire witch, 'a woman notoriously famed for a witch, . . . had so powerful hand over the wealthiest neighbours about her, that none of them refused to do anything she required; yea, unbesought they provided her with fire, and meat from their own tables; and did what else they thought would please her'.[120] It is likely that many of the 'innocent' old women who were the subject of a breach in neighbourly obligation were indeed those who used their reputation as a weapon in the battle for survival.[121] Reginald Scot, sometimes quoted in support of the Thomas–Macfarlane thesis, was actually describing the scenario of the refusal of a reputed witch rather than that of any innocent old woman:

These miserable wretches are so odious unto all their neighbors, and so feared, as few dare offend them, or denie them anie thing they aske: whereby they take upon them; yea, and sometimes thinke, that they can doo such things as are beyond the abilitie of humane nature. These goe from house to house, and from doore to doore for a pot full of milke, yest, drinke, pottage, or some such releefe; without the which they could hardlie live . . . It falleth out many times, that neither their necessities, nor their expectation is answered or served,

---

117. T. Ady, *A Candle in the Dark* (London, 1656), pp. 114–15.
118. A point made in recent critiques of Thomas/Macfarlane: J. Barry, 'Introduction: Keith Thomas and the problem of witchcraft', in Barry, Hester, and Roberts (eds), *Witchcraft*, p. 9; R. Briggs, *Witches and Neighbours: the Social and Cultural Context of European Witchcraft* (London, 1996), p. 142.
119. Ady, *Candle*, p. 129.   120. Grainge (ed.), *Daemonologia*, p. 34.
121. This argument did not escape Thomas, but it was not a central part of his thesis: Thomas, *Religion and the Decline of Magic*, pp. 674–5.

in those places where they beg or borrowe; but rather their lewdnesse is by their neighbors reproved. And further, in tract of time the witch wareth odious and tedious to hir neighbors; and they againe are despised and despited of hir: so as sometimes she curseth one, and sometimes another ... Thus in processe of time they have all displeased hir, and she hath wished evill lucke unto them all; perhaps with curses and imprecations made in forme. Doubtlesse (at length) some of hir neighbours die, or fall sicke; or some of their children are visited with diseases ... Which by ignorant parents are supposed to be the vengeance of witches ... The witch on the other side expecting hir neighbours mischances, and seeing things sometimes come to passe according to her wishes, curses, and incantations ... being called before a Justice, by due examination of the circumstances is driven to see hir imprecations and desires, and hir neighbors harmes and losses to concurre, and as it were to take effect: and so confesseth that she (as a goddes) hath brought such things to passe. Wherein, not onelie she, but the accuser, and also the Justice are fowlie deceived and abused ...[122]

Many of those (eventually) formally accused of witchcraft had been accounted witches for years, if not decades. The eighteenth-century witch Jane Wenham had been 'suspected of being a witch these twenty year'.[123] Narratives often refer to the accused as having 'an ill name' or 'very bad fame', long suspected 'for a Witch'. One of the Yorkshire witches came into the area with 'an evil report for witchcraft', while others were described respectively as 'reputed a witch for many years', 'long esteemed witches', and 'notoriously famed for a witch'.[124] Such women survived in their communities for years, known but never officially punished; and they may never have surfaced in the criminal records or the witchcraft literature at all if nearby well-publicised trials, the zeal of local gentry and ministers, or the intervention of witch-finders had not stimulated action against them. One of the Lancashire witches had been a witch for fifty years before she fell foul of a county justice.[125]

VII

Interestingly, Scot's account of the social context of witchcraft allegations referred also to the witch's 'imprecations and desires'.

122. R. Scot, *Discoverie of Witchcraft* (London, 1584), pp. 7–8.
123. Guskin, 'Context of witchcraft', p. 50.
124. *True and exact Relation*, pp. 15, 22; Grainge (ed.), *Daemonologia*, pp. 31, 33, 34.
125. Potts, *Wonderfull Discoverie*, sig. Bv. For elite initiative, see Holmes, 'Women', pp. 52–9.

It is this psychological element in the narratives of witchcraft that recent scholarship has begun to explore: the ability of witchcraft beliefs to foster and expose fantasy.[126] There have been studies of witchcraft confessions as expressions of the insecurities and hostilities of motherhood and housewifery, and as projections of the psychological conflict between mother and child: 'in early modern culture the figure of the witch was closely intertwined with that of the mother'.[127] Stories of witchcraft were a way for some women to 'negotiate the fears and anxieties of housekeeping and motherhood'. Female anxieties were projected onto the witch figure of the 'other', the anti-housewife or anti-mother: women such as Ursula Kemp. 'For women, a witch was a figure who could be read against and within her own social identity as housewife and mother.'[128]

Lyndal Roper has claimed recently that witch trials were not merely sites where accused women were forced to conform passively with stereotypes already plotted for them, but that the accused witches – even when tortured – were able to construct narratives to bring shape to their lives, and to make sense of 'their unbearable hatreds, agonies, jealousies'.[129] Diane Purkiss writes too of women accused of witchcraft 'shaping their own stories'.[130] This seems to me to be a very useful way to look at witchcraft confessions. In them the witch looks back over years of interaction with her neighbours and family, and is forced to confront her secret (and not so secret) 'imprecations and desires'.

Yet what these studies have not recognised sufficiently is the striking retrospective nature of many of the witchcraft narratives. It was this aspect of the accounts – witnesses' statements as well as the

126. Briggs, *Witches and Neighbours*, pp. 163, 387. See also Barry, 'Introduction', pp. 42–5.

127. L. Roper, *Oedipus and the Devil: Witchcraft, Sexuality and Religion in Early Modern Europe* (London, 1994); L. Jackson, 'Witches, wives and mothers: witchcraft persecution and women's confessions in seventeenth-century England', *Women's History Review* 4 (1995), 63–83; D. Purkiss, 'Women's stories of witchcraft in early modern England: the house, the body, the child', *Gender and History* 7 (1995), 408–32. For the quote, see D. Willis, *Malevolent Nurture: Witch-hunting and Maternal Power in Early Modern England* (Ithaca, NY, 1995), p. 17. While the witch as 'monstrous mother' has much to recommend it, Willis is inclined to rather bizarre claims. Of a victim of witchcraft whose pig would not let its young suckle, she says: 'Alice [the victim of witchcraft] perhaps saw in the pig the retaliatory mother whom she had unconsciously attacked and projected the image onto Joan [the witch]; the first sow in particular enacted a fantasy of maternal retaliation quite explicitly' (p. 51).

128. D. Purkiss, *The Witch in History: Early Modern and Twentieth-century Interpretations* (London, 1996), chs 4–5 (quotes from pp. 93, 94).

129. Roper, *Oedipus and the Devil*, p. 20.

130. Purkiss, *Witch in History*, p. 145. See ch. 6: 'Self-fashioning by women: choosing to be a witch'.

confessions of the accused – which gave such depth and force to their fantasies. They were histories of conflict, uncertainty, and malice which spanned five, seven, ten, twenty, thirty, fifty, sixty years.[131] Witchcraft statements repeatedly outline events from the distant past. Witchcraft narratives were deadly histories, where accuser, witch, and community looked back on their lives to chart their desires, temptations, and fantasies. Dreams and hidden impulses were realised in memory; and the tensions and fantasies revealed in these narratives were not limited to issues of motherhood.

As was suggested earlier in the chapter, vengeance lies at the heart of the witchcraft fantasies. The Flower women carried out a campaign of revenge against the family of the Earl of Rutland when one of their number was dismissed from the countess's service. They obtained gloves worn by the earl and countess's sons, pricked holes in them and, in a form of imitative magic, buried them in the ground to rot so that the wearers 'might never thrive'. Determined 'to bewitch the Earle and his Lady, that they might have no more children', they obtained wool from a household mattress (associated with the Rutlands' sexual activity and fecundity), boiled it in blood and performed rituals with it, 'saying the Lord and the Lady should have more Children, but it would be long first'.[132] Anne Chattox, one of the Lancaster witches, said that the Devil had told her that if she would give him her soul she would 'be revenged' upon whomever she wanted.[133] Rebecca West confessed that 'she had familiarity with the Devil, who came to her in the likeness of a young Man, promising her that she should be revenged of all her Enimies . . . if she would deny God and wholy trust to him'.[134]

Chattox and West were also told that they would 'want nothing' and have what they desired. Material gain is an important motive in the witchcraft narratives. The Lancaster examinations refer to demonic promises of 'worldly Wealth' and food and drink.[135] Learned commentators recognised the twin temptations of revenge and

---

131. See Potts, *Wonderfull Discoverie*; Stearne, *Confirmation*; J. Davenport, *The Witches of Huntingdon* (London, 1646); *True and exact Relation*. Ironically, the longevity of the witchcraft scenarios undermines one of the arguments for witchcraft as fantasy. Deborah Willis's recent Kleinian analysis of the witch as 'malevolent mother' rests on the observation that the typical witchcraft case began with the falling out between an older (the mother-figure) and younger woman. While this is true to some extent, such cases often represent the culmination of years of suspicions and accusations, stretching back to a time when the accused was far from elderly: Willis, *Malevolent Nurture*, pp. 30, 43.

132. *Wonderful Discoverie*.   133. Potts, *Wonderfull Discoverie*, sig. D3.

134. *Full Tryals*, p. 2.   135. Potts, *Wonderfull Discoverie*, sig. B4v.

wealth. People were susceptible to the wiles of Satan when they were 'impatient of poverty' or 'inraged with anger, plotting revenge'.[136] The Devil promised food to the poor and vengeance to the aggrieved.[137]

Confessions could also become narratives of an accused witch's life as wishes and fantasies were fulfilled in retrospect, and evil thoughts became evil actions. Some of the stories have a fairytale appearance. Elizabeth Francis, the Chelmsford witch, said that she had learned witchcraft at the age of 12, tutored by her grandmother. She had a familiar, a cat called Sathan or Satan, who fulfilled her wishes. She wanted to be rich, so Satan brought her sheep (but they died). Then she wanted a husband, and the cat brought her a 'man of some wealth'. But he got her pregnant and then refused to marry her, so Elizabeth 'willed Satan' to waste his goods, take his life, and abort her unwanted child. The man died, and the familiar 'bade her take a certain herb and drink it, which she did, and destroyed the child forthwith'. She then desired another husband, which the cat provided, although this one was 'not so rich as the other'. She had premarital sex with this man too, but he married her and the child was born three months into the marriage. 'After they were married they lived not so quietly as she desired', so Elizabeth 'willed' Satan to kill the child and lame her husband. She then passed on Satan to a neighbour (another accused witch) and this woman used the familiar to kill her husband because they lived 'somewhat unquietly'.[138] Here was a spirit, the suggestively named Satan, which could rid the world of unwanted husbands and children, but which was clearly the projection of a woman's desires and guilt – a baby aborted, and lovers and children wished dead.

The psychological element of these deadly narratives is particularly strong in the 1640s when accused women reinterpreted their pasts in the light of the more distilled demonology of the witchhunters Matthew Hopkins and John Stearne. A Suffolk woman said that the Devil had appeared to her thirty years earlier in the shape of a 'black boy' and drew blood from her against her will. She covenanted to give him her body and soul in return for money and vengeance against those who angered her.[139] Another claimed that about twenty years before three things had come to her, one like a rat, one like a mole, and one like a mouse. The mole 'spoke to her with a great hollow voyce' and asked her to give her soul to him;

---

136. Bernard, *Guide to Grand-Jury Men*, pp. 99–100.   137. Ibid., p. 106.
138. Rosen (ed.), *Witchcraft*, pp. 73–7.
139. C.L. Ewen, *Witch Hunting and Witch Trials* (London, 1929), p. 292.

in return 'he told her she should never want, but be avenged of all her enemies'. She consented, and 'confessed that her wishes came to passe': 'she wished one goodman Garneham might be lame, and so he was, and that Master Lockweed might have Lice, because he formerly accused her for sending, or causing him to have some when she did it not, and so he had'.[140] Like her earlier Lancashire counterpart, the accused Suffolk witch gave her soul to the Devil so that he would 'provide for her against all want', and she could 'be avenged of all her enemies'.[141]

Thomazine Ratcliffe confessed 'that it was malice that had brought her to that she was come to'. Soon after her husband's death, a man had come to her bed and told her in a hollow shrill voice that he would 'be a loving husband to her, if she would consent to him', and he promised he would 'revenge her of all her enemies'.[142] Another woman claimed that the Devil had appeared in the likeness of a calf and asked for the use of her body. She had denied him, but then consented when he appeared as a 'handsome yonge gentleman wth yellow hayre and black cloaths & often times lay wth her and had the carnall use of her'.[143] It is difficult to know whose sexual fantasies the material reflects – those of the hunters or the witch – but the narratives of the 1640s contain a definite sexual element. The Devil repeatedly appeared to women in their beds at night (sometimes with cloven feet) and had 'the use of' their bodies: 'at his next appearance he lay wth her. She saw not his shape but onely felt round . . . and cold like a stone.'[144] The Huntingdon woman Elizabeth Weed was approached by three spirits as she said her evening prayers. She signed a covenant (with her own blood), promising her soul to the Devil at the end of twenty-one years. The role of one of the spirits (a black puppy) was to hurt cattle, the role of the other (a white puppy) was to hurt people, while 'the office of the man-like Spirit was to lye with her carnally, when and as often as she desired, and that hee did lye with her in that manner very often'.[145] Mary Skipper was visited by the Devil after her husband's death; he had 'constantly had the use of her ever since'.[146] One woman even observed the proprieties of courtship: she married the Devil and only had sex 'after she wer married'.[147]

---

140. Stearne, *Confirmation*, p. 28.   141. Ewen, *Witch Hunting*, pp. 298, 299.
142. Stearne, *Confirmation*, p. 22; Ewen, *Witch Hunting*, p. 300.
143. Ewen, *Witch Hunting*, p. 306.   144. Ibid., p. 299.
145. Davenport, *Witches of Huntingdon*, pp. 1–2.
146. Ewen, *Witch Hunting*, p. 313.   147. Ibid., p. 304.

These were retrospective fantasies in which demonology gave meaning to long-vanished wishes. Susanna Stegold knew that the Devil had come to her because when she wished her husband dead, he died, and that 'what so ever she wished came to pass'.[148] Priscilla Collit and Susannah Smith knew that they had been approached by Satan because they had been tempted to kill their own children – 'or else so shold allways continue poore'.[149]

VIII

This sort of analysis emphasises the agency of the witch, her role in the construction of the final confession. Yet it was obviously not an equal interaction, so it is worth pausing to consider the actual process of discovering a witch once a case had been brought to the attention of the legal authorities. It is true that in his influential advice to grand juries Bernard advised caution; it was better to put 'Ignoramus' on an indictment than 'Billa vera' 'and so thrust an intricate case upon a Jury [the Petty Jury] of simple men, who proceed too often upon relations of meere presumptions, and therefore sometimes very weake ones too, to take away mens lives'.[150] They were advised to be wary of counterfeits, to distinguish carefully between the supernatural and the natural, to seek learned advice from physicians, and to be alert to the fact that fear and imagination made 'many Witches among countrey people'.[151] He provided his readers with a list of the true signs of possession and the various attributes of the Devil and his agents. But the core impulse in Bernard's advice was to prove 'a league made with the Devil. In this only act standeth the very reality of a Witch.'[152] Those who examined witches were to be well versed 'in treatises of witchcraft, to know how to proceed understandingly in detecting them, and to bee able to judge when the witnesses speake to the point'. Detection was to proceed from what Bernard termed weak conjectures, through strong presumptions, to sufficient proofs and final confession.[153]

The impression given in this weighty guide is of advised checks, balances and caution, existing alongside a relentlessly blinkered logic which urged confession. Those involved in the case were to be

---

148. Ibid., p. 298.   149. Ibid., p. 296, 299. See also, Jackson, 'Witches'.
150. Bernard, *Guide to Grand-Jury Men*, pp. 24–5.   151. Ibid., p. 22.
152. Ibid., p. 212.   153. Ibid., pp. 222–3.

examined separately. First, the victim(s), those afflicted by witch-craft, were asked about the circumstances and nature of their bewitchment; whether they had sought a physician's advice; why they considered their affliction the result of witchcraft and not a natural ailment or the direct work of Satan; whom they suspected and on what grounds? Then it had to be determined whether a search had been made of the suspect to see if she (more rarely he) had the tell-tale witch's mark, insensitive to pain. If no search had been made, one had to be arranged.[154] Neighbours were then questioned along with others involved directly in the case, including 'suspected adversaries' of either the witch or the victim. If a physician or a white witch had been consulted by the bewitched, they were called in for questioning too. The suspect's family was central to the process, and indeed the testimony of a young child against a mother could bring about a confession. The authorities meanwhile searched the witch's house for physical signs of witchcraft: images, powders, bones, knots, receptacles for the witch's spirits, charms, books of witchcraft.

While all this was going on, a 'godly divine' was preparing the witch for the final confrontation and confession. Clearly there was pressure to confess: 'have a godly and learned Divine, and some-what well reade in the discourses of Witchcraft and impieties thereof, to bee instructing the suspected, of the points of salvation, of the damnable cursednesse of Witchcraft, and his or her fearefull state of death eternall, if guilty and not repentant'.[155] Finally, the suspect was examined – alone at first – and forced to answer the allegations of the witnesses. This was a moment of high drama as mothers were confronted by the denunciations of their own children, and many must simply have despaired and confessed. As the examinations proceeded, the questioners were to note the reactions of the witch: her demeanour (fear, down-cast looks!); how she answered (did she lie or contradict herself?). If the witch refused to confess during this private interrogation, he or she had to face her accusers – one by one, including her own family – in another stage of ritualised drama. If this still failed to bring the desired result, 'then such as have authority to examine, should begin to use sharpe speeches, and to threaten them with imprisonment and death'.[156] And then, when the case actually went to court (with or without a confession)

154. For searching, see Holmes, 'Women', pp. 65–75.
155. Bernard, *Guide to Grand-Jury Men*, p. 233.   156. Ibid., pp. 235–6.

a judge might well exert what has been described as inquisitorial pressure in an effort to secure a conviction.[157]

During the 1640s, in an 'inquisition of the body', the East Anglian hunters arranged humiliating searches for so-called witches' teats, immersed their victims in water (the swimming test), kept them without sleep, and walked them up and down throughout the night.[158] Matthew Hopkins denied putting words into the witches' mouths, yet his definition of a valid confession does little to undermine suspicions of undue pressure:

> when a Witch is first found with teats, then sequestered from her house . . . and so by good counsell brought into a sad condition, by understanding of the horribleness of her sin, and the judgements threatned against her; and knowing the Devils malice and subtile circumventions, is brought to remorse and sorrow for complying with Satan so long, and disobeying Gods sacred Commands, doth then desire to unfold her mind with much bitterness, and then without any of the before-mentioned hard usages or questions put to her, doth of her own accord declare what was the occasion of the Devils appearing to her, whether ignorance, pride, anger, malice, &c. was predominant over her, she doth then declare what speech they had, what likeness he was in, what voice he had, what familiars he sent her, what number of spirits, what names they had, what shape they were in, what imployment she set them about to severall persons in severall places (unknowne to the hearers) all which mischiefes being proved to be done, at the same time she confessed to the same parties for the same cause, and all effected, is testimony enough against her for all her denyall.[159]

Such evidence suggests a grid of persuasion, that the accused witches were certainly not free agents in the trial process. This is not to argue against any agency on the part of the defendant. The process of investigation and confession was one of negotiation (albeit on unequal terms) as women told their stories in histories only partly of their own making. Readers of 'witchcraft narratives' need to remember the rather forceful 'Meanes to bring him or her to confesse' which could lurk behind the brief witchcraft confessions tabled before the courts and/or relayed in printed accounts of trials.[160] The chaplain of Newgate prison, whose job it was to prepare the convicted Elizabeth Sawyer for execution in a 'theatre of

157. C.R. Unsworth, 'Witchcraft beliefs and criminal procedure in early modern England', in T.G. Watkin (ed.), *Legal Record and Historical Reality* (London, 1989), pp. 91–2.
158. Ibid., p. 93.   159. Hopkins, *Discovery*, p. 8.
160. Bernard, *Guide to Grand-Jury Men*, p. 235.

punishment' aimed at edifying and awing a much wider audience, remarked that her final confession (after conviction) had been 'extorted' 'with great labour'. Her confession – whose printing was part of this theatre – came as question-and-answer rather than free-flowing narrative, he explained, because he was 'inforced to speake unto her, because she might understand me, and give unto me answere, according to my demands, for she was a very ignorant woman'. His first question was: 'By what meanes came you to have aquaintance with the Divell?'[161]

IX

In an essay on one of the victims of the witch-hunter Hopkins, Malcolm Gaskill has argued that it is possible that the woman, Margaret Moore, who sold her soul to the Devil to protect her child, actually came to believe that she had the malevolent powers attributed to her by her neighbours and that these powers became part of a fantasy of revenge and reversal of oppression. She believed that she was a witch.[162] It is an interpretation very similar to that of the witch of Edmonton, who is forced into becoming a witch because she is treated as one:

> And why on me? Why should the envious world
> Throw all their scandalous malice upon me?
> 'Cause I am poor, deformed and ignorant,
> And like a bow buckled and bent together
> By some more strong in mischiefs than myself,
> Must I for that be made a common sink
> For all the filth and rubbish of men's tongues
> To fall and run into? Some call me witch,
> And, being ignorant of myself, they go
> About to teach me how to be one, urging
> That my bad tongue, by their bad usage made so,
> Forspeaks their cattle, doth bewitch their corn,
> Themselves, their servants and their babes at nurse.
> This they enforce upon me, and in part
> Make me to credit it.

161. Goodcole, *Wonderfull discoverie*, sigs B4, C. For the theatre of punishment, see J. Sharpe, ' "Last dying speeches": religion, ideology and public execution in seventeenth-century England', *Past and Present* 107 (1985), 144–67.

162. M. Gaskill, 'Witchcraft and power in early modern England: the case of Margaret Moore', in J. Kermode and G. Walker (eds), *Women, Crime and the Courts in Early Modern England* (London, 1994), ch. 6.

This witch became a witch because she thought that it was all one, 'To be a witch as to be counted one.' She then turned to the Devil because she wanted to be revenged upon those who mistreated her.

> Would some power, good or bad,
> Instruct me which way I might be revenged
> Upon this churl, I'd go out of myself
> And give this fury leave to dwell within . . .

It was her thirst for vengeance which provided the point of entry for Satan.[163]

Yet lurking in the background of most of the modern historiography of witchcraft is the assumption that the majority of accused witches were innocent. To quote one of the most influential recent texts, 'The majority of accused witches did not practise any sort of magic at all but were either accused of causing harm by magical means when unexplained misfortune struck one of their neighbours or when they were named as the accomplices of other witches in the course of a large witch-hunt.'[164] I am sceptical of this view of early modern society. As I hope this chapter has suggested, those accused of witchcraft when neighbourly relations were breached, or who narrated their deadly histories of temptation and malice, were not chosen randomly. They were those who had cultivated a reputation of witchcraft as a means of survival, who were linked to such people by blood or household ties, or who actually thought that they practised the art of black or white witchcraft. They were innocent in the sense that they could not help their inheritance, or because we would say they could not really bewitch or unwitch. But they were not innocent in terms of being totally unconnected with witching: they were not random victims. This explains the paucity of actual accusations of witchcraft in comparison to the numbers of those in the general population who fell out with their neighbours, or who had malevolent thoughts or misgivings about their husbands or motherhood. Those accused were the witch-prone.

This chapter has also argued that it is essential to take seriously the mental world of the witches. The *Strand Magazine* for 1900 contains an article by the writer Arthur Morrison about an Essex white witch known as Cunning Murrell who died in 1860. He was consulted over matters of the heart, the recovery of lost and stolen goods, to tell fortunes, heal animals, and to combat black witchcraft. His papers – astrological and geomantic notebooks, viewed by

---

163. Corbin and Sedge (eds), *Three Jacobean Witchcraft Plays*, pp. 159, 162.
164. Levack, *Witch-hunt*, p. 12.

Morrison but unfortunately destroyed in 1956 – contained numerous conjurations. There was one to summon the angel Raphael to assist Murrell in his work, another to call upon the angels to afflict those who harmed his patients. An 'immensely long conjuration' invoked 'the great Tetragrammaton and the whole host of Heaven to "drive out from Sarah Mott all evil spirits in the service of the Devil and to punish the witch who had put the harm upon her, but ten thousand times more to scarify and torture all the spirits of evil and bitterness of Great Wrath"'. Murrell is a perfect example of the ambivalences of white witchcraft. Although he was a good witch, both he and his patients believed that he had powers to inflict harm. Murrell's son, still living when the article was researched, insisted on his father's goodness: 'You know now about my father, sir, . . . Remember, sir, he were a good man – enemy to all witches, an the devil's master. He never *put on* – he took off. Remember that, sir.' Yet the author noted that many of the villagers were very careful not to displease Cunning Murrell's son.[165]

The account of Murrell contains many of the themes of early modern witchcraft, the need to be wary of a witch, the ambiguities of white witchcraft, the fusion of the discourses of demonology and primary witchcraft. It also provides a reminder that the world of the witches did not vanish with the last recorded witch trial in 1717. Hunting stopped in the early eighteenth century, but belief in witches continued.[166]

165. A. Morrison, 'A Wizard of Yesterday', *Strand Magazine* 20 (1900), 433–42; E. Maple, 'Cunning Murrell', *Folklore* 71 (1960), 37–43.

166. B. Bushaway, ' "Tacit, unsuspected, but still implicit faith": alternative belief in nineteenth-century rural England', in T. Harris (ed.), *Popular Culture in England, c. 1500–1850* (London, 1995), ch. 9; Sharpe, *Instruments of Darkness*, pp. 276–84; O. Davies, 'Cunning-folk in England and Wales during the eighteenth and nineteenth centuries', *Rural History* 8 (1997), 91–107. Ian Bostridge has shown that learned attitudes were slower in changing than has previously been thought: I. Bostridge, 'Witchcraft repealed', in Barry, Hester, and Roberts (eds), *Witchcraft*, ch. 12; I. Bostridge, *Witchcraft and its Transformations c. 1650–c. 1750* (Oxford, 1997).

CHAPTER FIVE

Festive Drama and Ritual

I

The autobiography of Samuel Bamford recalled ritual life in the north of England at the end of the eighteenth century. Although he was aware of the historical construction of ritual – indeed hypothesised about the origins of some of the local customs he described – Bamford's principal concern was with cultural transformation. His theme is of customs, 'time out of mind', undergoing great change in the space of his own lifetime (the first half of the nineteenth century). 'Thus we are enabled distinctly to perceive the great change which, in a few years, has taken place in the tastes and habits of the working classes.'[1] He therefore provides a rather static picture of the rites which he describes up until the very moment of their supposed rapid transformation. He also has political axes to grind. In his youth, he wrote, the poor sympathised with the poor, 'their sympathy not being of that description which in these times froths out in rabid speeches to starving multitudes, but was expressed by action as well as by word'.[2] When recounting Christmas holiday festivities, he outlined the reciprocities of poverty, the treating of neighbours to ale, food, or money. 'Thus the weaver and the collier would reciprocate their good wishes, which is better after all, more manly, and more in the old English way, more respectfully kind, than the vaunted French mode of fraternization.'[3] Such patriotic and masculinist subtexts were part of a view of the past that was romantic in essence, even pastoral. Allowing for these biases, Bamford's version of the rituals of his youth – at the very

---

1. S. Bamford, *Early Days* (London, 1849), p. 132.
2. Ibid., pp. 135–6.   3. Ibid., p. 136.

end of our period of interest – provides a useful snapshot of the types of activity which will be the subject of this chapter.

Bamford described a society in which customary rites were integrated into the rhythms and patterns of work, leisure, religion, and community. In Middleton, a weaving community of several thousand people not far from Manchester, it was the custom for the families of weavers to be set a quota of work to be completed before Christmas festivities commenced. This period of concentrated work was an important build-up to the relaxation of the Christmas holidays, which began (after Christmas Day) on the first Monday after New Year's Day. Like Lent and carnival – in reverse – the phase of heightened labour was a necessary counterpoint to the indulgence and idleness that followed. But this period of work and denial had its own rituals. Singing (hymns and carols in Methodist homes) kept participants awake during 'whole nights . . . spent at the loom'. 'A few hours of the late morning would perhaps be given to rest; work would then be resumed, and the singing and rattle of shuttles would be almost incessant during the day.'[4] When, after several weeks, the important Monday finally arrived, the cuts were prepared for dispatch to the warehouse, the loom-room swept, house and furniture cleaned, 'and the holidays then commenced'.[5] Festivities included football (for the boys) and ice-sliding for both sexes. Young men and women would gather in groups at night, in one another's homes or in the loom-houses, to play games and to tell ghost stories. There was also the conviviality alluded to earlier, with groups of people going from house to house: the church ringers and the colliers were two groups which Bamford particularly remembered. '[G]ood neighbourship' was demonstrated by the provision of 'a jug of ale and a present in money'. Dissenters gave to the church; weavers gave to miners.[6]

The rest of the year was also punctuated by ritual. At Shrovetide there was more visiting, and those who could not eat their pancakes were 'stanged', that is carried on a pole in a good-humoured ritual of humiliation, and deposited on a midden or rubbish tip. At mid-Lent, Cymbalin Sunday was observed, particularly in Bury, with more feasting: the eating of a round spiced cake called cymbalin and the drinking of mulled ale.

At Easter, 'all work was abandoned, good eating, good drinking, and new clothing were the order of the day'. 'Men thronged to the alehouses, and there was much folly, intemperance, and quarreling,

4. Ibid., p. 133.   5. Ibid., p. 134.   6. Ibid., p. 135.

amidst the prevailing good humour.' Children would go from door to door on Good Friday, 'peace egging'. On Easter Monday it was the turn of young men, 'grotesquely dressed', some in female attire, who would go in companies led by a fiddler. 'At some places they would dance, at others they would recite quaint verses, and at the houses of the more sedate inhabitants, they would merely request a "peace-egg".' [7] They were provided with the customary doles of money and ale. Bamford is almost certainly alluding here to what is known as the hero-combat form of the mummers' play, widespread throughout England in the nineteenth century.[8]

At night-time on Easter Tuesday, the alehouse culture provided a mock mayor, 'some unlucky fellow who had got so far intoxicated as not to be able to take care of himself', elected by the labourers and craftsmen of Middleton. In this mock election, the face of the candidate was daubed with soot and grease, his hair dusted with soot and flour,

> a pig-tail made from a dish-clout would be appended behind, a woman's kirtle, a cap, a hat without crown, an old jacket, an old sack, or any other dress which the imagination of his lordship's robers could construe, either into an article of adornment or deformity, would be placed upon him so as to have its greatest effect. He would then be taken into the street, placed on a chair, or in an arm-chair if too far gone to sit upright, and proclaimed 'Lord Mayor of Middleton', with every demonstration of drunken and mischievous glee.

Under cover of darkness, the 'mayor' was then paraded through the streets of the town, on a chair, pole, ladder, or the back of a donkey, as his supporters knocked on doors to request payment: 'Come deawn, milord wants his dues.'[9] Bamford noted a similar custom in nearby Ashton-under-Lyme, where a man clad in black was paraded through the town. This rite was called 'riding the Black Lad'. Bamford conjectured that the rituals had common origin in fifteenth-century derision of the injustices of the local lord of the manor, Raphe Assheton, the 'Black Knight', a sheriff of Yorkshire, and that the Middleton protest had originally been carried out under cover of darkness because of the proximity of the ritual's target and thus fear of repercussion. The blacking of Middleton's mayor, he thought, was, in effect, a disguise. The protestors at

7. Ibid., p. 138.

8. See A. Helm, *The English Mummers' Play* (Woodbridge, 1981), esp. ch. 5 and pp. 67–71.

9. Bamford, *Early Days*, p. 138.

Ashton, outside the immediate scrutiny of the lord, were able to express their 'hatred and contempt' more openly.[10]

On Easter Wednesday, Middleton held the 'White Apron Fair', 'an occasion for the young wives and mothers, with their children, and also for the young marriageable damsels, to walk out to display their finery and to get conducted by their husbands, or their sweet-hearts, to the alehouse, where they generally finished by a dance'.[11]

The next festive day in the calendar was 1 May. The night of May Day was termed 'Mischief-neet', the time for carnivalistic settling of old scores, when 'any one having a grudge against a neighbour was at liberty to indulge it, provided he kept his own counsel'. Gates and fences were pulled down, gardens trampled on, and carts upset. 'Mischief-neet' also occasioned a highly gendered, symbolic scrutiny of community morality. A mop would appear outside a home that needed cleaning; a ragged garment indicated that the woman of the house was a poor needle-worker. 'If a young fellow wished to cast a slur on a lass, he would hang a rag containing salt at her parents' door, or he would cast some of the same material on her door step, as indicative of gross inclinations.' A gorse bush was a sign of 'a woman notoriously immodest'. A holly indicated secret love. A ram's horn was a badge of adultery. As day broke, the iconography of popular morality was revealed to the community, and the round of gossip, recrimination, and retribution began.[12]

Whitsuntide was marked by the remnants of the 'Whitsun ales', a time of drinking, once closely associated with the church, but long since moved to the alehouse – a good example of the secularisation of popular rites which we will return to later.[13] However, the 'great feast of the year' was 'Rush-bearing', held later in August, on the anniversary of the dedication of the church, though barely con-nected with church ritual in Bamford's day. Middleton was the focus for a series of satellite hamlets and settlements which provided rush carts for the celebrations during wakes week. It was a time of courtship, inter-community rivalry, and merry-making; Bamford could recall the jangle of morris bells 'along the lanes and field roads'. He also implies a gendered division of labour: the men responsible for the actual cutting of the rushes for the carts and for the drawing of the heavy load; the women engaged in the design and construction of the colourful, ribboned clothing, the garlands, and the extravagantly ornamented banners or sheets, which would

10. Ibid., pp. 141–3.   11. Ibid., pp. 143–4.
12. Ibid., pp. 144–5.   13. Ibid., pp. 145–6.

be displayed proudly on the front of the pageant rush carts. As Robert Poole has explained, the carts represented the pride and prosperity of each participating community.[14] Amidst dancing, playing of music, and the ringing of morris bells, the carts perambulated the town, stopping at every public house, before ending up at the church. The ritual fiction was that the rushes were for the interior of the church, but in fact they were either given to the church for disposal or sold off to the highest bidder. The participants – Bamford implies mainly young men and women – then repaired to the beer houses for a night of drinking and dancing. The next day, a Sunday, saw the display of the wakes banners and garlands at church, followed by yet more drinking. It was a day of hospitality when visitors and friends were treated. At nearby Oldham, the wakes were even more ambitious, with festivities lasting for the whole week. On Sunday 'all would be over, and sobered people going to church or chapel again, would make good resolutions against a repetition of their week's folly. And thus would have passed away the great feast of "The Wakes".'[15]

Finally, there was 5 November, the anniversary of the discovery of the Gunpowder Plot. 'Most people ceased from working in the afternoon, and children went from house to house begging coal to make a bon-fire.' 'In addition to these contributions, gates and fences suffered, and whatever timber was obtainable from the woods and plantations, was considered fair game "for King George's sake".' At night, 'the country would be lighted up by bonfires'. Children were given cake and sweets, and the older members of the community had '"a joynin" in some convenient dwelling'. Young men, donated coal by the lord of the manor, were responsible for the main bonfire, lit near the church. This fire lasted all night and for much of the following day. 'The young fellows also joined at ale from the public-house, and with drinking, singing, and exploding of fire-arms, they amused themselves pretty well, especially if the weather was favourable.'[16]

II

Some of the rituals described by Bamford would have been recognisable to the inhabitants of sixteenth- and seventeenth-century

14. R. Poole, 'Samuel Bamford and Middleton rushbearing', *Manchester Region History Review* 8 (1994), 15.

15. Bamford, *Early Days*, pp. 146–55.   16. Ibid., pp. 159–60.

England.[17] Although the precise timing of Middleton's Christmas holiday was different, the themes of feasting, story-telling, and games were very similar to descriptions of the early modern Twelve Days of Christmas.[18] In sixteenth- and seventeenth-century England, groups of mummers, cross-dressed youth of both sexes, went around the parish seeking handouts of food and drink.[19] The first Monday after Twelfth Night was known as Plough Monday, a further opportunity for ritual largesse, involving the ceremonial dragging of the plough through villages by ploughmen in fancy dress (the ritual antecedent of the nineteenth-century mummers' Plough Play).[20] Shrovetide was likewise an important date on the early modern ritual calendar. Though a moveable feast, it always fell in February, traditionally a time of feasting and play before the various restrictions on the flesh during Lent. It involved pancake-eating as well as recreations: cock-fighting, cock-throwing, and camping and hurling, rather violent and unruly regional variants of folk football.[21] In London, Shrovetide was associated with almost ritualistic attacks on brothels (and sometimes playhouses) by crowds of apprentices. Charles II is reputed to have responded to the apprentice sacking of the bawdy houses, 'Why do they go to them then?' But this was surely the whole point. The clients of brothels were ritually closing them before the bodily strictures of Lent.[22]

Then there was mid-Lent or Mothering Sunday (Bamford's Cymbalin Sunday), essentially a regional festival. Observed either as a time when the family gathered, or as a holiday for those in service, and associated with the consumption of simnel (cymbalin) cake, it probably dates from the seventeenth century and was limited to

17. For the calendar rituals of early modern England, see C. Phythian-Adams, *Local History and Folklore: a New Framework* (London, 1975); F. Laroque, *Shakespeare's Festive World: Elizabethan Seasonal Entertainment and the Professional Stage* (Cambridge, 1991); and R. Hutton, *The Stations of the Sun: a History of the Ritual Year in Britain* (Oxford, 1996).

18. Hutton, *Stations of the Sun*, ch. 2.   19. Ibid., p. 21.

20. Ibid., ch. 11; A. Howkins and L. Merricks, 'The ploughboy and the Plough Play', *Folk Music Journal* 6 (1991), 187–208.

21. Hutton, *Stations of the Sun*, ch. 15. For the recreations, see also N. Elias and E. Dunning, 'Folk football in medieval and early modern Britain', in E. Dunning (ed.), *The Sociology of Sport* (London, 1971), ch. 7; R.W. Malcolmson, *Popular Recreations in English Society 1700–1850* (Cambridge, 1973), pp. 34–40, 48–9, 120–1, 139–45; D. Dymond, 'A lost social institution: the camping close', *Rural History* 1 (1990), 165–92.

22. This is a point that seems to escape most historians. For the riots against the brothels, see P. Griffiths, *Youth and Authority: Formative Experiences in England 1560–1640* (Oxford, 1996), pp. 151–61 (quote at p. 154). And for apprentices as clients of brothels and prostitutes, ibid., pp. 213–21.

the west, west midlands, and northwest of England. It is, of course, the precursor of Mother's Day, reinvented in the USA in the twentieth century.[23]

Easter was the next of Bamford's 'principal games, pastimes, and observances of the rural population of Middleton and its vicinity'.[24] It had long been an important folk and church festival. As we saw in Chapter 3, Ronald Hutton has argued that the beliefs associated with the pre-reformation religious rites of Easter were transformed into the folklore surrounding the festival. Thus it was a common popular belief in the nineteenth century that the hot-cross bun, baked on Good Friday and marked with the sign of the cross, had protective or curative powers.[25] Traditionally, of course, Easter came at the end of Lent, and it is somewhat ironic that Middleton's Easter, long after the abolition of Lent in Protestant England, had much more of a carnivalistic atmosphere about it than what we know of early modern practices. Although the actual rituals were more highly, and locally, developed in Middleton with the pace- or peace-egging, and the ritual licence of its mock mayor, the main themes are comparable to those of the earlier period. Easter was a time of ritualised begging, merriment, misrule, sports, and fairs. It was probably at Easter revelries in Shropshire in 1621 that a Rushbury man danced in the churchyard with a hobby-horse, 'running, playing at stool ball, leaping, and jumping'. When challenged by the parson, who said that he was breaking the graves with his heels, he replied that he could take him before the chuch courts if he wanted but the punishment 'was but the wearing (of) a sheet', and then proceeded to mock the parson by jumping after him.[26]

Easter merged with the inversions of Hocktide, which commenced two weeks later. During Hocktide, at its height in the late medieval period, women caught and bound men, releasing them in return for a payment which went to the church. This day or two of gender reversal and misrule was another casualty of England's reformations; its institutional endorsement disappeared rapidly in the early modern period. However, the ritual of capture remained in the Welsh borderlands and midlands in the eighteenth century in the custom of 'heaving' or 'lifting'.[27]

23. Hutton, *Stations of the Sun*, pp. 174–7.   24. Bamford, *Early Days*, p. 160.
25. Hutton, *Stations of the Sun*, pp. 192–3.
26. J.A.B. Somerset (ed.), *Records of Early English Drama: Shropshire, Vol. 2 Editorial Apparatus* (Toronto, 1994), p. 561. The incidents happened on 15 and 22 April.
27. Hutton, *Stations of the Sun*, ch. 20; S.B. MacLean, 'Hocktide: a reassessment of a popular pre-Reformation festival', in M. Twycross (ed.), *Festive Drama* (Cambridge, 1996), pp. 233–41; K.L. French, '"To free them from binding": women in the late medieval English parish', *Journal of Interdisciplinary History* 27 (1997), 387–412.

It is likely that the misrule of May Day (Bamford's next recorded festival), so similar to the licence associated with 1 April, was unique to the north and a product of the eighteenth and nineteenth centuries – indeed, Bamford provides the earliest reference to the rite.[28] Yet the spirit of Middleton's 'festivities' was not too far removed from the tropes of early modern May. May was a time of renewal and growth, the change-over point between winter and summer. It was a time when milk and cheese became plentiful in the dairying areas. May was also associated with courtship and celebration of sexuality. All these themes were proclaimed in the iconography of greenery, garlands, and may poles.[29] The godly Philip Stubbes complained of the May celebrations:

> all the young men and maides, olde men and wives run gadding over night to the woods, groves, hils & mountains, where they spend all the night in plesant pastimes, & in the morning they return bringing . . . birch & branches of trees, to deck their assemblies withall . . . But the cheifest jewel they bring from thence is their May-pole, which they bring home with great veneration . . . this May-pole (this stinking Idol rather) which is covered all over with floures, and hearbs bound round about with strings from the top to the bottome, and sometime painted with variable colours, with two or three hundred men, women and children following it with great devotion. And thus beeing reared up, with handkercheefs and flags hovering on the top, they straw the ground rounde about, binde greene boughes about it, set up sommer haules, bowers and arbors hard by it. And then fall they to daunce about it like as the heathen people did at the dedication of the Idols.[30]

As the reactions of Stubbes suggest, and as David Underdown and others have shown, an important key to the history of sixteenth- and seventeenth-century England lies with the humble may pole, for it became the symbolic focus for England's cultural wars. Banned in a succession of Puritan towns in the late sixteenth and early seventeenth centuries, outlawed during the mid-seventeenth-century era of godly rule, may poles resurfaced like saplings at the Restoration in 1660.[31]

28. Hutton, *Stations of the Sun*, p. 233.

29. C. Phythian-Adams, 'Milk and soot: the changing vocabulary of a popular ritual in Stuart and Hanoverian London', in D. Fraser and A. Sutcliffe (eds), *The Pursuit of Urban History* (London, 1983), ch. 4.

30. P. Stubbes, *The Anatomie of Abuses* (London, 1583), sig. M3v.

31. J. Goring, *Godly Exercises or the Devil's Dance? Puritanism and Popular Culture in Pre-civil War England* (London, 1983); D. Underdown, *Revel, Riot, and Rebellion: Popular Politics and Culture in England 1603–1660* (Oxford, 1985); Hutton, *Stations of the Sun*, ch. 23.

Bamford's neglect of Whitsun is out of step with the calendar year of the early modern period. The festivities of May merged with those of Whitsun (beginning on the seventh Sunday after Easter). Until 1575, Chester was the site of religious drama, the Whitsun Plays, announced by a horseman on St George's Day, and, at their height, consisting of twenty-four pageants, arranged by the various companies or guilds of Chester, reducing 'the whole historye of the bible into englishe storyes in metter'.[32] Hutton sensibly includes his discussion of May games and Whitsun ales in the same chapter, for festivities tended to stretch from May through June and well into the summer.[33] May games at South Kyme in Lincolnshire in 1601 were still going in August.[34] May and June were the peak months for fairs.[35] This was also the period of the church ales, a parish feast used by the church for fund-raising for church maintenance and poor relief, and involving a great deal of drinking: 'swilling and gulling, night and day, till they be as drunke as Apes, and as blockish as beasts'.[36]

Although the picture is somewhat unclear, it is likely that the church ales were a stronger institution in the south of England than in the north, where the fixed wake (or parish dedication feast) may always have been ritually dominant. Steve Hindle has recently presented compelling evidence for the strength of the early modern Cheshire wakes, with their resilient culture of drinking, dancing, minstrelsy, and bull- and bear-baiting.[37] The church ales were relatively common in the fifteenth and sixteenth centuries, but (like the may pole) fell foul of enthusiastic Protestant influences. Hutton has argued that ales were institutionally dead before the 1640s. The focus for communal festivity that they had provided then moved (as Bamford claimed of Middleton) to the wakes or church dedication feasts. The shift was 'only relative, as May games and Whitsun feasts long continued to flourish in what may be termed the private sector'.[38] In other words, both church and community continued to be involved in these early summer festivities, but whereas the church

32. L.M. Clopper (ed.), *Records of Early English Drama: Chester* (Toronto, 1979), pp. liii–lviii, 238–9.

33. Hutton, *Stations of the Sun*, ch. 24.

34. N.J. O'Conor, *Godes Peace and the Queenes* (London, 1934), pp. 110, 114.

35. J.A. Chartres, 'The marketing of agricultural produce', in J. Thirsk (ed.), *The Agrarian History of England and Wales: Volume V, ii. 1640–1750: Agrarian Change* (Cambridge, 1985), pp. 434–5.

36. J.M. Bennett, 'Conviviality and charity in medieval and early modern England', *Past and Present* 134 (1992), 19–41; Stubbes, *Anatomie of Abuses*, sig. M4v.

37. S. Hindle, 'Custom, festival and protest in early modern England: the Little Budworth wakes, St Peter's Day, 1596', *Rural History* 6 (1995), 155–78.

38. Hutton, *Stations of the Sun*, ch. 24 (quote at p. 257).

had been organisationally central to their performance in the late medieval period, they increasingly became folk customs.

As intimated earlier, May and Whitsuntide festivities could continue until Midsummer (24 June), the end of what has been termed the ritual half of the year.[39] Midsummer in the towns was marked by the Midsummer shows or watches, urban pageants or parades, common before the ravages of reformed Protestantism.[40] The only Midsummer show to survive until the end of the seventeenth century was at Chester. It is particularly intriguing because the characters of the abolished Chester cycle of medieval guild drama lingered on in the Midsummer parades. Thus the Chester shows included shepherds on stilts from the 'The Shepherds' Play' of the painters, the feathered devil of the butchers' 'The Temptation of Christ', the cross-dressed alewife from the innkeepers' 'The Harrowing of Hell', as well as a dragon, giants, hobby-horses, morris dancing, model beasts, and naked boys. The Puritan mayor Henry Hardware got rid of the giants, the dragon, the devil, the transvestite, and the naked boys in the early seventeenth century, in an effort to reshape the ritual to reformed sensibilities.[41]

The wakes, revels, or hoppings (the terms varied regionally) were parish feasts held on the anniversary of the foundation of the church. As we have seen, they were probably common in the north throughout the early modern period, and strengthened in the south as they replaced church ales. They were certainly ubiquitous by the eighteenth century: some 70 per cent of Northamptonshire parishes in the early 1720s had an annual feast.[42] Although technically the dedication could fall at any time of the year, wakes tended to concentrate, as in Middleton, in the late summer and autumn, and are probably best seen in combination with the other carnivalistic festivity of those months, the harvest celebrations and a plethora of fairs, including the hiring fairs around Michaelmas (29 September). Nearly 60 per cent of the wakes in early eighteenth-century Northamptonshire were held between mid-August and early November.[43] They represented a break from the labours of harvest in

39. C. Phythian-Adams, 'Ceremony and the citizen: the communal year at Coventry', in P. Clark and P. Slack (eds), *Crisis and Order in English Towns 1500–1700* (London, 1972), pp. 70, 74–5.

40. Hutton, *Stations of the Sun*, pp. 314–15.

41. Clopper (ed.), *Records of Early English Drama: Chester*, pp. lii–liii, 198–9, 252–3; D. Mills, 'Chester's Midsummer Show: creation and adaptation', in Twycross (ed.), *Festive Drama*, pp. 132–44.

42. Malcolmson, *Popular Recreations*, p. 17.

43. Malcolmson, *Popular Recreations*, ch. 2; Hutton, *Stations of the Sun*, ch. 34. The Northamptonshire figures come from my re-working of the table in Malcolmson, *Popular Recreations*, p. 18.

a predominantly rural economy, 'As toil comes every day & feasts but once a year.'[44] A late seventeenth-century antiquary noted that many wakes were celebrated at Michaelmas when 'a vacation from the labours of harvest and the plough' permitted festivity.[45] They were also linked to the rushbearing customs of the north, the precursors of Middleton's ceremony. In the market town of Congleton (Cheshire) musicians headed a procession of 'gaily dressed' young women and men who carried garlands of flowers and rushes to strew on the church floor. The day ended in dancing, drinking, and feasting.[46] One observer of the wakes complained that it was a day when 'every dissipation and vice which it was possible to conceive could crowd upon a villager's manners and rural life'. Robert Malcolmson has described them more appositely as petty carnivals, a time of feasting, dancing, sports, and a range of other diversions.[47] The defenders of wakes saw them as an opportunity for popular hospitality, 'for preservation of mutuall amytie . . . and allayinge of strifes, discordes and debates between neighbour and neighbour'.[48]

It is fitting that Bamford finished his account with 5 November, a day on the ritual calendar which dates from the period with which we are concerned. Established as an anniverary of thanksgiving for deliverance from the gunpowder attempt on parliament in 1605, it became a bonfire night towards the middle of the seventeenth century, and remained a truly popular festival throughout the seventeenth and eighteenth centuries.[49] It was closely associated with early modern anti-popery, Queen Elizabeth I's accession day (commemorated on 17 November), and with the colourful Whig-organised Pope-burning processions in London in the 1670s and 1680s.[50] This ritual propaganda included mock papal ceremonies and processions, and the burning of effigies of the Pope filled with live cats. Audience and procession merged: 'people actually dressed up as devils and catholic priests and acted out the pageants themselves'.[51]

44. John Clare, 'The Village Minstrel', in E. Robinson and D. Powell (eds), *The Early Poems of John Clare 1804–1822*, Vol. 2 (Oxford, 1989), p. 161.

45. Malcolmson, *Popular Recreations*, p. 25.

46. Hutton, *Stations of the Sun*, pp. 323–6; Hindle, 'Custom', p. 158.

47. Malcolmson, *Popular Recreations*, p. 19.

48. F. Heal, *Hospitality in Early Modern England* (Oxford, 1990), p. 360.

49. Hutton, *Stations of the Sun*, ch. 39.

50. S. Williams, 'The Pope-burning processions of 1679, 1680 and 1681', *Journal of the Warburg and Courtauld Institutes* 21 (1958), 104–18; O.W. Furley, 'The Pope-burning processions of the late seventeenth century', *History* 44 (1959), 16–23; T. Harris, *London Crowds in the Reign of Charles II: Propaganda and Politics from the Restoration until the Exclusion Crisis* (Cambridge, 1987), pp. 103–6.

51. Harris, *London Crowds*, p. 106.

Like all ritual forms, the rites of 5 November were open to a range of readings and intentions. As Hutton has pointed out, the intriguing thing about the celebrations during the reign of the Catholic James II was that they could 'conceal a gesture of detestation of his religion within one of loyalty to his person'.[52] Others would have used the day as an opportunity for winter merry-making and dole-seeking.

Clearly there was a vast repertoire of ritual activity in early modern England. Tom Pettitt has recently described such popular cultural forms as 'customary drama'.[53] This helpful category explodes disciplinary demarcations and privileging, thus enabling the historian to group together such seemingly disparate activities as lord mayors' shows, royal entries, guild pageants, miracle plays, summer games, morris dances, charivaris, and the range of calendar customs and seasonal observances discussed in the pages above. I now want to move from general descriptions of the ritual calendar to focus more analytically on two pairings of customary drama which could be interpreted as standing at opposite ends of the ritual spectrum: the officially organised civic pageantry associated with the inauguration of mayors and the visits of royalty; and the folk-ordered summer games and charivaris.

III

The civic pageantry connected with royalty was an occasional rite rather than a calendar ritual. Pageants occurred to register significant moments in the lives of monarchs, or as part of their royal progresses when they toured their kingdom, marking out their domains (in Clifford Geertz's memorable description) like territorial wolves.[54] They varied in frequency from monarch to monarch: Charles I's failure to exercise this cultural representation of political authority, it has been argued, weakened his charisma and hence his control of London in the 1640s.[55]

52. Ibid., p. 396.
53. T. Pettitt, 'Customary drama: social and spatial patterning in traditional encounters', *Folk Music Journal* 7 (1995), 27–42.
54. C. Geertz, 'Centers, kings, and charisma: reflections on the symbolics of power', in S. Wilentz (ed.), *Rites of Power* (Philadelphia, 1985), p. 16.
55. R.M. Smuts, 'Public ceremony and royal charisma: the English royal entry in London, 1485–1642', in A.L. Beier, D. Cannadine, and J.M. Rosenheim (eds), *The First Modern Society* (Cambridge, 1989), ch. 2.

The reception of Elizabeth I at Norwich in 1578 provides a good indication of the atmosphere of these events.[56] Over the week of her visit in August she was presented with a series of pageants, allegories, architectural declarations, speeches, and a variety of dramatic devices. Some of the envisaged dramaturgy never materialised because of the intervention of the weather, but the designers' printed accounts of the visit – in themselves part of the glorification – provide details of what might have been if everything had gone according to schedule.

Elizabeth was met outside Norwich by the mayor and, on horseback, sixty 'of the most comelie yong men' clad in black satin, purple taffeta, and silver lace. This welcoming procession also consisted of a man representing King Gurgunt, a mythical king of England, companies of gentlemen and wealthy citizens clad in velvet, city officials in scarlet, and the sheriffs in their violet gowns. 'Then followed divers others, to keepe the people from disturbing the array aforesaide. Th[u]s every thing in due and comely order.'[57] The mayor delivered an oration in Latin, and the queen responded, but Gurgunt's speech, which referred to the monarch's father's breach with Rome, 'that purple whore', was prevented by a shower of rain.[58] When the queen entered the newly painted and redecorated gates of the city, she passed the first pageant, a stage with children and men engaged in spinning, knitting, and weaving against a painted backdrop celebrating the cloth industry of Norwich. Above the artwork was painted the message:

> The causes of this common wealth are,
> God truely preached.
> Justice duely executed. The people obedient.
> Idelnesse expelled. Labour cherished.
> Universall concorde preserved.[59]

The next stage was at the entrance of the market. It consisted of a structure of gates, posterns, chambers (filled with musicians), and an over-arching stage, the whole structure simulating jasper and marble. The main characters in this pageant were 'five personages apparelled

---

56. The two descriptions of Queen Elizabeth's visit, Bernard Garter's *The Joyfull Receyving*, and Thomas Churchyard's *A Discourse of the Queenes Majesties entertainment*, both published in 1578, are reprinted in D. Galloway (ed.), *Records of Early English Drama: Norwich 1540–1642* (Toronto, 1984), pp. 243–390. D.W. Bergeron briefly discusses the visit in his *English Civic Pageantry 1558–1642* (London, 1971), pp. 37–44.
57. Galloway (ed.), *Records of Early English Drama: Norwich*, pp. 248–9.
58. Ibid., p. 253.   59. Ibid., p. 254.

like women': the City of Norwich, Deborah, Judith, Esther, and
Martia ('sometime Queene of Englande'). Each delivered a speech,
and then one of the musicians sang to the queen:

> The Sunne doth shine where shade hath bin,
> long darkenesse brought us day,
> The Starre of comfort now coms in,
> and heere a while will stay.
> Ring out the belles, plucke up your sprightes,
> and dresse your houses gay,
> Runne in for floures to straw the streetes,
> and make what joy you may.
> The deaw of heaven droppes this day
> on dry and barren ground...[60]

She then progressed to the cathedral, but paused by a stage outside
the home of one of the aldermen, where 'an excellent Boy' in a
long white taffeta robe, with a crimson and gold turban and garland about his head, made another speech.[61] After a service at the
cathedral, Elizabeth went to her lodgings at the bishop's palace,
and remained there the following day, a Sunday, 'when Princes
commonly come not abroade (and tyme is occupyed wyth Sermons,
and laudable exercises)'.[62]

Over the following days, Elizabeth was treated to a range of
shows. A coach with Mercury ready to deliver verse lingered outside
her bedroom window in the hope that she would appear. The designer was particularly proud of this device sent at speed by the gods
to address England's queen. The 'people... marvelled, and gazed
very much' at the winged horses and Mercury's coach, 'covered
with Birdes, and naked Sprites hanging by the heeles in the aire
and cloudes, cunningly painted out, as thoughe by some thunder
cracke they had bene shaken & tormented, yet stayed by power
devine in their places, to make the more wonder and miraculous
Shew'. The coach had a golden, jewelled tower, with a white plume
on the top. Mercury was clothed in blue satin and gold cloth, and
held a rod with serpents around it, 'wriggling or scrawling' as if
alive.[63] On another day, the queen was presented with a play celebrating her chastity. The designer had to predict the monarch's
movements, assemble his 'boys and men' in their coaches (followed
by a curious throng of the 'common people'), and practically am-
bush the monarch on her way to dinner.[64]

---

60. Ibid., p. 298.   61. Ibid., pp. 298–9.   62. Ibid., p. 299.
63. Ibid., p. 303.   64. Ibid., pp. 304–5.

On one occasion, the master of the Norwich grammar school delivered a speech in Latin in front of the gates of Norwich Hospital. 'We certeinly nowe inhabite, and lead our lives in those most happie Ilands of the which Hesiodus maketh mention, which not only abounde with all manner of graine, woll, cattel, and other aydes of mans life, but much more with the moste precious treasure of true religion and the worde of God, in the which onely the mindes of men have rest and peace.' On this day, Elizabeth was accompanied by three French ambassadors and several English lords, whom she called to her and 'willed them to harken'. [65]

Thomas Churchyard attempted to show his pageant, 'The Nymphs', and his play, 'Manhood and Desert', but was rained out. The nymphs' device involved a large pit dug in the ground and covered with canvas to make it appear as if the earth was opening. The nymphs themselves were boys with long golden tresses, and looked so beautiful that even those who knew the actors well 'tooke them to be yong girles and wenches, prepared for the nonce, to procure a laughter'. The play, 'Manhood and Desert', involved combat over a woman called 'Beauty', played by a boy dressed in 'very goodly garmentes', and appears to have featured much severing of bloodied limbs. [66]

On the day of the court's departure, the streets were decorated with herbs and flowers, 'with Garlands, Coronets, Pictures, rich clothes, and a thousand devices'. A stage was erected at the exit gate, 'very richly apparelled with cloth of Golde, & crimsen velvet', from which the farewell speeches were made. Time was running out, so the mayor's speech on this occasion was presented in writing to the queen. [67] Churchyard, dressed as a water sprite himself, was finally able to use his boy nymphs in a fairy dance, performed with tambourines on the route of the queen's departure. 'Their attire, and comming so strangely out, I know made the Queenes highnesse smyle and laugh withall.' [68]

The London lord mayor's shows, on the other hand, which flourished in the sixteenth and seventeenth centuries, were firmly linked to the calendar. They took place every year on 29 October at the inauguration of the new lord mayor. They were much like the royal progresses, involving similar iconographic use of spectacle, pageantry, drama, human sculpture, scenery, and music, but with the ritual focus on the mayor and his company instead of the

65. Ibid., pp. 270–1.   66. Ibid., pp. 315–17.
67. Ibid., pp. 276, 278.   68. Ibid., pp. 327–8.

monarch.[69] Fittingly, the Thames was a central stage for this annual declaration of civic pride; the mayor and the livery companies travelled the great river in barges to Westminster, passing land or water pageants en route. A seventeenth-century ballad captured something of the spectacle, singing of

> The glory of this City fair,
> you yearly may behold,
> For once a year they chuse Lord Mayor,
> whose train doth flame with gold.
> In'th morning as they go to Court,
> the Thames with wood is cover'd,
> Loud Musick plays, Guns give report,
> the Sun with smoak is smother'd.[70]

The civic rituals were secular morality plays where the virtues of order, loyalty to monarch, civic and guild pride were impressed through dramaturgy and spectacle upon a variety of audiences. They celebrated city and guild history: the fourteenth-century mayor William Walworth was resurrected from his tomb in a mayor's show in 1616. They complimented the guild or company of the elected mayor. A fishing boat and a giant crowned dolphin for the fishmongers; ships laden with ingots, and a mountain of gold for the goldsmiths; for the drapers, a land-drawn ship filled with woollens, a pageant personifying all sectors of the drapery industry, and the Argo carrying Jason and the Argonauts to fetch the golden fleece; and an island with a mine, and Mulciber (the god of mines and metals) for the ironmongers: such were the devices employed by Anthony Munday in the shows he designed between 1605 and 1623. The pageants also invoked symbols of national pride. The popular heroes, St George and Robin Hood, appeared in the shows of 1609 and 1615. Some employed animal symbolism. The pelican indicated loyalty to one's young: the mayor as 'a nursing father'. Other shows just played with words and images, using a lemon tree when the mayor's name was Leman.[71]

69. For the lord mayors' shows (and royal progresses and entries), see Bergeron, *English Civic Pageantry*; M. Berlin, 'Civic ceremony in early modern London', *Urban History Yearbook* (1986), 15–27; R. Dutton (ed.), *Jacobean Civic Pageants* (Keele, 1995); and L. Manley, *Literature and Culture in Early Modern London* (Cambridge, 1995), ch. 5.

70. W.G. Day (ed.), *The Pepys Ballads*, 5 vols (Cambridge, 1987), Vol. 4, p. 339.

71. All these examples come from D.M. Bergeron (ed.), *Pageants and Entertainments of Anthony Munday* (New York, 1985). The pelican also represented Christ's sacrifice: see M. Rubin, *Corpus Christi: the Eucharist in Late Medieval Culture* (Cambridge, 1991), pp. 310–12.

Peter Burke has discussed the awareness of the shows' organisers that their audience consisted of the 'multitude' as well as the 'sharp and learned', and of the unwillingness of some to concede to the ignorant. Burke argues that the shows drew on different icono-graphical traditions: the learned, classical tradition, and the pop-ular tradition of the crafts and companies.[72] Yet the craft allegories could be as complex as any classical metaphor, so it is likely that the cultural discriminations were more multi-layered than Burke has suggested. The complexity of pageant metaphor and allegory was open to multiple readings then as now. It has also been argued that the pageant organisers, John Tatham and Thomas Jordan, added a more popular element to the shows during the Restora-tion, that their aesthetic shifted after 1660, savouring more of the fairground than the artistry of Jonson. Entertainment became a governing motive.[73] Yet, as with the ballad literature discussed else-where, the vignettes of working life and the (mocking) dialogue of rustics may well have appealed to the city's elite. There was still a multiplicity of meanings.

The Norwich royal entry provides evidence of the multiple readings of this kind of ritual. It has been said that this form of pageantry is particularly suited to transmitting the messages of mon-archy to a non-literate audience, that 'pageantry by its very nature was the most socially and artistically inclusive form of discourse'.[74] But this is to seriously underestimate the sophistication of this cul-tural mode. As with commercial theatre, discussed in Chapter 2, there were different levels of understanding. The setting of the events and imagery in print soon after the performance itself was part of the process. The entry did not merely consist in the physical presence of the monarch (or the mayor in the mayor's show), but in the rep-resentation of the events. Print enabled the explanation of obscure metaphors, the restating of speeches missed in the jostle of perform-ance, the Englishing of Latin or Greek discourse, the linking of performance experienced in fragments, and the reinstatement of panegyric missed because of the weather or the unpredictable movements of the subject of the celebrations.

72. P. Burke, 'Popular culture in seventeenth-century London', in B. Reay (ed.), *Popular Culture in Seventeenth-century England* (London, 1985), pp. 44–5.

73. K. Richards, 'The Restoration pageants of John Tatham', in D. Mayer and K. Richards (eds), *Western Popular Theatre* (London, 1977), ch. 3.

74. J.P. Montano, 'The quest for consensus: the lord mayor's day shows in the 1670s', in G. MacLean (ed.), *Culture and Society in the Stuart Restoration: Literature, Drama, History* (Cambridge, 1995), p. 36.

Obviously the learned would get more from the five Latin orations, four Latin poems (including a pastoral dialogue), the Greek tags within Latin orations, and the Greek poem which formed part of the queen's welcome to Norwich in 1578. They would understand the constant invocation of classical, historical, and biblical mythology, the textual references to Homer, Hesiod and Plato, the significance of Mercury kissing the steps of England's queen. Those in Norwich in 1578 who were able to read would have been able to decipher the written captions as well as looking at the paintings and the actors in the pageant proclaiming Norwich's industriousness. No doubt most observers (literate or non-literate) would have understood the imagery of the looms on that stage, but how many would have realised that the 'prettie Boy richly apparelled' who spoke to the monarch in verse represented 'the Common welth of the Citie'? Some may just have been taken with the pretty boy/woman.

During Elizabeth's passage through London in 1559, one of the devices was a scene where the characters representing 'Pure religion', 'Love of subjects', 'Wisdom', and 'Justice' were trampling 'Superstition and ignorance', 'Rebellion and insolence', 'Folly and vainglory', and 'Adulation and bribery'. The spectators were supposed to be able to determine the respective virtues and vices by their apparel, but a speaker also interpreted the scene as the queen drew near. Further explanation was provided in a later pamphlet account. Even so, there were different ways of reading the scene, as we know from comparing the pamphlet account to the recorded reactions of the Venetian ambassador. It could be seen as a general prescription for a successful reign, or a more pointed comment upon recent history.[75] Another pageant played with the metaphor of the state as a garden. Two hills stood in contrast to one another: one was cragged, stony, and barren, with a withered tree (a decayed commonwealth); the other was fresh, green and flowered, with a flourishing tree (a thriving commonwealth). The trees contained tablets inscribed with explanations of their respective states. The unlearned would not have needed to read the Latin caption to understand what *Ruinosa Republica* represented, or to grasp the symbolic significance of Truth's presentation of the Bible to Elizabeth in the pageant. But by the same token, we should not assume that everyone fully grasped the connection between the two kingdoms and the role of the English Bible in government.[76]

---

75. Bergeron, *English Civic Pageantry*, pp. 17–18.   76. Ibid., pp. 19–21, 276–8.

Ben Jonson's triumphal arch at Fenchurch in 1604, designed for
James I, would also have appealed to a range of cultural levels. It
was covered with a curtain of silk, painted to look like a cloud, and
as the king approached, the curtain (the cloud) was drawn. Jonson
explained the allegory: 'those clouds were gathered upon the face
of the Citie, through their long want of his most wished sight: but
now, as at the rising of the Sunne, all mists were dispersed and
fled'. Most observers would have grasped this simple but effective
complimentary allegory, and would have understood the carvings
of the City on the top of the arch. But there were many other layers
of meaning conveyed in the figures Theosophia, Tamesis, and the
six daughters of Genius, the Latin inscriptions on the arch, and the
language of its classical architecture.[77]

In fine, like most cultural forms, civic rituals operated at a range
of levels. They included emblematic use of classical figures in ways
that would have escaped many contemporaries: Pallas (wisdom) as
an appropriate role model for rulers; Ulysses as a wise and discreet
magistrate; Orpheus able to govern discord.[78] But they also provided pageantry, imagery, and entertainment which potentially had
wider appeal. Those who had attended parts of the royal entry and
who were able to purchase and read accounts (with translations) of
the dramaturgy and speeches would be able to learn, say, that the
'pretty boy' in the Norwich pageant represented the City, and probably achieved a better sense of the whole than those who drifted in
and out of the week's performances without reading the printed
account afterwards, or those who read about the events without
visually or aurally experiencing them. But really any notion of wholes
is a fictive ideal; the pageants and progresses were experienced in
ritual fragments.

Clearly there were multiple audiences too. Apart from the monarch or mayor, who was the central focus of performance, as well as
being part of the show himself or herself, there were foreign observers, the civic elite, elites from other cities, and ordinary citizens.
To distinguish between actual performers and those lining the streets
or hanging from windows is also a somewhat artificial distinction;
all were part of the pageant. An observer of the lord mayor's show
in 1679 referred to spectators in the balconies watching activity in the
streets, and vice versa: 'in brief they were Shows to one another'.[79]

---

77. Ibid., pp. 75–7, and Plate 2.   78. For classical imagery, see ibid., ch. 11.
79. B. Klein, ' "Between the bums and the bellies of the multitude": civic pageantry and the problem of the audience in late Stuart London', *London Journal* 17
(1992), 21.

We are told that the 'people' marvelled at the Norwich spectacle, followed Mercury's coach in 'flockes and multitudes', and
cheered loudly for the queen. One of the functions of the royal
progress and mayor's show was to proclaim order. The processions
of gentlemen and civic dignitaries were visual representations of
hierarchy: 'every thing in due and comely order', as it was said of
the Norwich royal entry. A Londoner who watched a royal entry,
writes R. Malcolm Smuts, would be 'forcefully reminded of his [*sic*]
subordination to a massive multi-layered system of authority, ascend-
ing from his wealthier liveried neighbours and employers, through
the Lord Mayor and the aldermen, to the resplendent royal court
and half-deified monarch'.[80] Thomas Churchyard published his
account of the Norwich shows, he said, 'for those people that dwell
farre off the Court, that they may see what majestie a Prince raigneth,
and with what obedience and love good Subjectes do receive
hir'.[81] And yet amidst all this ritualised order, disorder constantly
threatened. The roses of York and Lancaster, painted on the gates
of Norwich to symbolise unity, were transposed in one of the printed
accounts.[82] The 'rudenesse of some ringer of belles' spoiled the
harmony of one pageant. The rain ruined sets and turned players
into 'drowned Rattes'.[83] Above all, the 'multitude' were there, an
unpredictable element capable of spoiling the decorum. Hence the
arrangements at Norwich 'to keepe the people from disturbing the
array'.[84] A satirical account of a late seventeenth-century mayor's
show stressed the unruliness of those in the streets, and a pamphlet
account of the show in 1679 wrote of 'the disorder'd People below
in the Street'.[85]

IV

The late spring/early summer, we saw earlier in the chapter, was a
time for games, cross-dressing, and the performance of forms of
folk drama which would be lost to the historian but for their occasional preservation in the papers of the church courts and records
of prosecution for libel. Thus we know of the Kendal men who
were in trouble in the 1620s for dressing in women's apparel in a

80. Smuts, 'Public ceremony', p. 74.
81. Galloway (ed.), *Records of Early English Drama: Norwich*, p. 293.
82. Bergeron, *English Civic Pageantry*, p. 38.
83. Galloway (ed.), *Records of Early English Drama: Norwich*, pp. 299, 317.
84. Ibid., p. 249.   85. Klein, 'Civic pageantry', pp. 21–2.

show 'before a summer rodd or Maypole', which included a character dressed like the devil.[86] The May revels and shows in Wells in 1607, which lasted into June, provide a celebrated, though somewhat exaggerated, example of the spirit of these summer games. Indeed it has been argued recently that the affair represented an attempt to reclaim traditional summer festivities.[87] Occasioned by an ale held to raise money for the parish church of St Cuthbert, the Wells celebrations seem to have included the lord and lady of the May (a gentleman and a barber's wife), morris dancers, singing, music, community dancing, charivaris, a play performed in the church, and a series of pageants and street shows containing many of the popular figures of ballad and chapbook (Robin Hood, the Pinder of Wakefield, St George and the dragon, and Mother Bunch) as well as some recognisable remnants of the medieval drama of Corpus Christi and Midsummer (Noah and his ark, giants, and even a naked, feathered boy). The festivities also provided the opportunity for libellous and dramatic mockery of a Puritan clothier and his reputed mistress – hence our knowledge of the whole affair. The Wells rituals, then, were a combination of church ale, charivari, May games, and, as James Stokes has shown, traditional Midsummer shows or guild processions.[88]

Another libel action in the Court of Star Chamber during the 1620s reveals a series of summer plays or interludes performed at Claverley in Shropshire for more than a decade. The characters in 1621 included a fool, a userer, a philosopher, and one 'Bravado', who managed to slip in a libellous line about a local minister's daughter. Evening prayer ended early to accommodate the performance, and the players, who were local tradesmen and craftsmen, took their act to neighbouring communities – Bobeton is mentioned. Another verse play, much more pointedly libellous, and which survives in text, was also performed (presumably in the streets) by a variety of actors, 'persons unknowne in severall other formes and fashions of attyer & they beinge all of them aparell and dysguised'. The focus of this drama was 'Jenny', a man dressed in

---

86. A. Douglas and P. Greenfield (eds), *Records of Early English Drama: Cumberland, Westmorland, Gloucestershire* (Toronto, 1986), p. 201.

87. J. Stokes, 'The Wells shows of 1607', in Twycross (ed.), *Festive Drama*, pp. 145–56.

88. C.J. Sisson, *Lost Plays of Shakespeare's Age* (London, 1970), pp. 162–85; Underdown, *Revel, Riot, and Rebellion*, p. 55; Stokes, 'Wells shows'. Until the careful work of Stokes, historians had not grasped the richness and complexity of the Wells shows: see now, J. Stokes (ed.), *Records of Early English Drama: Somerset, Vol. 1 The Records* (Toronto, 1996), pp. 261–367; J. Stokes (ed.), *Records of Early English Drama: Somerset, Vol. 2 Editorial Apparatus* (Toronto, 1996), pp. 709–28.

women's clothing and padded to simulate pregnancy. The other main character was 'Jocky', her (his) lover. Although women were involved in the devising of this libel against the sexual probity of the daughter of the minister of Claverley, men played the main female part. In one performance, the role of Jenny was acted by a dyer, and Jocky by a blacksmith. This short play, a combination of verse, song, transvestism, drama, and probably dance, hinges on the identity of the father of the heavily pregnant Jenny's twins. Its *dramatis personae* consisted of the main couple, two other lovers of Jenny's, a constable and his assistant, and a midwife and her helper.[89]

The South Kyme May games in 1601 included a ride on horseback to a neighbouring village to 'dine' in an alehouse. The company had reeds tied together to simulate spears, with painted flags, and drummers. As the reference to horseback indicates, these were by no means humble participants – they included esquires and yeomen. The games, which became entangled in a gentry family feud, included a play performed beside the may pole on the parish green, after evening prayer, to an audience of 100 or so. The drama, which marked the ritual burial of the summer lord at the end of the games, and had a devil and a fool as well as the lord, was wide open for libellous use. The lord affected the 'person . . . speches and gesture' of the Earl of Lincoln; and the performance concluded with a mock minister delivering a pretend sermon and prayer for the 'dead' lord, and then attaching a written libel to the may pole. This was carnival, but misrule carefully contained within gentry feuding. The author of the play and principal actor was from a leading local gentry family. An earl was mocked, but by one of his own class. Social upheaval was never threatened.[90]

The Robin Hood 'plays' – a series of games, fund-raising parish processions, and possibly folk drama featuring the popular hero, Robin Hood – were also associated with May and Whitsun, and often formed part of the festivities of the summer kings or lords and ladies of the May.[91] The best description we have of these revelries is that of a critic, Philip Stubbes:

> all the wilde-heds of the Parish, conventing togither, chuse them a Graund-Captain (of all mischeefe) whome they innoble with the title of my Lord of Mis-rule, and him they crowne with great solemnitie,

89. Sisson, *Lost Plays*, pp. 140–56; J.A.B. Somerset (ed.), *Records of Early English Drama: Shropshire, Vol. 1 The Records* (Toronto, 1994), pp. 23–39.

90. O'Conor, *Godes Peace*, pp. 108–26.

91. D. Wiles, *The Early Plays of Robin Hood* (Cambridge, 1981); Hutton, *Stations of the Sun*, ch. 25.

and adopt for their king. This king anointed, chuseth forth twentie, fortie, threescore or a hundred lustie Guttes like to him self to waighte uppon his lordly Maiestie, and to guarde his noble person. Then everie one of these his men, he investeth with his liveries, of green, yellow or some other light wanton colour. And as though that were not (baudie) gaudie enough . . . they bedecke them selves with leafs, ribons & laces hanged all over in golde rings, precious stones & other jewels: this doon, they tye about either leg xx. or xl. bels, with rich handkercheifs in their hands, and sometimes laid a crosse over their shoulders & necks, borrowed for the most parte of their pretie Mopsies & loving Besses, for bussing them in ye dark. Thus all thinges set in order, then have they their Hobby-horses, dragons & other Antiques, togither with their baudie Pipers and thundering Drummers to strike up the devils duance withall, then marche these heathen company towards the Church and Church-yard, their pipers pipeing, their drummers thundring, their stumps dancing, their bels jyngling, their handkerchefs swinging about their heds like madmen, their hobbie horses and other monsters skirmishing amongst the route: & into the Church (though the Minister be at praier or preaching) dancing & swinging heir handkercheifs over their heds, in the Church, like devils incarnate . . . Then the foolish people, they looke, they stare, they laugh, they fleer, & mount upon fourmes and pewes to see these goodly pageants . . .

After parading around the church a number of times, writes Stubbes, the revellers march into the churchyard, where they have erected their halls and bowers, and commence the feasting that will last all night.[92] The audience is drawn into the proceedings through the purchase of lord's badges which the buyer wears as a pledge of allegiance. The churchwardens' accounts of early sixteenth-century Kingston-upon-Thames record the preparation of 2,000 badges or 'small liveries' and 2,000 pins for one year's celebrations.[93]

Stubbes's 'devil's dance' was the morris, a ubiquitous but rarely described early modern dance, commonly performed at May and Whitsun festivals.[94] A group of Shrewsbury morris dancers, who found themselves in court after a fracas in 1619, were led by a man described as the 'lord of misrule'; they performed on 30 May, the Sunday after Corpus Christi, dancing well into the evening.[95] The symbiosis between church and the rituals of misrule, of which Stubbes disapproved, was in the process of disintegration under the

---

92. Stubbes, *Anatomie of Abuses*, sigs M2–M3.

93. Wiles, *Early Plays of Robin Hood*, p. 13.

94. For the morris's ubiquity, see Laroque, *Shakespeare's Festive World*, index: 'morris dance'.

95. Somerset (ed.), *Records of Early English Drama: Shropshire, Vol. 1*, pp. 310–11; *idem, Records of Early English Drama: Shropshire, Vol. 2*, p. 405. Hutton makes a point of

pressures of reformed Protestantism – indeed, his text is part of that very process. But it is an interesting link. The Articles of Enquiry of Bishop Richard Neile for the Diocese of Coventry and Lichfield found it necessary to enquire in 1610 whether the ministers of churchwardens under their jurisdiction had 'suffered any Feastes, Banquets, Churchales, or Drinkinges in the Church, or any Lords of Misrule, or Summer Lord or Lady, or any disguised persons: any Players, or May-games, or any Moris dauncers at any time to come unreverently into the Church or Church-yarde, and there to daunce or play, or shew themselves disguised in the time of common prayer'.[96] And there are several examples of morris dancing in and around the church in the west midlands in the seventeenth century.[97] In 1619 a group of Shropshire morris dancers fell foul of the church courts when they used the communion cloth of Clee St Margaret as a flag for their Whitsun dances. The group, all men, came from Clee St Margaret and nearby settlements, and their dance included a drummer, a sword-carrier, and men playing the parts of 'the friar', 'the hobby horse', 'the lord's fool', and 'the lord's shepherd'. Although he is not directly mentioned, the list of characters implies that the dancing was linked to a lord of misrule.[98] The use of the communion cloth is interesting, for we have a similar reference from sixteenth-century Berkshire.[99] Communion symbolised the communicant's unity with the social as well as the spiritual community, and it may well have been in this vein that the morris made use of the iconography of the communion cloth. The fact that some were prosecuted for doing so is further evidence of the gap between religious and secular ritual.

V

Charivari, a dramatic popular form of ritual justice, similarly left its archival imprint only when participants fell out with the

---

confining the term 'lord of misrule' to winter rites, but the descriptions of Stubbes and the Shrewsbury case indicate that the term was used of the summer lords as well (Hutton, *Stations of the Sun*, pp. 249, 252).

96. Somerset (ed.), *Records of Early English Drama: Shropshire, Vol. 1*, pp. 3–4.

97. E.C. Cawte, 'It's an ancient custom – but how ancient?', in T. Buckland and J. Wood (eds), *Aspects of British Calendar Customs* (Sheffield, 1993), pp. 48–9.

98. Somerset (ed.), *Records of Early English Drama: Shropshire, Vol. 1*, pp. 40–50; *idem, Records of Early English Drama: Shropshire, Vol. 2*, pp. 523–31.

99. A.F. Johnston, '"All the world was a stage": records of early English drama', in E. Simon (ed.), *The Theatre of Medieval Europe: New Research in Early Drama* (Cambridge, 1991), pp. 121–2.

authorities.[100] Although used against wife-beaters in the nineteenth century, the overwhelming target in the surviving cases from the early modern period was the woman who dominated or cuckolded her husband – contemporaries did not distinguish between the two. Though we call the ritual form charivari, it was known at the time by its regional variants: skimmington (in the south-west), riding the stang (in the north), or simply riding. The ritual varied according to circumstance, but, as the name implies, usually involved a riding, on a pole or a cowl-staff (used for carrying water), or backwards on a horse, either of the offenders, an effigy or effigies, or someone (a neighbour) playing the part of the skimmington (the word was used to describe both victim and ritual). The imagery of inversion was further pursued in the transvestite dress of the participants or in other disguises such as the blacking of their faces. This ritual of public humiliation, for that is what it was, proclaimed community disapproval of the alleged activity of the accused. Their offence was declared mimetically, usually to the accompaniment of the beating of pots and pans, ringing of bells, blowing of horns, or discharging of fireworks and guns, what is termed 'rough music'. Indeed, Edward Thompson has used the description 'rough music' as a generic term for British ritual forms of charivari.[101] There was also a folk symbolism in the actions that is sometimes difficult for the historian to decode, although horns obviously denoted cuckoldry and grain stuffed in the mouth indicated a scold.

Sometimes the parade was accompanied by a written or sung libel of the sort encountered in Chapter 2. In fact charivari was part of a 'wide and flexible' repertoire of mockery which included individual acts of insult involving crudely constructed pudenda and horn motifs as well as folk drama and libels.[102] At Westonbirt in Gloucestershire in 1716, a group of people, mainly men, enacted a piece of folk theatre to shame the sodomy of a farm servant by a local farmer. The drama was a 'mock groaning' in which the farm

---

100. The best accounts for early modern England are M. Ingram, 'Ridings, rough music and the "reform of popular culture" in early modern England', *Past and Present* 105 (1984), 79–113; M. Ingram, 'Ridings, rough music and mocking rhymes in early modern England', in Reay (ed.), *Popular Culture*, ch. 5; D.E. Underdown, 'The taming of the scold: the enforcement of patriarchal authority in early modern England', in A. Fletcher and J. Stevenson (eds), *Order and Disorder in Early Modern England* (Cambridge, 1985), ch. 4. For a wider perspective, see B. Palmer, 'Discordant music: charivaris and whitecapping in nineteenth-century North America', *Labour/Le Travailleur* 3 (1978), 5–62; J. Le Goff and J.-C. Schmitt (eds), *Le Charivari* (Paris, 1981).

101. E.P. Thompson, *Customs in Common* (London, 1991), ch. 8.

102. Ingram, 'Ridings, rough music and mocking rhymes', pp. 166–7.

servant himself took part, dressed as a woman in a mantua petti-
coat, and giving birth to a child, '*viz.* a wad of straw made up and
dressed with clothes in that form'. The child, a male, was delivered
by another man, a blacksmith, dressed as the midwife. '[T]he company drank plentifully and rejoiced up exceedingly at the birth.'
The baby was christened 'George Buggarer or Buggary' by 'a scan-
dalous fellow', a mason, who played the part of the parson. Amidst
music and dancing, the 'baby' was then paraded around the village
towards his father, the farmer's house, 'tost about', and eventually
'torn to pieces'.[103] It is difficult to characterise the subject of David
Rollison's fascinating case study. The organisation of the event has
the hallmarks of a church ale; yet the 'groaning' was the actual
occasion for the gathering. There was a parade of sorts and the
implements for rough music; but the drama was pre-eminent. It
approaches the classic charivari, but is probably best described as
charivaresque.

The Westonbirt 'groaning' stood at one end of the spectrum, then,
closest to charivaris. At the other end were cases like the woman
who erected a stage in her backyard to act out the infidelities of
nearby residents, and those who threw dildoes and 'merkins' over
their neighbour's wall with the intention of defaming.[104] Charivari
was merely a more organised form of disapprobation: the target was
still the individual or couple but the theatre of mockery involved
the crowd and took the form of a central procession.

In Aveton Gifford in 1737, for example, a group estimated at
more than 100

> Assembled before the doors of the dwelling house of Charles Jones,
> Gent. did make an Assault upon Mary his wife and in a sporting
> manner did demand where the black Bull was, meaning the said
> Charles Jones, and in such Riotous manner did run up and down the
> Church Town of Aveton Gifford with black and Disguised Faces
> carrying a large pair of Rams Horns tipt like Gold and adorned with
> Ribbons and Flowers with a mock child made of raggs, and having
> an Ass whereon the said John Macey [a miller] and John Pinwell
> [a labourer] rid, dressed in a Ludicrous manner, back to back, with
> beating of Drums and winding of Hunting Horns and throwing of
> lighted Squibbs, and Reading a Scandalous Libellous paper, making

103. D. Rollison, 'Property, ideology and popular culture in a Gloucestershire
village 1660–1740', in P. Slack (ed.), *Rebellion, Popular Protest and the Social Order in
Early Modern England* (Cambridge, 1984), ch. 14, esp. pp. 296–8, 314–15.
104. These examples come from Ingram, 'Ridings, rough music and mocking
rhymes', p. 166; and Day (ed.), *Pepys Ballads*, Vol. 4, p. 287. The word 'merkin' is
probably 'murkin', as in dark, indicating the female private parts.

loud Huzzahs Hallows and out Cries and so continuing for the space of 5 hours.[105]

The focus seems to have been upon the morality of the husband, Charles Jones, rather than that of his wife, and the reference to the mock child almost certainly refers to a discovered illegitimate child. But the themes of charivari are there in Aveton Gifford: the public parade, the effigy, the horns, the actors, disguise and transvestism, riding backwards, and even a libellous paper. The tenor of the riding should be familiar to readers of this chapter, for it is very similar to the festive milieu of folk drama described earlier: Christmas, Easter, the summer games, the lords of misrule.[106] In fact all the ingredients of the custom are present in the calendrical rites discussed earlier. In a sense, charivaris were punitive applications of festive ritual. The Quemerford skimmington, discussed below, occurred in May, and there are other examples stemming from church ale, Whitsun, and Plough Monday festivities.[107]

Martin Ingram's description of charivari as a mix of the penal and the festive captures its duality perfectly. He has written that it is essential to grasp this festive element: 'They plainly drew some of their vitality from the fact that they were a form of festivity in their own right.'[108] The aim of charivari was to provoke laughter. People were told to 'make merry with Skimmington' in one Somerset episode.[109] It is true that for the participants charivaris were miniature carnivals. They would have derived fun from the mock groaning at Westonbirt, acting out the rituals of childbirth. There was also a festive feel about the skimmington at Quemerford in Wiltshire in 1618, when a band of several hundred men from the nearby market town of Calne marched behind a man on a red horse who was casting brewing grain upon the crowd. The horseman had 'a white night cap upon his head, two shoeing horns hanging by his ears, a counterfeit beard upon his chin made of a deer's tail, a smock upon the top of his garments'. When the band arrived outside the home of their victim, Agnes Mills, a cutler's wife, 'the gunners shot off their pieces, pipes and horns were sounded, together with

105. M.G. Dickinson, 'A "skimmington ride" at Aveton Gifford', *Devon and Cornwall Notes and Queries* 34 (1981), 290–2.

106. Ingram also makes this connection: Ingram, 'Ridings, rough music, and the reform of popular culture', p. 94.

107. Underdown, *Revel, Riot, and Rebellion*, p. 102; Underdown, 'Taming of the scold', pp. 131, 133.

108. Ingram, 'Ridings, rough music, and the reform of popular culture', p. 96.

109. Underdown, *Revel, Riot, and Rebellion*, p. 102.

lowbells and other small bells . . . and rams' horns and bucks' horns, carried upon forks, were then and there lifted up and shown'.[110] In a skimmington in Brislington (Somerset) in the 1630s, a man was hired from Bristol to beat a drum, and another, dressed in women's apparel, rode behind a mop 'made like a man', beating it with a basting ladle (hence the term skimmington). The marchers' ensign was an apron tied to a long staff.[111]

But laughter was at the expense of those being ridiculed. We should not neglect the disciplining purpose of charivaris, the role of violence and humiliation. A child was killed by a stone in the Brislington skimmington. The skimmington riders at Quemerford were not content with mere effigies or actors, they wanted Agnes Mills herself, and they stormed the house, dragged her through the mud, and beat her, in an unsuccessful attempt to set her up behind the disguised horseman to ride her to Calne to 'washe her in the cuckinge stoole, & if she would not be still & sitt quietly, then to stuffe hir mouth wth greines'.[112] The festive element may have been uppermost for the band from Calne, but it was hardly a factor for the victim and her family, or for those who opposed the skimmington.

The issue of the nature of violence in charivaris is particularly interesting. It could be argued that the use of acting and effigies muted the actual physical violence, deflecting it away from the culprits; that violence was contained through ritual.[113] Yet we have seen (in the case of Agnes Mills) that it was easy for brutality to predominate when the alleged offender or his or her supporters resisted. In Burton-upon-Trent in Staffordshire in 1618, a couple who were accused of living together immorally were hauled out of their house in the late evening, led through the streets 'with greate noyce and with ringing of cow bells, basons, candlesticks, frying-pannes and with the sounde of a drumme', set in the stocks, and then dragged by their feet back through the street and left lying 'amased and hurte'. Dirt was thrown at them, and they were publicly proclaimed to be 'a whore and a knave, a whore, a whore'. Again, there was no attempt here to use effigies or substitutes. The offenders themselves were publicly shamed, as one of the leaders of

110. B.H. Cunnington, '"A skimmington" in 1618', *Folklore* 41 (1930), 287–90; Ingram, 'Ridings, rough music, and the reform of popular culture', p. 82, corrects Cunnington's transcription.

111. Stokes (ed.), *Records of Early English Drama: Somerset, Vol. 1*, pp. 61–2; *idem, Records of Early English Drama: Somerset, Vol. 2*, pp. 768–9.

112. Cunnington, 'Skimmington', pp. 289–90.

113. Thompson, *Customs in Common*, p. 486.

the crowd put it, 'to make soe notorious an abuse exemplarye whereby others evill disposed might be discoraged from comittinge the like'.[114] But even when such open savagery was absent, charivaris were far from benign folk justice.[115] The young Westonbirt farm servant seems to have avoided violence by colluding in the groaning, including a lying-in after the birth, attended by some of the village women.[116] But even if this participation helped him to cope with the ignominy, and the real target of the ritual was his penetrator, the farmer, the hidden injuries of ridicule must have been very strong. The very violence of charivaris resided in its ritual, the public nature of its message, and identification; in short, in its shaming. Charivari, to quote Edward Thompson, 'is a public naming of what has been named before only in private'.[117]

Another issue in studies of charivari is the custom's community role. Thompson has pointed out that charivari will only be effective if the target is sufficiently integrated into the community to be affected by the mockery, and if the message of the rite reflects 'the consensus of the community – or at least of a sufficiently large and dominant part of the community'.[118] Yet the consensus of a community and the pressure of a vocal or aggressive group within that society are not the same. Charivari were also a site of disharmony. The Quemerford incident represented community discord as much as any expression of shared morality. Earlier in the day, a smaller band of three or four men and ten or twelve boys, led by a drummer, had been thwarted by a group of women who 'understanding' that the drummer and his company 'came thither for a Skimmington' had cut the young man's drum.[119] The Quemerford incident was unusual in the openly gendered nature of the antagonism: the marchers were male – men and boys – but it was women who initially stopped the charivari, presumably because they identified with the victim. Elsewhere, as far as we know (historians

---

114. J.R. Kent, ' "Folk justice" and royal justice in early seventeenth-century England: a "charivari" in the midlands', *Midland History* 8 (1983), 70–85.

115. N.Z. Davis comes close to this view with her descriptions of French charivaris as 'a boisterous mixture of playfulness and cruelty', 'local folk justice as a source of control, of amusement, and of solidarity': N.Z. Davis, 'Charivari, honor, and community in seventeenth-century Lyon and Geneva', in J.J. MacAloon (ed.), *Rite, Drama, Festival, Spectacle* (Philadelphia, 1984), pp. 42–57 (quotes on pp. 42–3). However, John Cashmere has argued that violence is integral to the rituals of charivaris: J. Cashmere, 'The social uses of violence in ritual: *charivari* or religious persecution', *European History Quarterly* 21 (1991), 291–319. I lean towards Cashmere.

116. See the description in Rollison, 'Property, ideology', p. 297.

117. Thompson, *Customs in Common*, p. 488.   118. Ibid., p. 490.

119. Cunnington, 'Skimmington', p. 289.

have not been strong on the gendered composition of charivaris), skimmington crowds were mixed, although tended to be male-dominated. The Aveton Gifford charivari contained women (real women) as well as men.[120] Whatever the sex of the participants, early modern English charivaris enforced a highly gendered morality. It was the 'women on top' and the cuckolded man (not vice versa) who were the principal objects of censure. It would be a mistake to read the fictive drama of community norms as the representation of a genuine consensus.

VI

This chapter began with a comparison between late eighteenth- and early nineteenth-century Middleton and our period of interest. We have seen both similarities and differences. There is much that is recognisable across the eras in terms of ritual form and annual rhythm. But we have also detected significant ruptures. The Puritan impact on civic ritual is superficially well known but more complic-ated in detail and chronology. Rituals were transformed everywhere in England's reformations, yet with interesting cultural overlaps, resistance, and compromise. The death of 'medieval' religious drama was a complex and attenuated process. The mystery, morality, and saints plays – not, it is worth noting, confined to large urban centres – lasted well into the sixteenth century.[121] The Coventry Corpus Christi plays were performed until 1579 – and, in modified Protestant form, slightly later: the Smiths' accounts for 1584 record payments for drink, drums, trumpets, bagpipes, and the painting and construction of scenery, to actors who played the parts of Jesus and Salome, and even for starch 'to make the storme in the pagente'.[122] Characters from the Wells and Chester drama, we have seen, were transported into the more secular watches and shows of urban Midsummer. The same was true of York.[123] But only the

120. Ingram, 'Ridings, rough music, and the reform of popular culture', p. 102, refers to women's 'back-up functions'; Dickinson, 'Skimmington ride'. The Burton episode seems to have been a predominantly male affair: Kent, 'Folk justice'.

121. For a recent survey of medieval theatre, see R. Beadle (ed.), *The Cambridge Companion to Medieval English Theatre* (Cambridge, 1994).

122. P. Collinson, *The Birthpangs of Protestant England* (London, 1988), pp. 100–1; R.W. Ingram (ed.), *Records of Early English Drama: Coventry* (Toronto, 1981), pp. 307–9; R.W. Ingram, 'Fifteen seventy-nine and the decline of civic religious drama in Coventry', in G.R. Hibbard (ed.), *The Elizabethan Theatre VIII* (Port Credit, 1982), pp. 114–28.

123. Collinson, *Birthpangs*, p. 101; R. Hutton, *The Rise and Fall of Merry England: the Ritual Year 1400–1700* (Oxford, 1994), p. 121.

Kendal Corpus Christi cycle lasted until the beginning of the seventeenth century.[124] In Norwich, St George and Lady Margaret were purged from the city's famous St George's Day parade in 1559, but the dragon survived for centuries, transferred to the mayoral inauguration parades.[125]

Although there is a recognition of ruptures (abolished rites) it has existed alongside a historiographical tendency which could be described as essentialist. That is, those rituals 'discovered' by antiquarians and folklorists in the nineteenth and early twentieth centuries are seen as survivors, traceable to a common (usually pagan) origin. They are seen as capable of being modified; they wane and are revived. But the central assumption is of some unchanging core, and the hunt for origins and influences stalks the literature of British calendar customs.

This reverse Whig view of the past is no longer tenable. British rituals were continually invented and reinvented.[126] The lord mayor's shows, for instance, essentially date from the late sixteenth century. When John Stow published his *Survey of London* in 1598, he had little to say about the shows, presumably because these 'recently invented traditions' had little place in his nostalgic invocation of ceremony and community. One could argue for a vague kind of ceremonial continuity in the historical shift in London's civic calendar, as Corpus Christi gave way to the Midsummer watches, which, in turn, were replaced by the shows. But the shows represented a different ideology, what Lawrence Manley has termed a new civic religion, celebrating the commercial wealth and power of the City's elite.[127] There are other examples of inventions and discontinuities. Welsh wakes effectively date from the Restoration, and end with the New Poor Law in the 1830s.[128] All Fool's Day (1 April) is a late-seventeenth-century import from the Continent.[129] The folk drama, the mummers' play, probably dates from no

124. Hutton, *Stations of the Sun*, p. 309.

125. Galloway (ed.), *Records of Early English Drama: Norwich*, pp. xxvi–xxvii; Hutton, *Stations of the Sun*, pp. 216–17.

126. Apart form the work of Hutton, cited throughout this chapter, see Buckland and Wood (eds), *British Calendar Customs*; and Pettitt's important article, 'Customary drama'.

127. See I. Archer, 'The nostalgia of John Stow', and L. Manley, 'Of sites and rites', in D.L. Smith, R. Strier, and D. Bevington (eds), *The Theatrical City: Culture, Theatre and Politics in London, 1576–1649* (Cambridge, 1995), ch. 1: 'John Stow's Survey of London'.

128. R. Suggett, 'Festivals and social structure in early modern Wales', *Past and Present* 152 (1996), 110.

129. Hutton, *Stations of the Sun*, p. 177.

earlier than the eighteenth century.[130] Sometimes the basic form continues, but its functions and meanings change. The principal site of the English morris dance, the main folk dancing form for much of the early modern period, moved from the fifteenth-century noble household, to the sixteenth-century town, and then to the seventeenth-century village. By the eighteenth century it was used by rural workers as a way of raising money. Hutton has argued that the history of the morris is far from that of some 'unchanging and ancient rite', but rather 'one of a triumph of versatility'.[131] Charles Phythian-Adams has charted the transformation of a May ritual in seventeenth- and eighteenth-century London, where the milkmaids who originally dominated the rites were ousted by the chimney sweeps. The imagery of femininity, milk, and purity was replaced by masculinity, soot, and dirt. The maid's garland gave way to the sweeps' 'Jack in the Green'.[132]

Hutton has raised considerable doubt about the assumed pagan origins of most rites. Only the use of fire, festival greenery, and the giving of gifts at New Year can be firmly established in the pre-Christian period. '[A]lthough some of the rituals and customs carried on in early Tudor communities were very old, many had either been introduced or embellished only a few generations before or even within living memory.'[133] A newer Protestant calendar, commemorating significant dates in the history of the early modern monarchy and church, provided ritual occasions for a greater awareness of national identity: King Charles's Day (30 January), Royal Oak Day (29 May), Gunpowder Treason Day (5 November), Queen Elizabeth's Day (17 November).[134]

Recent work on British folklore is moving towards establishing a chart of historical change, with booms in ritual observation in the late medieval period and the eighteenth century.[135] From the fifteenth century onwards, seasonal rituals and festivities were used as a means of raising church money: the church was thus closely associated with the rituals of popular festivity. However, England's

130. Ibid., ch. 7.

131. J. Forrest and M. Heaney, 'Charting early morris', *Folk Music Journal* 6 (1991), 169–86; Hutton, *Stations of the Sun*, p. 276.

132. R. Judge, *The Jack in the Green: a May Day Custom* (Cambridge, 1978); Phythian-Adams, 'Milk and soot'.

133. Hutton, *Rise and Fall of Merry England*, pp. 51, 61.

134. D. Cressy, *Bonfires and Bells: National Memory and the Protestant Calendar in Elizabethan and Stuart England* (London, 1989); D. Cressy, 'The Protestant calendar and the vocabulary of celebration in early modern England', *Journal of British Studies* 29 (1990), 31–52.

135. Hutton, *Stations of the Sun*, p. 426.

reformations gradually severed these ties. By the eighteenth century such rituals had moved more firmly into the secular sphere. Another change was in the dole-providing function of seasonal rites. Although there were handouts at earlier festivals, the dole-giving role of British rites was particularly strong in the eighteenth and nineteenth centuries. The regionalised begging customs of St Thomas's Day (21 December), a doling day par excellence, seem to originate in the eighteenth century.[136] The ubiquity of the 'ritualized begging' of the later period is in marked contrast to the situation in early modern Britain.[137] It was as if the community – or sections of the community – rather than the church became the recipient of ritual largesse.

VII

It is important to stress the variety of ritual occasions in early modern England, the multiple rhythms of festivity. Until 1752, the civil year in England started on the 25 March. The liturgical year, however, began on 1 January, and there were both fixed and moveable dates in the church calendar. Added to this was the fact that the agricultural year followed its own tempo. When Thomas Tusser wrote his advice book, *A Hundreth Good Pointes of Husbandrie*, he began in August and ended in the following July, with the harvest providing the focus for his tips for the whole agricultural year.[138] The rural rhythm also varied with types of agriculture; arable and pastoral districts had different patterns of marriage seasonality and labour hiring and therefore of the festivity and ritual associated with these important moments in people's lives.[139]

There were also strong local variations. Rituals such as the Abbot's Bromley Horn Dance, although containing thematic elements common to other popular rites – in this case, the morris,

---

136. Ibid., pp. 58–60.
137. Ibid., p. 422. See also, B. Bushaway, *By Rite: Custom, Ceremony and Community in England 1700–1880* (London, 1982), esp. pp. 180–90, for the prevalence of dole-seeking in the eighteenth and nineteenth centuries; although he was unaware of discontinuities with the sixteenth and seventeenth centuries.
138. T. Tusser, *A Hundreth Good Pointes of Husbandrie* (London, 1557) (repr. Theatrum Orbis Terrarum, Amsterdam, 1973).
139. D. Cressy, 'The seasonality of marriage in old and new England', *Journal of Interdisciplinary History* 16 (1985), 1–21; A. Kussmaul, *A General View of the Rural Economy of England, 1538–1840* (Cambridge, 1990); J. Thirsk, 'A time to weed, a time to wed', *Times Higher Educational Supplement*, 16 November 1990.

hobby-horse, and doling – were unique in the detail of their actual performance.[140] Local interests continually dictated that national commemorations could be used to settle specific grievances, and would be invested with local rather than national significance. Thus in the nineteenth century 5 November was used as an opportunity for mockery of unpopular local figures.[141] Oak Apple Day merged with local May customs and the traditional right to gather wood.[142] The various calendars of the English ritual year provide ample evidence of regional variety.[143] Furthermore, as well as being important sites for a range of calendrical rites and festivities, towns had their own rituals and ceremonies, influenced by the occupational structure of their inhabitants and the ceremonies of local politics. The symbolic presentation of urban community and hierarchy in the religious pageantry of the medieval guild processions faded during the sixteenth century. However, ritual (and community and hierarchy) found expression in other ways. Peter Borsay has demonstrated a flourishing of ritual and ceremony in the English towns of the late seventeenth and eighteenth centuries.[144] In short, there were 'many calendars'.[145]

The carnivalesque was central to early modern English culture. The elite had their own form of carnival by the eighteenth century in the form of the masquerade, the masked fantasy world of sexual licence.[146] But we have seen that they also participated in a range of popular festive drama and ritual. The themes of patriarchy and momentary gender or social inversion were by no means alien to elite culture. Henry Oxinden, member of the Kent gentry, said that ridings were 'a harmless pastime, which according to the opinion of honest divines is not only lawful but in some sort necessary'.[147] The Aveton Gifford skimmington included a wide social range of

140. E.C. Cawte, *Ritual Animal Disguise* (Cambridge, 1978), pp. 65–79.
141. R.D. Storch, '"Please to remember the Fifth of November": conflict, solidarity and public order in southern England, 1815–1900', in R.D. Storch (ed.), *Popular Culture and Custom in Nineteenth-century England* (London, 1982), ch. 4.
142. Bushaway, *By Rite*, pp. 74–80, 209–10; Hutton, *Stations of the Sun*, ch. 27.
143. See A.R. Wright, *British Calendar Customs*, 3 vols (London, 1936–40); C. Hole, *A Dictionary of British Folk Customs* (London, 1984).
144. P. Borsay, '"All the town's a stage": urban ritual and ceremony 1660–1800', in P. Clark (ed.), *The Transformation of English Provincial Towns 1600–1800* (London, 1984), ch. 7.
145. R. Poole, '"Give us our eleven days!": calendar reform in eighteenth-century England', *Past and Present* 149 (1995), 97.
146. T. Castle, *Masquerade and Civilization: the Carnivalesque in Eighteenth-century English Culture and Fiction* (London, 1986). However, I cannot agree with her that the masquerade was socially inclusive (other than including prostitutes).
147. Ingram, 'Ridings, rough music, and the reform of popular culture', p. 105.

participants: gentry, yeomen, a variety of craftsmen and tradesmen, their wives and daughters, as well as the labourers, who were a minority of those accused.[148]

The term carnivalesque is fully justified in this context of festive ritual. Again and again, we see moments of indulgence and excess in sex, eating, drinking, and play.[149] These were times of mirth, misrule, inversion, and (we should not forget) brutality. We have seen that there were many uses of festive drama and ritual, and multiple meanings. There were mock lords and ladies, mock births, mock elections, and mock sermons. There was ridicule of an earl. There was raillery against unruly women – misrule against misrule! Dramatic ritual was employed against Catholics as well as Puritans. It was wielded against those who broke sexual codes. And it was linked to popular protest: some of the local leaders of anti-enclosure riots in the west of England in the 1620s and 1630s were known by the aliases 'Lady Skimington' and 'Skimington'.[150] Transvestism was a common, if inherently unstable, common ingredient. Men dressed as women – the prevailing form – could arouse fear, laughter, or even same-sex desire, depending on the context (and, presumably, the aesthetic appeal of the actor).[151]

Mikhail Bakhtin has interpreted carnival as 'the second life of the people, who for a time entered the utopian realm of community, freedom, equality and abundance': 'one might say that carnival celebrated temporary liberation from the prevailing truth and from the established order; it marked the suspension of all hierarchical rank, privileges, norms, and prohibitions. Carnival was the true feast of time, the feast of becoming, change, and renewal. It was hostile to all that was immortalized and completed.'[152] Natalie Davis has similarly argued that the theme of the 'woman on top' may have provided a brief glimpse of an alternative to the prevailing gender order.[153] While not denying the ambivalence of festive rites – indeed, the possibilities of disruption are one of this chapter's themes – the structures of English society severely curtailed

148. Dickinson, 'Skimmington ride'.
149. Compare D.A. Reid, 'Interpreting the festival calendar: wakes and fairs as carnivals', in Storch (ed.), *Popular Culture*, ch. 6.
150. B. Sharp, *In Contempt of All Authority: Rural Artisans and Riot in the West of England, 1586–1660* (Berkeley, 1980), pp. 97–107.
151. For a recent discussion of cross-dressing, see D. Cressy, 'Gender trouble and cross-dressing in early modern England', *Journal of British Studies* 35 (1996), 438–65.
152. M. Bakhtin, *Rabelais and His World* (Bloomington, 1984), pp. 9–10.
153. N.Z. Davis, 'Women on top', in her *Society and Culture in Early Modern France* (Stanford, Calif., 1975), ch. 5.

Bakhtinian potentials. Bakhtin's grand claims, so influential in twentieth-century cultural studies, do not describe the capacities of the English carnivalesque. The only moments when these forms were truly threatening were at times of genuine crisis in the social order, and such moments were rare in early modern England. The weight of festive ritual was towards social conservatism, the reinforcement of male dominance and social hierarchy. After all, most of the dramatised 'women on top' were men in drag. The very absurdity of the 'world upside down' confirmed normality. The ritualised begging which peppered the English calendar might lean towards coercion of social superiors by their inferiors, but it operated within the parameters of a firm recognition of dominance and deference.

This is not to question the significance of festive drama and ritual during the period 1550–1750. Peter Burke has written of the 'repudiation of ritual' in early modern Europe, a shift in attitudes, a struggle against ritual: 'the early modern period was . . . extremely important in the articulation and development of the propensity to repudiate ritual'.[154] However, I think that this chapter has demonstrated the strength of ritual in early modern popular culture. In the words of Alexandra Johnston, 'to engage in mimetic imitation . . . was as common as engaging in trade'.[155] English rites were dynamic. Rituals changed; they were continually invented and reinvented, shaped and reshaped. But the centrality of ritual is scarcely in doubt. It would be more appropriate to write of the resilience of ritual than of its repudiation.

154. P. Burke, *The Historical Anthropology of Early Modern Italy: Essays on Perception and Communication* (Cambridge, 1997), ch. 16: 'The repudiation of ritual in early modern Europe'. Quote at p. 225.
155. Johnston, 'All the world was a stage', p. 123. She is referring to the period before the 1640s.

CHAPTER SIX

Riots and the Law

I

The clothing area of Dewsbury (Yorkshire) was the scene of a series of riots in 1740. On 27 April, a Sunday, at about 6 p.m., a number of people, some armed with clubs, arrived at a Thornhill mill. They told the millman that if he did not open his door they would break it down. They entered and destroyed his bolting mill. They then went to the man's house, and, when he refused them access, lifted a woman up onto the roof so that she could remove slates for them to gain entry. Rather than having his roof destroyed, the millman decided to let the protesters in. The crowd entered and took several packs of flour and meal, as well as some food and alcohol (so their victim deposed). The next day, 'a great Number of persons came to his house again under pretence to buy Corn of him & offer'd him a low price for the same'. This group (one assumes the same crowd as the previous day) did not merely remove the grain; they offered to purchase it at a lower price than that asked by the dealer. They 'told him that if he would not take their own price, they would take it by force & accordingly they took away & destroyed about 3 loads . . . for wch they left this informant ten shillings'. The miller was able to identify two of the men: one from Dewsbury and one from Batley. A mill in Dewsbury was attacked about the same time, and in much the same manner, with a woman climbing up onto the roof to effect an entry. The rioters shattered the bolting mill, and appropriated sacks of wheat-flour, bran, and beans. Some of the sacks were ripped open, and their contents thrown either on the mill floor or in the river; others were taken for food. A clothier told the justices that he saw one man scattering bran dust on the river, and a man and his wife carrying off wheat flour. The rioting was also accompanied by more generalised threats and intimidation. One grain dealer had to leave the area after three women had threatened his life – he hired another man to carry on his trade. The women who threatened him included the tile-remover.[1]

These riots were part of more widespread disturbances which occurred in eastern England, north of the Thames, a crisis provoked by the crop-damaging rains of the previous harvest and a severe winter. The aim of the rioters was to prevent export of grain at a time of anticipated shortage. It was reported that the protesters in the Dewsbury region attempted 'to prevent the Badgers from making Wheat Meal or Flower, to send into other Countries, alledging that such Practice would cause a Scarcity in Yorkshire, and much advance the Price of Corn'.[2] The riots took place before the harvest of 1740, but the prospect of another bad harvest and associated hoarding had already forced prices up. In Newcastle, a town without a strong tradition of food rioting, the price of oats and rye had doubled by June. The result, after more moderate protest escalated, was the sacking of the Guildhall. Action included the blocking of the movement of grain through the town, the seizing of grain and bread, negotiation with magistrates and merchants in an effort to reduce prices on a range of food items, and an attempt to commandeer a ship-load of rye. Women and children were prominent in the disturbances, but they were joined by contingents of pitmen, keelmen, and ironworkers as the food protest merged with discontent over wages and labour conditions (of which Newcastle did have a tradition).[3]

The protests of 1740, towards the conclusion of our period of interest, introduce some of the more salient aspects of the subject of this chapter: the role of riot in popular culture.

II

During the period before 1750, food riots and anti-improvement or anti-enclosure disturbances were the most important forms of overt protest. Buchanan Sharp has said that these forms of protest

1. Public Record Office, ASSI 45/21/4/91-5: North-East Circuit Assize Depositions.
2. R.W. Malcolmson, '1740', in A. Charlesworth (ed.), *An Atlas of Rural Protest in Britain 1548–1900* (London, 1983), p. 83.
3. J. Ellis, 'Urban conflict and popular violence: the Guildhall riots of 1740 in Newcastle Upon Tyne', *International Review of Social History* 25 (1980), 332–49.

were to the pre-industrial economy what strikes are (or were) to the industrial era.[4] Food rioting punctuates the history of the period, with concentrations in 1551, 1586–7, 1594–8, 1605, 1608, 1614, 1622–3, 1629–31, 1647–8, 1662–3, 1674, 1681, 1693–5, 1709–10, 1727–9, 1739–40, 1756–7, 1766–8.[5] In other words, in terms of what historians have defined as impact at a national level, there were riots about every decade. Yet other than providing this vague sense of occurrence, it is extremely difficult to count riots. An influential study of grain riots in the period from 1585 to 1660 counted forty, but these were riots which came to the attention of the central authorities.[6] Some historians follow the Riot Act of 1715 in defining a riot as a disturbance involving twelve or more people; others set the crowd limit at fifty or more.[7]

There was regional variation. Food riots were confined to market towns, towns, and ports rather than villages; clothmaking areas were also relatively riot-prone. Certainly there was no simple correlation between hardship and riot: the population of the north west of England in the sixteenth and seventeenth centuries literally starved to death without overt protest of this type.[8] The maps of the geography of food riots indicate that they were confined to south of a line drawn from the Wash to the Severn for the period up to the 1730s, but with disturbances in the midlands, the Welsh borders, Yorkshire, and the north-east Tyne and Tees areas in 1740 and 1756–7.[9] Experiences, and hence the repertoires of protest, must have varied immensely. In 1630–1 there were grain riots in Somerset, Wiltshire, Hampshire, Berkshire, Hertfordshire, Suffolk, Kent, and Sussex.[10] It is easy for the student – and the historian – to be dazzled by the dotted maps of protest. But the point is that large

4. B. Sharp, 'Popular protest in seventeenth-century England', in B. Reay (ed.), *Popular Culture in Seventeenth-century England* (London, 1985), p. 274.

5. M. Beloff, *Public Order and Popular Disturbances 1660–1714* (London, 1963 edn), ch. 3; Sharp, 'Popular protest', p. 274; J. Stevenson, 'The "moral economy" of the English crowd: myth and reality', in A. Fletcher and J. Stevenson (eds), *Order and Disorder in Early Modern England* (Cambridge, 1985), ch. 8; J. Stevenson, *Popular Disturbances in England, 1700–1832* (London, 1992 edn), p. 114.

6. J. Walter and K. Wrightson, 'Dearth and the social order in early modern England', in P. Slack (ed.), *Rebellion, Popular Protest and the Social Order in Early Modern England* (Cambridge, 1984), p. 112.

7. J. Bohstedt, *Riots and Community Politics in England and Wales 1790–1810* (Cambridge, Mass., 1983), p. 4.

8. Sharp, 'Popular protest', pp. 274–7; A.B. Appleby, *Famine in Tudor and Stuart England* (Stanford, Calif., 1978), chs 8–9.

9. See maps 18–23 in Charlesworth (ed.), *Atlas of Rural Protest*, pp. 73, 75, 78, 81, 84, 87.

10. Walter and Wrightson, 'Dearth and the social order', p. 112.

areas of the nation, whatever the period, were riotless. 'Despite the predictions of contemporaries and presumptions of historians,' John Walter has noted, 'years of harvest failure were not marked by widespread and frequent food riots.'[11] Essex, for example, involved both in the grain trade and the cloth industry, reported only ten grain riots between 1585 and 1660.[12] Even in those nodes of food rioting, the market towns, 'one food riot per century would have been a sanguine expectation'.[13]

The background to the food riot was often – though not necessarily – harvest failure or anticipated failure, with their associated impact on prices. Unemployment was also a contributory factor. Crises in the English cloth industry were likely to promote unrest: clothmaking areas and English clothworkers were prominent in food riots. Riots in the 1620s, for example, corresponded to a slump in the cloth trade.[14] Bread was the staple diet of the majority of the English population. From 50 to 60 per cent of a working family's budget each week would go on food; and the main item of this expenditure was on cereals (bread, flour, meal).[15] The supply of grain was therefore extremely important; and harvests, as historians of the early modern period continually point out, formed the pulse or heartbeat of the nation. Food riots were directed at those involved in the various stages of getting the grain out of the fields and onto the table: farmers, dealers, millers, mealmen, merchants, and bakers, middlemen, and speculators who held back grain at a time of shortage (to force up or capitalise on increasing prices), sent grain or other food stuffs outside the immediate area (grain on the move was always viewed with suspicion), those who were considered to be making unjust profits from a perceived crisis, or taking advantage of the situation by selling underweight bread or adulterated food. Wiltshire craftsmen in 1614 urged 'the reformation of the intollerable abuses used by maltsters millards Badgers & drivers for their excessive buyinge hordinge & forestalling of Corne & other p[ro]visions w[hi]ch we truly knowe to be the originall

11. J. Walter, 'The social economy of dearth in early modern England', in J. Walter and R. Schofield (eds), *Famine, Disease and the Social Order in Early Modern England* (Cambridge, 1989), ch. 2 (quote at p. 76). Walter explores the lack of crises of subsistence in early modern England.

12. Walter and Wrightson, 'Dearth and the social order', pp. 112–13.

13. D.E. Williams, 'Morals, markets and the English crowd in 1766', *Past and Present* 104 (1984), 70.

14. B. Sharp, *In Contempt of All Authority: Rural Artisans and Riot in the West of England, 1586–1660* (Berkeley, 1980), ch. 2: 'Food riots, 1586–1631'.

15. C. Shammas, *The Pre-industrial Consumer in England and America* (Oxford, 1990), ch. 5, provides the most sophisticated discussion of this topic.

cause of dearthe'.[16] Riots in Worcester in 1693 began when factors arrived 'to buy up corne, bacon and cheese to export them'.[17]

Tactics varied. In a riot at Stratford on Avon in 1674, 'sluices on the river were broken to prevent the corn-laden barges from moving'.[18] Carts and barges carrying grain were stopped in the western counties in the sixteenth and seventeenth centuries.[19] The maps of Andrew Charlesworth's *Atlas of Rural Protest* indicate that seizure of food was the most common means of protest in the period before 1660, followed by attacks on dealers and storehouses and the prevention of the transportation of food. The order was reversed after the Restoration, with the obstruction of the movement of food as the most prevalent means of protest from 1660 to 1740. This tactic was followed closely by attacks on warehouses, granaries, dealers, and millers, while 'seizure of foodstuffs' had slipped to less preferred status.[20] There are problems with this type of categorisation, as the example of the riots in Dewsbury in 1740 indicates. They involved attacks on mills – indeed are plotted as firm black dots, indicating 'Attack on mills', on the atlas's map for 1740. Yet we saw that these attacks included seizure of food and a pre-emptive strike against the export of processed grain – hence the breaking of machinery. It is sometimes difficult to separate categories, then. The distinction between the seizure of food and attacks on storehouses is likely to be somewhat artificial. However, the maps do indicate broad trends. The staying of transport was more common after 1660 than during the period before. We also know that the foray of protesters into the countryside to force farmers to sell their products at 'agreed' (i.e. coerced) prices was a tactic of the second half, particularly the end, of the eighteenth century.[21]

III

Anti-enclosure and anti-improvement riots, as their names suggest, were directed against the visible forms of enclosure or land improvement, or the property of those pursuing such schemes. Hence rioters levelled or destroyed hedges or fences on acreage which

---

16. Walter and Wrightson, 'Dearth and the social order', p. 116.

17. Beloff, *Public Order*, p. 61.   18. Ibid., pp. 59–60.

19. D. Underdown, *Revel, Riot, and Rebellion: Popular Politics and Culture in England 1603–1660* (Oxford, 1985), pp. 116–17.

20. Calculated from maps 18–23 in Charlesworth (ed.), *Atlas of Rural Protest*, pp. 73, 75, 78, 81, 84, 87.

21. For these forays, see Bohstedt, *Riots*, ch. 2.

was considered to be common land, and, in the case of the fens, attacked drainage works or the homes of those engaged in the new drainage schemes. The regional distribution of anti-enclosure riots varied according to period. Roger Manning's sample of over 200 enclosure riot cases during the reigns of Elizabeth and James shows a concentration in the midlands and the south, but the period from the mid-1620s onwards represents a shift in such protest to the geographical areas of East Anglia and the west.[22] We know most about the larger waves of protest: 1548–52, 1596, the midland revolt of 1607, the western rising of 1626–32, the fenland disturbances of the late 1620s and the 1630s, unrest during the 1640s and 1650s, 1670, 1689, 1699, 1710, 1748–51.[23]

But these 'risings' are merely tips of icebergs of more widespread local resistance. The miners of the Forest of Dean waged a continuous war of attrition against enclosure, for example, with disturbances recorded in 1612, 1629–32, 1640, 1659, 1670, 1688, 1696, 1707, and 1735.[24] When we note historians' general agreement about the quiescence of the period after the Restoration, we need to qualify this claim with the vital rider that rioting is not the only place to look for resistance. J.M. Neeson has argued that riot was probably the least common and least effective way of opposing enclosure, and she has explored tactics of 'non-compliance, foot-dragging and mischief' employed in eighteenth-century Northamptonshire. Small farmers, landless labourers, shopkeepers, and craftsmen resisted enclosure through a combination of threat, refusal to sign agreements, petitions, theft of field books, destruction of markers, and fence-breaking.[25]

The common land was extremely important to the household economies of the early modern period for grazing as well as providing access to a range of food and fuel. Commons or manorial wastes, woods, and meadows provided pasture for cattle, horses, pigs, sheep, and geese. Woods and heaths yielded a range of building material and fuel. The product varied with the locality: sand,

22. See tables in R.B. Manning, *Village Revolts: Social Protest and Popular Disturbances in England 1509–1640* (Oxford, 1988), pp. 325, 327; and the maps in Charlesworth, *Atlas of Rural Protest*, ch. 2.

23. Charlesworth, *Atlas of Rural Protest*, ch. 2; Stevenson, *Popular Disturbances*, pp. 51–3.

24. Stevenson, *Popular Disturbances*, p. 53.

25. J.M. Neeson, 'The opponents of enclosure in eighteenth-century Northamptonshire', *Past and Present* 105 (1984), 114–39. This became chapter 9 of her *Commoners: Common Right, Enclosure and Social Change in England, 1700–1820* (Cambridge, 1993): 'Resisting enclosure'.

stone, coal, wood, peat, turf, gorse or furze, fern, rushes.[26] The commons supplied food too: nuts, fungi, herbs (used in healing as well as eating), berries, fish, birds, game. All had considerable value for consumption or sale. The marshland, peat, and silt areas of the fens, for example, supplied turf for fuel; reeds for thatching; rushes for baskets, mats, and lighting; alders and willows for basket-making; hemp and flax for spinning and weaving; fish and wildfowl for food and feathers; and fertile common pasture for feeding cattle, horses, and sheep.[27] The miners of the Forest of Dean claimed the right to mine the king's soil for coal and iron ore, and resisted enclosures which limited their access. But the Forest also supported a population of woodworkers, and others who made a living quarrying grindstones and millstones.[28] During times of unemployment the supplemental value of access to the commons was even greater, and rioting could result from this added pressure. The fens drainage schemes, which cut great lines across the landscape, were also blamed, with some justice, for disturbing the ecological balance of local subsistence economies. A libellous song encapsulated such fears:

> Behold the great design, which they do now determine,
> Will make our bodies pine, a prey to crows and vermine:
> For they do mean all Fens to drain, and waters overmaster,
> All will be dry, and we must die, 'cause Essex calves want pasture.
>
> Away with boats and rudder, farewell both boots and skatches,
> No need of one nor th'other, men now make better matches;
> Stilt-makers all and tanners, shall complain of this disaster,
> For they will make each muddy lake for Essex calves a pasture.
>
> The feather'd fowls have wings, to fly to other nations;
> But we have no such things, to help our transportations;
> We must give place (oh grievous case) to horned beasts and cattle,
> Except that we can all agree to drive them out by battle.[29]

The royal forests of Gloucestershire, Wiltshire and the Wiltshire–Dorset border saw sustained action against enclosure and disafforestation in the 1620s and early 1630s. Although these protests consisted of independent riots, their sheer intensity ensured that they became known as the western rising. In incidents in the Forest

26. See Manning, *Village Revolts*, chs 1, 10; E.P. Thompson, *Customs in Common* (London, 1991), ch. 3; and especially the marvellous account in Neeson, *Commoners*, ch. 6: 'The uses of waste'.

27. H.C. Darby, *The Draining of the Fens* (Cambridge, 1956), ch. 2; K. Lindley, *Fenland Riots and the English Revolution* (London, 1982), Introduction.

28. Sharp, *In Contempt of All Authority*, ch. 7.   29. Ibid., p. 55.

of Dean in 1631, hundreds of rioters 'did with two drummes, two coulors and one fife in a warlike and outragious manner assemble themselves together armed with gunnes, pykes, halberdes and other weapons' and, carrying an effigy of one of the projectors responsible for exploiting the forest, marched on recently enclosed land. They fired on the home of a developer's agent, burned houses, destroyed hedges and ditches, and filled in ore pits.[30]

IV

Historians have stressed the orderly, controlled nature of these forms of popular protest. John Bohstedt has referred to the 'protocol of riot'; the food riots of eighteenth-century Devon were 'remarkable in their discipline'.[31] The price-fixing riots, sometimes referred to as *taxation populaire*, were, in effect, popular forms of price control. Rioters would coerce the sale of food or grain at what they decided was a just price. There were various ways of achieving this. By their very presence, a crowd could compel dealers to comply with their price. In 1693, 'the poore in Oxford by clamoring brought the price of corne from 9s. to 6s. 2d.'.[32] Or they took more direct action in the sense of seizing the grain but paying for it as they took it. In Northampton in 1693, wheat seized from the carts of corn-dealers was sold at the market at 5s. a bushel.[33] The point about this form of protest is that it was not simple theft: rather than stealing it, the rioters paid for the grain, albeit at a lower price than that asked by the seller(s). In eighteenth-century Exeter, a crowd of forty or fifty seized food and forced its sale. They asked 7s. 6d. a bushel for wheat instead of 9s. 6d., and 8d. a peck for potatoes instead of 10d.[34]

Their mobilisation was orderly too. Some protesters marched in companies, like the militia or army, to the beat of the drum. Several riots were led by a 'captain' or a 'major'.[35] 'Captain Dorothy' Dawson led female protesters on Thorpe Moor in 1607.[36] Anti-enclosure rioters in seventeenth-century Wiltshire, who kept up their protests for five years, and who included women and children as well as men, wore red badges and feathers in their caps and marched in companies when they levelled hedges.[37] Others in Bedfordshire,

30. Sharp, *In Contempt of All Authority*, pp. 94–6.   31. Bohstedt, *Riots*, p. 27.
32. Beloff, *Public Order*, p. 62.   33. Ibid., pp. 63–4.
34. Bohstedt, *Riots*, pp. 27–8.   35. Manning, *Village Revolts*, p. 83.
36. Ibid., p. 281.   37. Ibid., p. 98.

also numbering women among their ranks, were divided into companies; the village constable organised their protest in the parish church and made a collection to fund their resistance to the Earl of Kent's enclosure of wasteland.[38]

Historians have argued that such rioters were limited in their objectives. They were 'pragmatic, not revolutionary'; 'most rioters confined their actions and objectives, their practical intentions, to the concrete, the particular, and the local'.[39] Their aim was to regulate, not to overturn. They wanted to regulate the price and flow of food and the impact of land improvement, and they wanted to ensure access to affordable grain and the produce of the commons. E.P. Thompson has described the ideology behind these forms of protest as the 'moral economy':

> these grievances operated within a popular consensus as to what were legitimate and what were illegitimate practices in marketing, milling, baking, etc. This in its turn was grounded upon a consistent traditional view of social norms and obligations, of the proper economic functions of several parties within the community . . . An outrage to these moral assumptions, quite as much as actual deprivation, was the usual occasion for direct action.[40]

Rioters acted in the name of the community. Riots were a form of 'community politics' in defence of what were perceived to be traditional rights and customs.[41] Rioters believed that it was the duty of the magistrates to enforce these rights. This is most clearly the case with food riots, for the laws were frequently there to regulate the grain trade during times of crisis. A series of statutes in the sixteenth and seventeenth centuries curbed the export of grain and other food, and even when controls were relaxed in the 1670s, official intervention, proclamations, and the invoking of earlier legislation against the abuses of middlemen meant that controls from the top were still exerted. The reprinted sixteenth-century *Book of Orders for the Relief of Dearth* likewise legitimated the notion of regulation. The *Book of Orders* was not officially reissued after 1630, and intervention, whether at the central or local level, declined thereafter.[42] But the popular feeling of official legitimation remained.

---

38. Ibid., pp. 100–1; Public Record Office, STAC 8/156/32: Star Chamber Proceedings, James I.

39. Bohstedt, *Riots*, pp. 221–2.   40. Thompson, *Customs in Common*, p. 188.

41. The phrase 'community politics' is Bohstedt's.

42. For official policy, see R.B. Outhwaite, *Dearth, Public Policy and Social Disturbance in England, 1550–1800* (London, 1991), ch. 3; P. Slack, 'Dearth and social policy in early modern England', *Social History of Medicine* 5 (1992), 1–17.

If the magistrate did not respond to the informal appeals or more formal petitioning which frequently preceded coercive behaviour, then it was the crowd's duty to persuade still further through riot.[43] Sharp has called riots an extreme form of petitioning.[44] If the magistrates remained inactive, then protesters would take matters into their own hands. At the end of the seventeenth century, Oxfordshire rioters 'took away the corne by force out of the waggons, as it was carrying away by the ingrossers, saying they were resolved to put the law in execution, since the magistrates neglected it'.[45]

Rioters therefore claimed that law and custom were on their side. A few invoked more exalted support. An Ely labourer recounted how he had visited Charles I; the king had leaned on his shoulder and wept when he heard the plight of the fenlanders.[46] One of the leaders of the 1607 rising, Captain Pouch, said that 'hee had authority from his majestie to throwe downe enclosures'.[47] Anti-enclosers in Blunham in Bedfordshire rioted with the cry, 'Now for King James and for the Comons of Blunham.'[48] Food rioters in Kent in 1631 took corn, saying that 'one half was for the king and the other for them'.[49]

Recent studies have demonstrated just how ubiquitous regulatory trading practices were. When protesters pressed for price control or action against middlemen and speculators, they were operating along, rather than against, the grain of a common culture of control and regulation. It was the middlemen who were out of step with what could be termed a cross-class ideology of market control.[50] The Oxford rioters who in 1766 fixed the prices not only of wheat and flour but of a whole range of groceries and farm produce were drawing on an established tradition of market control by the university and colleges, dominant players in the political economy of the town and its hinterland.[51]

43. See Walter and Wrightson, 'Dearth and the social order'.

44. Sharp, *In Contempt of All Authority*, p. 42.

45. R.B. Westerfield, *Middlemen in English Business* (New Haven, 1915), p. 148.

46. Lindley, *Fenland Riots*, p. 103.   47. Manning, *Village Revolts*, p. 233.

48. Ibid., p. 101; Public Record Office, STAC 8/156/32.

49. P. Clark, 'Popular protest and disturbance in Kent, 1558–1640', *Economic History Review* 29 (1976), 370.

50. See the important collection of case studies: A. Randall and A. Charlesworth (eds), *Markets, Market Culture and Popular Protest in Eighteenth-century Britain and Ireland* (Liverpool, 1996).

51. W. Thwaites, 'Oxford food riots: a community and its riots', in Randall and Charlesworth (eds), *Markets*, ch. 7.

V

The description of riot as 'community politics' is further under-scored by the prevalence of women in this form of protest. They were there in the Axholme riots in 1629, several hundred of them, on 'divers dayes and tymes', throwing down the banks and drainage works, and burning building material and workmen's tools.[52] Preg-nant women destroyed enclosures on Enfield Chase (Middlesex) in 1589 – a number of them actually gave birth in Newgate Gaol while awaiting trial.[53] In Maldon in 1629, women and children boarded a Flemish ship and took grain. One of the leaders of this riot, Ann Carter, later hanged for her role in the events of that year, helped to mobilise a second riot of clothworkers, predominantly men, who seized more grain.[54] Most of those named as participants in the Cumberland food riots of 1740 were also women.[55]

These are examples where women were dominant or pivotal, of course, and they are not meant to be representative. It is impossible to quantify the role of women in riots – the sources simply do not lend themselves to this type of counting.[56] Often protest was male-dominated. However, it is clear that the presence of females was commonplace in both food and anti-enclosure riots.[57] Historians have disagreed over the significance of this political role in a soci-ety where women played little formal part in the civic sphere. It has been claimed that female protesters were directed by the men and were deliberately used either because of a mistaken notion that women (and children under the age of discretion) could not be punished for such activity, or due to the more grounded belief that the law would treat them more leniently.[58] It was alleged that some

---

52. S.R. Gardiner (ed.), *Reports of Cases in the Courts of Star Chamber and High Commission* (Camden Society, 1886), p. 63.

53. Manning, *Village Revolts*, p. 69.

54. J. Walter, 'Grain riots and popular attitudes to the law: Maldon and the crisis of 1629', in J. Brewer and J. Styles (eds), *An Ungovernable People: the English and their Law in the Seventeenth and Eighteenth Centuries* (London, 1983), ch. 2.

55. Public Record Office, ASSI 45/21/4/64B-C.

56. Compare J. Bohstedt, 'Gender, household and community politics: women in English riots 1790–1810', *Past and Present* 120 (1988), 88–122; and Thompson, *Customs in Common*, pp. 305–36.

57. Clark, 'Popular protest', pp. 368, 369, 370, 376; Underdown, *Revel, Riot, and Rebellion*, p. 117; Lindley, *Fenland Riots*, pp. 41, 72, 75, 77, 84, 85, 86, 92–3, 118, 120, 123, 125, 127–8, 173, 221, 248; Walter, 'Grain riots', pp. 62–3; R.A. Houlbrooke, 'Women's social life and common action in England from the fifteenth century to the eve of the civil war', *Continuity and Change* 1 (1986), 171–89; Manning, *Village Revolts*, pp. 64, 69, 92, 96–101, 115–16, 230, 281.

58. Lindley, *Fenland Riots*, pp. 63, 254; Houlbrooke, 'Women's social life', pp. 182–3; Manning, *Village Revolts*, pp. 96–8.

Lincolnshire husbandmen had encouraged their wives to regain enclosed pastures in Waddingham in 1608: 'they the said persons, thinkeing as yt should seeme that the castinge downe of the ffences and hedgs of the said closes would be a gretter offence and more greevously punished in them, then if yt should be done by weomen, . . . did . . . move, persuade and procure diverse weomen to the number of fortie or thereabouts to go to cast downe the said hedge and ffences.'[59] The women, led by Dorothy Dawson, who levelled enclosures on Thorpe Moor as well as attacking the Earl of Derby's workmen, were said to have taunted that 'the wyves of Thorpe had long before that tyme done the like against the Earle of Derbyes Auncestors and were nevr. punished'.[60]

But we need not put too much store in theories of manipulation as the main motive. The explanation of the role of women in food and enclosure rioting is much more straightforward. They were involved in community politics because of the vital part they played in the early modern economic community. Protest flowed directly out of the role of women in the social economies of commons, marketplace, and household.[61]

There has also been some debate about the class composition of the rioting crowd. The languages of orders or sorts can certainly be found in the documentation of early modern riot.[62] Petitions, statements, allegations, and defences, spoke and wrote of 'the common sort of people', 'men of mean and weak understanding and small estates', the 'poorest and meanest sort', 'baser sort', 'of so inferior and mean condition', 'miserable poor and base', 'the poor people', 'of poor and mean condition', 'the meaner sort of people', 'poor husbandmen', 'ignorant men', 'a very rude Kind of People', 'men of small estates', 'poor labouring men', 'the ruder sort'. Those above them in the social scale were described as 'the better sort', 'rich men', 'the great ones', those of 'better condition and quality', 'sufficient men'.[63] However, riot was certainly not a simple theatre

59. Manning, *Village Revolts*, p. 97.
60. A. Wood, 'The place of custom in plebeian political culture: England, 1550–1800', *Social History* 22 (1997), 56.
61. Walter, 'Grain riots', pp. 62–3; Houlbrooke, 'Women's social life', pp. 184–6; W. Thwaites, 'Women in the market place: Oxfordshire c. 1690–1800', *Midland History* 9 (1984), 23–42; Bohstedt, 'Women in English riots', pp. 93–8, 121–2; Thompson, *Customs in Common*, pp. 314–22; B. Capp, 'Separate domains? Women and authority in early modern England', in P. Griffiths, A. Fox, and S. Hindle (eds), *The Experience of Authority in Early Modern England* (London, 1996), ch. 4.
62. For the language of sorts, see K. Wrightson, 'Estates, degrees and sorts in Tudor and Stuart England', *History Today* 37 (1987), 17–22.
63. These examples all come from Lindley, *Fenland Riots*, pp. 32, 38, 39, 40, 45, 61, 75, 92, 97, 104, 106, 107, 109, 115, 119, 125, 159, 179, 202.

for conflict between rich and poor. Indeed, propaganda in the fens was quite capable of arguing that the rich benefited from both customary rights and innovation.[61] In some fenland communities the 'better' sort supported or consented to drainage and enclosure schemes, and the 'poorest and meanest sort' resisted: in others, the opposite situation prevailed.[65]

The social profile of the crowd depended upon the local context and the type of grievance. Food riots were more uniformly plebeian than anti-improvement protests. Agricultural labourers played little part in the sort of activity which we have been discussing, particularly in food riots. This reflects the urban bias of the food riots, commented upon earlier, but it was probably due also to problems of mobilisation and the fact that their means of survival may have depended on theft (or perks) rather than open confrontation.[66] The lower and middle sorts of people, as they were known, were certainly active. Labourers and those earning a living in the crafts and trades took part in food riots. The same groups and small farmers rioted against enclosure. There were also middle- and lower-rank leaders: 'Captain' Pouch in the midlands in 1607; 'Captain' Ann Carter in Maldon in 1629; and the various Skimmingtons and Lady Skimmingtons, the symbolically named leaders of local riots in the west.[67]

The western riots against disafforestation were an affair of the artisan and the landless with little participation by smallholders and gentry.[68] But elsewhere, the anti-enclosure, drainage, and forest disputes were more likely to cut across class to include wealthier farmers and even the gentry. Gentry were among the Welsh border inhabitants who in 1678 forcibly removed felled wood from the Marquis of Worcester's enclosures in Wentwood Forest.[69] The Staffordshire commoners who dug up the Earl of Uxbridge's rabbit warrens on Cannock Chase in the mid-eighteenth century, in a festive slaughter of 10–15,000 rabbits, included not only colliers and labourers but also wealthy farmers.[70] Cottagers and poor women

64. Lindley, *Fenland Riots*, p. 5.   65. Ibid., p. 61.

66. Stevenson, *Popular Disturbances*, pp. 311–12.

67. K. Wrightson, *English Society 1580–1680* (London, 1982), p. 178.

68. Sharp, *In Contempt of All Authority*, pp. 126–34, 155. But even here there is evidence of the involvement of yeomen and husbandmen. See the comments of Underdown, *Revel, Riot, and Rebellion*, pp. 108–9.

69. M. McClain, 'The Wentwood Forest riot: property rights and political culture in Restoration England', in S.D. Amussen and M.A. Kishlansky (eds), *Political Culture and Cultural Politics in Early Modern England* (Manchester, 1995), ch. 5.

70. D. Hay, 'Poaching and the game laws on Cannock Chase', in D. Hay, P. Linebaugh, J.G. Rule, E.P. Thompson, and C. Winslow, *Albion's Fatal Tree: Crime and Society in Eighteenth-century England* (Harmondsworth, 1977), pp. 228–9.

comprised the rank and file of protest at Thorpe Moor in 1607, but the leaders, 'Captain Dorothy' Dawson and her companions, were the wives of 'substantial tenants and freeholders'.[71] Sustained protest in Great Wishford, in Wiltshire, included a clergyman, gentlemen, and yeomen.[72] The gentry, yeomen, and richer husbandmen were pivotal in many of the fenland riots.[73] Some of the leaders in the Isle of Axholme riots at Haxey in 1628 and 1629, for example, were wealthy yeomen, and one of the women, fined by the Court of Star Chamber for her role in the violent disturbances, later married a local minister.[74] In Kent in 1606, it was husbandmen and yeomen from Boughton-under-Blean and surrounding parishes who defended their right to common access by pulling down fences and filling in ditches in opposition to a London merchant's enclosure of the Blean Woods.[75] Constables were sometimes identified as ringleaders.[76] Furthermore, some of the fines handed out to those selected for prosecution indicate the involvement of the more substantial sectors of rural society. Star Chamber fined the prosecuted Haxey commoners up to £1,000 each, crippling sums even for a yeoman.[77] Again, it would seem the term 'community politics' is appropriate.

VI

Historians have also referred to the 'intense legalism of popular politics'.[78] We can see this quite clearly in a petition from the inhabitants of Hanworth and other Middlesex villages who, in the late 1640s and early 1650s, protested enclosure and the creation of a new river through Hounslow Heath to the king's residence at Hampton Court. After explaining that the new river 'drowned the corn fields, dwellings, and commons, and ruined and rotted cattle and sheep', the petitioners outlined how they had

71. Manning, *Village Revolts*, p. 281.   72. Ibid., p. 98.
73. Lindley, *Fenland Riots*, pp. 63, 255; C. Holmes, 'Drainers and fenmen: the problem of popular political consciousness in the seventeenth century', in Fletcher and Stevenson (eds), *Order and Disorder*, pp. 179–86.
74. Gardiner (ed.), *Reports of Cases in the Courts of Star Chamber*, pp. 59–65; Holmes, 'Drainers and fenmen', p. 183.
75. Clark, 'Popular protest', p. 369.
76. E.g. Manning, *Village Revolts*, pp. 101, 102, 281.
77. Gardiner (ed.), *Reports of Cases in the Courts of Star Chamber*, pp. 64–5.
78. Underdown, *Revel, Riot, and Rebellion*, p. 119.

sought redress from Parliament, but as, on account of other urgent occasions, they could obtain no answer, they were forced to make stoppage of the river; they are confident that their present governors will little countenance the oppression of the former, and humbly desire that what was done may not be taken as an affront to any lawful authority, and pray that the river may not be allowed to run again to the ruin and undoing of so many poor inhabitants.[79]

Their action, they told the Council of State in another petition, 'was not done in Affronte to any lawfull authoritie but of necessitye for if it had Continewed wee Could not have Subsisted but must of necessitye have left our Farmes and dwellings'.[80]

Commoners in the Isle of Epworth in the Lincolnshire fens claimed that a fourteenth-century charter, kept under lock and key in a chest in the Haxey church, protected their right to the commons, even from the encroachments of the king. When they acted against the drainers, they said that it was the developers rather than the commoners of Epworth who were legally the rioters.[81] Some of those who gathered in Cotesbach in Leicestershire in 1607 asserted that the law was not being enforced against those disobeying James's law against depopulating enclosures; in other words, when they levelled hedges they were merely enforcing the act.[82] And the anti-enclosers of Wentwood Forest in the 1670s claimed legal right to the common, dating back to the thirteenth century. They said that they had only taken action because their opponent, the Marquis of Worcester, had refused to test the case at law; the rioters intended to prevent the destruction of the wood by the marquis's workmen before a legal decision had been made.[83] Again 'rioters' were claiming the legal high ground.

John Walter has observed a popular awareness of legal prescription and practice in relation to the marketing of grain. The fact that governors responded to this type of popular pressure – as they did in Maldon in 1629, withdrawing grain export licences and purchasing grain from dealers to prevent it from leaving the area – reinforced both the effectiveness and the quasi-legality of such protest.[84] This awareness was probably more in the form of a general mindfulness than detailed knowledge of the varying administrative

79. *Seventh Report of the Royal Commission on Historical Manuscripts: House of Lords MSS 1648–1665* (London, 1879), p. 77; House of Lords Record Office, Main Papers, 25 July 1653.
80. House of Lords Record Office, Main Papers, 29 August 1653.
81. Lindley, *Fenland Riots*, pp. 26–7.   82. Manning, *Village Revolts*, p. 231.
83. McClain, 'Wentwood Forest riot', p. 117.
84. Walter, 'Grain riots', is an important case study.

rules; certainly there was a willingness to read prescription as a wide-ranging legitimation of control, including the crowd's own intervention in market regulation. The periodic judicial punishment of engrossers, and the issuing of proclamations against the export of grain, meant that rioters could claim that they were acting to remind magistrates of their duties. The Kent rioters mentioned earlier, who spoke of half of the corn being for them and half for the king, were referring directly to a proclamation against the illegal export of grain.[85] Rioters in St Dunstan's in Canterbury, in 1596, certainly exercised legal care, seeking out advice from one of their number about the legality of stopping grain; they were told that it was all right to stop wagons, 'in her Majesty's behalf', but must not 'touch the corn'.[86]

As the Hanworth protesters demonstrated, direct action could occur when petitioning was not heeded. Other rioters in the fens and Lancashire acted during the transfer of rule from Elizabeth to James in 1603, claiming that 'until the King was crowned there was no law wherefore they might do what they would for that the Parliament would clear all'.[87] In 1640, during the Short Parliament, Lindsey Level commoners drove cattle onto disputed land, 'boasting that what they do will be pardoned by the general pardon usually granted at the end of the parliament'.[88] Others, in Huntingdonshire in 1641, refused to obey orders from the House of Lords, saying that 'that order was only or but from the Upper House and that the Lower House was not acquainted therewith'. Lindsey Level protesters seized harvested grain, hemp, and flax in the same year, reiterating such sentiments: the Lords' orders were worthless, but if they had an order from the House of Commons, they would observe it.[89] Rioters also attempted to exploit the common law definition of riot as involving three or more people in force or violence against the peace. The Yorkshire women who opposed coal mining on Thorpe Moor in 1607 worked in groups of two to avoid prosecution for riot, as did Lincolnshire anti-enclosers in 1651.[90] As we have seen, protesters also made use of the ambivalent legal attitude towards women. Such uses of the law were characterised by a mix of myth, opportunism, retrospective justification, and genuine conviction which it is difficult to disentangle.

85. Walter and Wrightson, 'Dearth and the social order', pp. 119–20.
86. Clark, 'Popular protest', pp. 374–5.
87. Lindley, *Fenland Riots*, p. 34; Manning, *Village Revolts*, p. 116.
88. Lindley, *Fenland Riots*, p. 109.   89. Ibid., pp. 117, 122, 126, 133.
90. Manning, *Village Revolts*, p. 281; Lindley, *Fenland Riots*, p. 197.

VII

The role of the law in rioting complements a literature which demonstrates the 'permeation of the law into the wider culture'.[91] In fact it is crucial to understand the wider legal context of rioting. To the modern mind, the early modern criminal law is a bizarre blend of vicious deterrent punishment and what has been termed 'practical flexibility'.[92] We should not forget the role of savage punishment in that society: about 800 people a year were hanged in 1600, and about 100 a year by 1750.[93] However, the day-to-day operation of the law lay with the unpaid parish officials, who, as Keith Wrightson has put it, acted as 'brokers between the demands of their governors and those of their neighbours'.[94] The diary of the eighteenth-century Sussex shopkeeper Thomas Turner, who served as churchwarden, overseer of the poor, surveyor of highways, and collector of taxes, provides an instructive glimpse at the demands and pressures of such community office-holding, the conflicts of interest brought on by neighbourhood interaction. On one occasion, he was pursuing a case on behalf of a man against whom he was taking action on another issue. The man, a labourer called Peter Adams, had helped Turner home after a drunken Whitsun binge (had indeed intervened to protect him from a beating). The next month, Turner was enforcing maintenance from Adams to support his illegitimate child. (Adams was also suspected of having had some connection with the suspicious death of an unmarried, pregnant local woman, possibly while attempting to abort her child. Adams, a married man, was alleged to have been the dead woman's lover.) On another occasion, Turner wrote a pleading letter on behalf of some smugglers, and gave 2s. 6d. to their father, noting in

91. J. Sharpe, 'The people and the law', in Reay (ed.), *Popular Culture*, ch. 7, is the best short account (the quote comes from p. 247). See also, J.A. Sharpe, *Crime in Early Modern England 1550–1750* (London, 1984); J.M. Beattie, *Crime and the Courts in England 1660–1800* (Oxford, 1986); C.B. Herrup, *The Common Peace: Participation and the Criminal Law in Seventeenth-century England* (Cambridge, 1987).

92. The phrase 'practical flexibility' comes from Herrup, *Common Peace*, p. 165.

93. For punishment, see P. Jenkins, 'From gallows to prison? The execution rate in early modern England', *Criminal Justice History* 7 (1986), 51–71. Jenkins observes that the execution rate in Tudor England 'finds its closest parallel among notorious repressions like the Argentine "dirty war" of the 1970s' (p. 53). The execution rate dropped dramatically over the period 1600 to 1750, although the actual number of offences carrying the death penalty had risen considerably.

94. K. Wrightson, 'Two concepts of order: justices, constables and jurymen in seventeenth-century England', in Brewer and Styles (eds), *An Ungovernable People*, p. 44.

his diary that he had purchased contraband drink from them and feared that they might inform against him.[95]

Investigation and prosecution in the early modern period lay with the general population rather than a professional police force. By the time a felon was hanged, as Cynthia Herrup has put it, 'as many as three dozen men had participated in the decision-making process that sent him to the gallows'.[96] It is also apparent that formal recourse to law was seen as something of a last resort after other ways of dealing with an offender had failed: private settlement, the mediation of friends, the intervention of an employer or a minister, or shame punishment organised by the community. Alternatively, initiating litigation was a means of provoking an out-of-court settlement or arbitration rather than an attempt to settle disputes through the often costly and time-consuming legal system.[97] When cases reached a justice, he often preferred informal settlement, as the eighteenth-century notebook of the Wiltshire JP William Hunt demonstrates: '28 May 1744. I granted a warrant upon the complaint of Joseph May, labourer, against Stephen Godwin and William Daniel, both of the parish of West Lavington, labourers, for an assault. But the parties agreeing between themselves, my warrant was returned without hearing it'; '3 June 1746. Granted a warrant on the complaint of Sarah Oram of Market Lavington against Mary Jones for an assault. They agreed it before some neighbours without coming before me.'[98] Nearly 60 per cent of his cases were settled informally.[99] The point about this informality and flexibility – to bring us back to the legal context of riot – is that it involved the community in the operation of the law and imbricated it into the everyday workings of local society. The

95. D. Vaisey (ed.), *The Diary of Thomas Turner 1754–1765* (Oxford, 1984), pp. xxii, xxxiv–xxxv, 44–5, 50–4, 56–9, 71, 122.

96. C. Herrup, 'Law and morality in seventeenth-century England', *Past and Present* 106 (1985), 107.

97. J.A. Sharpe, 'Enforcing the law in the seventeenth-century English village', in V.A.C. Gatrell, B. Lenman, and G. Parker (eds), *Crime and the Law: the Social History of Crime in Western Europe since 1500* (London, 1980), ch. 4; Wrightson, 'Two concepts of order'; Wrightson, *English Society*, ch. 6; J.A. Sharpe, '"Such disagreement betwyx neighbours": litigation and human relations in early modern England', in J. Bossy (ed.), *Disputes and Settlements* (Cambridge, 1983), ch. 7; C. Herrup, 'New shoes and mutton pies: investigative responses to theft in seventeenth-century east Sussex', *Historical Journal* 27 (1984), 811–30.

98. E. Crittall (ed.), *The Justicing Notebook of William Hunt 1744–1749* (Devizes, 1982), pp. 28, 51.

99. R.B. Shoemaker, *Prosecution and Punishment: Petty Crime and the Law in London and Rural Middlesex, c. 1660–1725* (Cambridge, 1991), pp. 42–3.

detection of crime and the operation of the law was communal; it rested upon popular participation.[100]

However, it is important to be aware that this permeation was socially variable. Describing the early modern criminal law as a 'multi-use right' is fine as long as it is recognised that its uses reflected the hierarchies of that society.[101] Below the level of the aristocracy and gentry, it was the middling sorts who were most at ease with the law. As manorial and leet court officials, parish constables, and churchwardens, they were prominent in the exercise of the law at the grass-roots level.[102] They made up the trial juries.[103] Either all or nearly all jurors in late-eighteenth-century Essex and Staffordshire were tradesmen, craftsmen, or farmers.[104] They were active in the local regulative courts too: the juries of sewers in the fens, the barmote juries of the mining areas.[105] J.M. Beattie discovered that the Kingston-upon-Thames tradesmen and craftsmen who served on the assize jury in the 1690s also held an impressive range of local offices and other jury positions.[106] Such individuals must have accumulated considerable legal knowledge over the years, as the diary of the shopkeeper Turner indicates.[107]

As owners of property and capital, and as employers of labour, the middle sections of society used the courts to punish, settle disputes, and protect their reputations. They were the social group most likely to take out warrants for the peace against those they were in dispute with; the practice of binding over was important in

100. Herrup, 'Investigative responses to theft', pp. 829–30.

101. The term is Peter King's: P. King, 'Decision-makers and decision-making in the English criminal law, 1750–1800', *Historical Journal* 27 (1984), p. 53.

102. M. Griffiths, 'Kirtlington manor court, 1500–1650', *Oxoniensia* 45 (1980), 260–83; W.J. King, 'Leet jurors and the search for law and order in seventeenth-century England: "galling persecution" or reasonable justice', *Histoire Sociale* 13 (1980), 305–23; J. Kent, 'The English village constable, 1580–1642: the nature and dilemmas of the office', *Journal of British Studies* 20 (1981), 26–49; J. Kent, *The English Village Constable 1580–1642: a Social and Administrative Study* (Oxford, 1986); M. Ingram, *Church Courts, Sex and Marriage in England, 1570–1640* (Cambridge, 1987), p. 324.

103. Herrup, *Common Peace*, pp. 138–41.

104. P.J.R. King, ' "Illiterate plebeians, easily misled": jury composition, experience, and behaviour in Essex, 1735–1815', in J.S. Cockburn and T.A. Green (eds), *Twelve Good Men and True: the Criminal Trial Jury in England, 1200–1800* (Princeton, 1988), p. 264; D. Hay, 'The class composition of the palladium of liberty: trial jurors in the eighteenth century', in Cockburn and Green (eds), *Criminal Trial Jury*, p. 344.

105. Holmes, 'Drainers and fenmen'; A. Wood, 'Custom, identity and resistance: English free miners and their law, c. 1550–1800', in Griffiths, Fox, and Hindle (eds), *Experience of Authority*, ch. 8.

106. Beattie, *Crime and the Courts*, pp. 387–8.

107. Vaisey (ed.), *Diary of Thomas Turner*, passim.

the maintenance of order in early modern England.[108] They comprised some 75 per cent of those who prosecuted in property cases at the Surrey and Essex quarter sessions in the eighteenth century.[109] They were the people who could afford the £1 to £5 that it cost to pursue a case at the quarter sessions or assizes.[110] They were the main social group to employ defamation suits in the ecclesiastical courts to protect their honour, costing anywhere from £2 to over £10, depending on the complexity of the case.[111]

Labourers also prosecuted at law. Labourers and the poor, including the female poor, sought and obtained warrants, summonses, and arbitration from the Wiltshire justice, Hunt, in their disputes with employers, overseers of the poor, and abusive husbands.[112] Thomas Turner's diary also refers to the poor using the law to enforce their right to relief.[113] Peter King has argued that the unpropertied labouring poor 'made extensive use of the courts for their own purposes'.[114] Nearly 20 per cent of those who prosecuted felonies in Essex in the second half of the eighteenth century were labourers; nearly 10 per cent in Surrey in the same period.[115] But this was largely after a mid-eighteenth-century act meeting the court costs of the poor in recognition of the financial barriers which existed throughout our period of interest. In fact it could be argued that the figures of 10 per cent and 20 per cent indicate the relative *exclusion* of the lower sort, even at this late stage. Prosecutions for assault are a better measurement of the use of the law at a labouring level, for the poor were more likely to be assaulted than stolen from. Here King's figures for eighteenth-century Essex show that just over 25 per cent of prosecutors at quarter sessions were labourers.[116] The occupational categories used in these measurements are very nebulous. The labels of tradesman, craftsman, and artisan include the poorer employee as well as the substantial employer, so these figures should be taken as the very minimum

108. S. Hindle, 'The keeping of the public peace', in Griffiths, Fox, and Hindle (eds), *Experience of Authority*, ch. 7.

109. Calculated from Table 4.10 in Beattie, *Crime and the Courts*, p. 193; King, 'Decision-makers', pp. 28–9.

110. Beattie, *Crime and the Courts*, pp. 41–7.

111. Ingram, *Church Courts, Sex and Marriage*, pp. 57 (for costs), 304; J.A. Sharpe, *Defamation and Sexual Slander in Early Modern England* (York, 1980), p. 17.

112. Crittall (ed.), *Justicing Notebook of William Hunt*, pp. 28, 31, 39, 40, 54, 59, 61, 67.

113. E.g. Vaisey (ed.), *Diary of Thomas Turner*, pp. 91, 121.

114. King, 'Decision-makers', p. 33.

115. Ibid., p. 29; and my calculation from the figures in Beattie, *Crime and the Courts*, pp. 193, 195.

116. King, 'Decision-makers', p. 29.

of labouring involvement in the courts. Labourers also appeared before the courts as witnesses: 40 per cent of witnesses in felony cases in the Essex quarter sessions in the second half of the eighteenth century were labourers.[117]

While we have focused on the criminal law, this was not the only forum for legal aquaintance. Craig Muldrew has demonstrated widespread debt litigation, pursued in the guildhall court of the seventeenth-century Norfolk town of King's Lynn. On his calculations, these credit suits involved a majority of the town's (male) household heads, and included the poor as plaintiffs as well as defendants. Although few of these cases went beyond the initial complaint – another example of the earlier-mentioned use of the courts to initiate an informal settlement – they suggest 'a surprisingly egalitarian and accessible institution'. It is probable that the situation in King's Lynn mirrored similar activity in other early modern towns.[118]

Despite all these caveats, the point remains that the criminal and civil legal systems reflected and reinforced the power structure of the wider society. Although work on civil litigation in the heavily used royal courts of King's Bench, Chancery, and Common Pleas is imprecise on the status of litigants below the level of gentry, it is unlikely that labourers made much use of courts where it cost from £6 to £8 to recover a debt.[119] It was primarily as the prosecuted, not prosecutors, that the labouring population experienced early modern justice. The majority of labourers mentioned in the notebook of the justice Hunt are alleged woodstealers rather than complainants.[120] As Douglas Hay has shown for Staffordshire in the 1780s, only 2 per cent of the accused would have been qualified to sit as jurors in the courts in which they appeared.[121] The history of petty crime in late seventeenth- and eighteenth-century London demonstrates similar parameters. Even though the costs of prosecuting a misdemeanour were cheaper than for felonies, Robert Shoemaker has argued that they were still a disincentive. Defendants were at a disadvantage too if they were poor, for pleading not guilty would cost a minimum of 12s. It was cheaper to plead guilty. When Elizabeth Linsey appeared in court in 1691, charged with assault, 'being

117. Ibid., p. 32, n. 16.
118. C. Muldrew, 'Credit and the courts: debt litigation in a seventeenth-century urban community', *Economic History Review* 46 (1993), 23–38 (quote at p. 36).
119. C.W. Brooks, *Pettyfoggers and Vipers of the Commonwealth: the 'Lower Branch' of the Legal Profession in Early Modern England* (Cambridge, 1986), p. 107.
120. Crittall (ed.), *Justicing Notebook of William Hunt.*
121. Hay, 'Trial jurors', pp. 350–1.

poor' she 'chose rather to submit herself to the court than to trouble [the justices] with a trial'.[122]

The greater familiarity of the middling sort with the law explains compelling evidence for the legal sophistication of the yeomen who spear-headed opposition to drainage and improvement schemes in the fens, including their recognition of the legality of those schemes which had received parliamentary approval.[123] Fenlanders drove cattle onto enclosed land so that they would be impounded, thus providing the opportunity for a legal challenge to determine whether or not trespass had been committed.[124]

VIII

The picture so far is rather benign. But there was another, less orderly and legalistic, more violent side to popular protest. Although anti-enclosure rioters killed few, it would be stretching credibility to view them as non-violent. Captain Dorothy's band threw stones and wielded coal knives.[125] In 1628, the Isle of Axholme rioters – women and men – stoned drainage workers, beat them, held them under water with long poles, and threatened to hang them on gallows which they had erected. They were alleged to have said that 'if the King was there they would kill him'.[126] Some of the western and fenland rioters carried firearms.[127] Violence was integral to the activities of the Windsor Blacks, whose deer-poaching and fishpond-cutting activities of the 1720s were enmeshed in resistance to encroachments upon long-accustomed rights of access to forest land.[128] It was central to food disturbances too. In the Northampton riots of 1693, a large crowd of women gathered in the market 'with knives stuck in their girdles "to force corn at their own rates"'.[129] And food rioters in Cumberland in 1740, with blackened faces, and wielding swords and pistols, entered the houses of grain dealers late at night, threatening one man 'that if he Stirred out of his Bed . . . death Should be his portion'.[130]

---

122. Shoemaker, *Prosecution and Punishment*, pp. 140, 152, 312–13, 316–17.
123. Holmes, 'Drainers and fenmen'.   124. Lindley, *Fenland Riots*, p. 32.
125. Manning, *Village Revolts*, p. 281.
126. Lindley, *Fenland Riots*, p. 72; *Reports of Cases in the Courts of Star Chamber*, pp. 59–65.
127. E.g. Sharp, *In Contempt of All Authority*, pp. 95, 224; Lindley, *Fenland Riots*, p. 179, 190, 231, 233.
128. E.P. Thompson, *Whigs and Hunters: the Origin of the Black Act* (Harmondsworth, 1977), chs 1–3.
129. Beloff, *Public Order*, p. 64.
130. Public Record Office, ASSI 45/21/4/64B-C.

It is true that it was usually the excess or incompetence of the magistrates, the militia, or the army, rather than the crowd which precipitated loss of life. But death or severe injury in one riot became a possible death in the next, injecting new menace into the interplay of resistance and reaction – on both sides of the confrontation. The killing in 1740 of a Newcastle rioter, and three men, two women, and a boy in bread riots in Norwich, would become part of the repertoire of negotiation.[131] One should not underestimate the psychological impact of the damage of property, either. Fenland rioters attacked the Huguenot settlement of Sandtoft, established on newly drained and disputed land. In a series of assaults in the 1650s, they impounded cattle, sacked the church, appropriated the minister's house, and destroyed over eighty homes, a mill, farm buildings, fences, and crops.[132]

It is also worth remembering that actual rioting was merely centre stage in a wider drama involving threats, libels, and intimidation. Thus the Dover labourers in 1618 who threatened to cut the throats of corn-buyers rather than quietly starve. Hence also the warning verse circulating at Wye (Kent) in 1630–1:

> The corn is so dear,
> I doubt [i.e. fear] many will starve this year;
> If you see not to this,
> Some of you will speed amiss;
> Our souls they are dear
> For our bodies have some care
> Before we arise
> Less will suffice.[133]

The largest category in Edward Thompson's sample of anonymous threatening letters was that of those sent in connection with prices and abuses relating to the marketing of food: 'if you don't stop carrin the Flower to Bristoll we will knock you ... in the Head'. 'God Damn you blood,' the mayor of Chester was told in 1767, 'your house shall be burnt down very soon if you don't look after the Markets better.'[134]

The stress upon familiarity with the law as an important ingredient in explaining the nature and context of popular protest should not be interpeted as implying a wide-eyed adherence to legal

131. *Gentleman's Magazine* 10 (1740), 355–6.
132. Holmes, 'Drainers and fenmen', p. 166.
133. Clark, 'Popular protest', pp. 369, 370.
134. E.P. Thompson, 'The crime of anonymity', in Hay, Linebaugh, Rule, Thompson, and Winslow, *Albion's Fatal Tree*, ch. 6 (quotes on pp. 270, 278).

prescription. The law was a contested terrain. Certain crimes – offences according to the letter of the law – were tolerated or actively justified by particular social groups or communities. Customary petty pilfering and minor frauds, the perquisites of every work process often winked at by employers during good times, could be redefined as theft with the force of legislation. What was considered legitimate and necessary appropriation for a worker was embezzlement for a master. Every trade had its customary benefits. Textile workers in the putting-out industry added oil or water to fibre to increase its weight and used other ways of appropriating material.[135] Sailors could carry cargo freight-free, and had 'socking', (appropriated tobacco). Shoemakers and hatters substituted bad material for good, called, respectively, 'clicking' and 'bugging'. Tailors had 'cabbage', the overcutting and purloining of cloth, mentioned in many an early modern ballad. Servants had their household vails (tips) and perquisites of food, broken items, and cast-off clothing. Silk-workers had wastage. Dockyard workers, lumpers, and lightermen had 'chips' (wood scraps) and spillage. Coopers had samplings. Miners had coal. We know mostly about these customary perks from eighteenth-century legislation against them, but as customs they had a much earlier history.[136]

There are numerous examples of clashes in concepts of the law. Gleaning, the right of the poor to gather the remaining crop after harvest, seen as an 'immemorial right', conflicted with farmers' notions of property.[137] Wood stealing/gathering was another area of conflict. Even when the law was clear, the force of custom – the tradition of customary right of access to wood gathering, often enshrined in older manorial law – ensured that wood 'stealing' was not considered to be theft by the offenders and many of their neighbours.[138] Poaching was yet another area of dispute – in fact

135. J. Styles, 'Embezzlement, industry and the law in England, 1500–1800', in M. Berg, P. Hudson, and M. Sonenscher (eds), *Manufacture in Town and Country Before the Factory* (Cambridge, 1983), ch. 7.

136. For customary appropriations, and the moves against them, see J. Rule, *The Experience of Labour in Eighteenth-century Industry* (London, 1981), ch. 5; and P. Linebaugh, *The London Hanged: Crime and Civil Society in the Eighteenth Century* (London, 1991), chs 5, 7–8, 11–12, from which the above examples come. For servants, see B. Hill, *Servants: English Domestics in the Eighteenth Century* (Oxford, 1996), ch. 4.

137. Sharpe, *Crime in Early Modern England*, p. 123; P. King, 'Gleaners, farmers and the failure of legal sanctions in England 1750–1850', *Past and Present* 125 (1989), 116–50, deals with resistance to later moves against gleaning.

138. R.W. Bushaway, 'From custom to crime: wood gathering in eighteenth-century England: a focus for conflict in Hampshire, Wiltshire and the south', in J. Rule (ed.), *Outside the Law: Studies in Crime and Order 1650–1850* (Exeter, 1982), pp. 65–101.

one which could ally farmer and labourer against gentry. The Game Act of 1671, restricting the hunting of hares, partridges, pheasants, and moor fowl to one social group, the gentry, was a blatant piece of class legislation.[139] Those who did not meet the criteria were not even permitted to hunt game on their own land. (Deer and rabbits (not game) were protected by other legislation.) The law clashed with a popular toleration and justification of poaching. As a Bedfordshire farmer put it, game was 'ordained from the beginning free for anyone who could over take them'. The lower orders were said to believe that game was 'the property of those who can take it', that there 'is no crime' in poaching.[140]

Other crimes were tolerated by communities rather than by social groups, although sometimes it is difficult to separate genuine support from fear and coercion. Smuggling was rife in some eighteenth-century Sussex and Kent communities. Tea and spirits were smuggled to the coast and transported across land by wagon and horse teams. Whole neighbourhoods were said to be implicated in the various branches of the trade. We can recall Thomas Turner's peripheral involvement in inland Sussex. Not only had he purchased contraband, but he was given confiscated brandy whenever his friend the excise officer seized a load from the smugglers.[141] The triviality of these links is the very point: smuggling was part of everyday life in such environments.[142] Wrecking enjoyed similar community sanction. Although sixteenth- and eighteenth-century acts prohibited such activity, there was a belief in the coastal areas of Britain – especially in Cornwall, the Isles of Scilly, Kent, Norfolk, and the Wirral – that the inhabitants had the right to shipwrecks and goods cast up by the sea. Wrecking was another customary activity, 'from time immemorial'. It was observed in 1818 that the Cornish had an inherited belief that they had 'a right to such spoils as the ocean may place within their reach, many of the more enlightened inhabitants secure whatever they can seize, without any remorse; and conclude without any hesitation, that nothing but injustice, supported by power and sanctioned by law, can wrench it from their hands'. This linking of injustice, power, and law, in

139. Hay, 'Poaching and the game laws'.
140. P.B. Munsche, *Gentlemen and Poachers: the English Game Laws 1671–1831* (Cambridge, 1981), pp. 6–7, 63–4. For the earlier period, see R.B. Manning, *Hunters and Poachers: a Social and Cultural History of Unlawful Hunting in England, 1485–1640* (Oxford, 1993).
141. Vaisey (ed.), *Diary of Thomas Turner*, pp. 282, 286, 310.
142. C. Winslow, 'Sussex smugglers', in Hay, Linebaugh, Rule, Thompson, and Winslow, *Albion's Fatal Tree*, ch. 3.

opposition to 'right', is telling. Wrecking, as John Rule has argued, is an example of the resilience of custom in the face of unambiguous legal prohibition.[143]

Finally there was coining. Coining, the clipping of the edges of legitimate currency (with large shears) and its fashioning into new coin, was not justified as a customary right. But it was tolerated, indeed was widespread, in particular communities. Though illegal, there was a lower- and middle-class legitimation of the trade, and a distinction was made between clipping, in a sense recycling, and the outright forging of base metal. Coining was rife on the border of Lancashire and the West Riding of Yorkshire, in and around the textile area of Halifax. The local community, as John Styles has shown, including merchants and manufacturers with access to large quantities of gold coin, was involved in various ways: from lending the money for clipping, to the clipping and rubbing of the clipped coin and coining itself, through to the laundering of the new product. The practice was clearly an integral part of the local economy in the eighteenth century, and some of the yellow traders, as they were known, were willing to resort to violence, and even murder, to protect their interests.[144] Earlier court records reveal humbler coining networks of some complexity in the 1670s and 1680s, centred on fairs, alehouses and trading contacts in the Wigan area of Lancashire, and extending into Cheshire and Staffordshire.[145] Another network of silver coining and clipping existed on the border areas of Cumberland, Westmorland, Yorkshire, and Lancashire, although this one included men of some substance.[146]

Such lawlessness was reflected in the actions of many rioters. In Cumberland they took money and silver as well as oatmeal.[147] The Newcastle crowd who wrecked the Guildhall removed over £1,000 from the coffers. Norwich protesters attacked the prison and released fellow rioters who had been imprisoned by the mayor.[148]

143. J.G. Rule, 'Wrecking and coastal plunder', in Hay, Linebaugh, Rule, Thompson, and Winslow, *Albion's Fatal Tree*, ch. 4 (p. 176 for quotes).

144. J. Styles, ' "Our traitorous money makers": the Yorkshire coiners and the law, 1760–83', in Brewer and Styles (eds), *An Ungovernable People*, ch. 5.

145. Public Record Office, PL 27/1: Information re. coin clipping, 4 July 1682. Those involved in the illegal trade were a corn and potato dealer and a pedlar, who used counterfeit money to buy their goods; a feltmaker, a painter, alehouse keepers, a cattle dealer, a shoemaker, skinners, and a carpenter; a miller who collected his master's rent money and replaced it with clipped coins; a bowling-green keeper, and watchmakers; and a constable who clipped the town's money which he had in his charge.

146. A. Macfarlane, *The Justice and the Mare's Ale* (Oxford, 1981), ch. 3.

147. Public Record Office, ASSI 45/21/4/64B-C.

148. *Gentleman's Magazine* 10 (1740), 355–6.

Indeed, a constant argument of early modern rioters was that necessity justified stepping outside the law: 'Necessity hath no law', as an anonymous letter warned Norwich magistrates in 1595.[149] Even when it was used in petitions or mild demonstrations, the phrase implied a threat. Necessity would force protesters to more extreme measures if the authorities refused to respond to their requests. 'We may as well all be hanged as starved to Death' was a desperate refrain found in seventeenth-century food riots and eighteenth-century threatening letters alike.[150] This sort of justification could override the legal niceties of adherence to the moral economy.[151]

Not all food rioters sought the orderly control of prices, either. *Taxation populaire* was effectively a practice of the second half of the eighteenth century. Most food riots before that century, and many during it, involved the simple seizure and division of grain or food, without payment, or the destruction of food or property as a punishment and/or warning to other traders.[152] Even in the riots at the end of the eighteenth century, the seizure of food without payment, and/or its destruction, were as common as orderly sale.[153] When payments were made, the amount given could be derisory. Rioters in the Isle of Ely in 1740 broke into the storehouses of Wisbech merchants, removing an estimated 2,000 bushels of wheat which they sold for as little as 1d. and 4d. a bushel – that is, from 1.5 to 5 per cent of the current market price! This was hardly a 'just price' by anyone's definition.[154]

IX

We have concentrated on two main forms of early modern riot, but it is possible to extend the logic of the moral economy to other forms of popular action. To quote Robert Malcolmson, 'Just as there was thought to be a "fair" maximum for food prices, so too there was a "fair" minimum for wages: a level determined by customary expectations and "normal" human needs. This commitment

149. J. Walter, 'A "rising of the people"? The Oxfordshire rising of 1596', *Past and Present* 107 (1985), 91.

150. The quote comes from an anonymous letter from the Manchester area, 1762, in Thompson, 'Crime of anonymity', p. 326; see also, Sharp, *In Contempt of All Authority*, p. 34.

151. J. Bohstedt, 'The moral economy and the discipline of historical context', *Journal of Social History* 26 (1992–3), 269–70.

152. Sharp, *In Contempt of All Authority*, pp. 32–3.

153. Bohstedt, 'Moral economy', pp. 274, 277.

154. Calculated from *Gentleman's Magazine* 10 (1740), 355, and 360 (for monthly prices).

to maintaining standards was central to industrial relations of the period.'[155] Adrian Randall has argued for an industrial moral economy, with eighteenth-century artisans striking to protect customary wages and working conditions. There was a comparable stress on custom, control, and protection of rights. Petitioning preceded more direct action.[156] Miners in Derbyshire rioted in the seventeenth century in defence of their right to free mining.[157] The colliers and carters of Kingswood Chase, near Bristol, opposed the eighteenth-century turnpike acts with the cry, 'King George and no turnpikes.' They claimed that the acts were illegal because the king had not set his hand to them. Those who demolished the turnpikes claimed that the new legislation (which also permitted turnpike trustees to encroach on the commons) would not have been necessary if the magistrates had performed their duties properly in the first place: that is, had enforced the laws for the upkeep of the highways.[158]

We have seen that notions of the rule of law and the moral economy are central to any understanding of early modern protest. This is in keeping with the new historiography of riot, restated forcefully by Charlesworth and Randall: 'It is above all else this orderliness, this sense of community solidarity and of legitimacy, which strikes the historian.'[159] The thesis of the moral economy is a welcome corrective to the conservative propensity to dismiss crowd action as 'devoid of political consciousness', 'sub-political', 'primitive', and 'manipulated'.[160] But the cumulative picture of the newer historiography is a little too orderly. We have also explored a darker side to popular protest. Riots were certainly a form of negotiation rather than rebellion; and, as we have seen, could be successful. Anti-enclosers were able to stop or modify draining schemes in the fens.[161] The justices issued an order against engrossers in response to the unrest of 1740.[162] However, violence or the threat of violence

155. R.W. Malcolmson, *Life and Labour in England 1700–1780* (London, 1981), p. 123.

156. A. Randall, 'The industrial moral economy of the Gloucestershire weavers in the eighteenth century', in J. Rule (ed.), *British Trade Unionism 1750–1850* (London, 1988), ch. 2.

157. A. Wood, 'Social conflict and change in the mining communities of north-west Derbyshire, c. 1600–1700', *International Review of Social History* 38 (1993), 31–58.

158. R.W. Malcolmson, ' "A set of ungovernable people": the Kingswood colliers in the eighteenth century', in Brewer and Styles (eds), *An Ungovernable People*, ch. 3.

159. A. Charlesworth and A. Randall, 'Morals, markets and the English crowd in 1766', *Past and Present* 114 (1987), 211.

160. These descriptions come from Manning, *Village Revolts*.

161. Holmes, 'Drainers and fenmen', pp. 172–4.

162. *Gentleman's Magazine* 10 (1740), 355.

was integral to the bargaining. Fear of Christopher Hill's 'many headed monster' of the crowd was crucial in shaping the response of the authorities.[163]

Describing riots as 'community politics' is a useful way to indicate the level at which negotiation and interaction occurred, the horizon of political concern. Yet it is a misleading ascription if it is taken to imply some sort of organic civic or parish unity. We saw that the social composition of the rioting crowd, and its support network, crossed gender and class lines. But this is not to deny the importance of lower-class commitment or social division in riot. Despite the rhetoric of petition and riot, protest represented community division, for in every local society there were those who would benefit from enclosure, 'improvement', or rising food prices. Fenland commoners were frequently divided over change, and 'community action' was sometimes the result of coercion rather than popular endorsement.[164] Of course projectors, developers, drainers, could be attacked as outsiders or – in the case of the fens – foreigners, but what about the workers who dug the drains, erected embankments, harvested the crops, mined the land, and cut the timber in the newly enclosed commons? Not all of the work was done by Dutch and French craftsmen, farmers, and labourers. The criss-cross of popular allegiances and divisions, including insider against outsider, was more complex than a simple contest between patrician and plebeian.

Popular protest is best viewed as a varied repertoire of action, a series of 'pragmatic tactics'.[165] As the case studies which began this chapter suggest, the women and men who rioted in the early modern period drew on a tradition where it existed, but they were perfectly capable of invention. They could oscillate from gentle negotiation to violent action, from adherence to the law to blatant illegality. They were as capable of pressing the magistrates to perform their duties as they were of carrying out their own forms of retribution. We gain a sense of the process of protest from events in Newcastle in 1740, when ironworkers from the Whickham area of the Durham coalfields were both persuaded *and intimidated* into entering the city. Delegates from the keelmen told them 'that unless they joined to Assist in Takeing what corn Remained in

163. C. Hill, 'The many-headed monster', in his *Change and Continuity in Seventeenth-century England* (London, 1991 edn), ch. 8.

164. Lindley, *Fenland Riots*, pp. 61–2, 88, 148, 238.

165. This is essentially the argument of Bohstedt, 'Moral economy', esp. pp. 274, 279.

Newcastle it would be ship'd of in the Night Time and they . . . would be starved for want of Bread as well as the Keelmen'. One of the mobilisers, a smith, 'strode around the square "with a naked sword in his hand"'. The delicate balance, indeed struggle, between discipline and disorder emerges from the post-riot statements of participants. One man, clearly a leader, had had a petition in his pocket, setting out suitable prices for corn. He made a speech, telling the workers that their aim was to go to Newcastle to 'Settle the price of corn', and that they were not to coerce drink or 'take any thing at [their] own hands'. The mere fact that he needed to stress control indicated that disarray was a possibility. The protesters' tactics included direct negotiation with the mayor, gentry, and a wharf official – to a backdrop of violent confrontation, capture of officials, and destruction of property. There were internal tensions between the ironworkers and keelmen. Two men complained that the keelmen were 'very Riotous . . . Committing Great Outrages'.[166]

Ironically, it was the period immediately following 1750, our rough cut-off point, that was the real age of rioting: 1756–7, 1766–8, 1772–3, 1783, 1795–6, 1799–1801. There were over 200 riots in 1800. But that, as they say, is not our period.[167]

166. This detail comes from D. Levine and K. Wrightson, *The Making of an Industrial Society: Whickham 1560–1765* (Oxford, 1991), pp. 382–9.
167. The best account of the later period can be found in Stevenson, *Popular Disturbances.*

CHAPTER SEVEN

Popular Cultures

I

The bipolar or binary model of the cultural make-up of early modern England has slowly been replaced by a newer interpretation which stresses diversity and multiplicity. Although the emphases have varied, and most accounts have allowed for overlap and interaction, the bipolar approach to cultural history saw the past in terms of a basic division between elite and popular. This polarity – to take us back to this book's introduction – was the starting point for historical analysis. It was a governing trope in two influential studies which appeared in the late 1970s: Peter Burke's *Popular Culture in Early Modern Europe* (1978), and Robert Muchembled's *Culture Populaire et Culture des Elites dans la France Moderne* (1978).[1] We can trace something of a turning point in the mid-1980s, a transitional phase represented by the internal tensions of the essays in two edited texts published in the same year: S.L. Kaplan's *Understanding Popular Culture* (1984), and Barry Reay's *Popular Culture in Seventeenth-century England* (1984). The binary approach is by no means jettisoned in these books (although it is stronger in Reay than in Kaplan), but both contain substantial rethinking of approaches.[2] More recent accounts, including an important article by Bob Scribner, Miri Rubin's awe-inspiring work on medieval culture, and Tim Harris's excellent edited collection, *Popular Culture in England,*

---

1. P. Burke, *Popular Culture in Early Modern Europe* (London, 1978, repr. 1994); R. Muchembled, *Popular Culture and Elite Culture in Early Modern France 1400–1750* (Baton Rouge, La., 1985) (first published in French in 1978).
2. S.L. Kaplan (ed.), *Understanding Popular Culture: Europe from the Middle Ages to the Nineteenth Century* (Berlin, 1984); B. Reay (ed.), *Popular Culture in Seventeenth-century England* (London, 1985 and 1988).

c. 1500–1850 (1995), have challenged the usefulness of viewing societies in terms of a simple cultural polarity.[3] As Harris has explained,

> The language we use often limits the questions we ask and structures the way we conceive the phenomena and processes we are seeking to understand. The use of the term 'popular culture' in the singular encourages us to think of the culture of those below the elite as if it were a coherent whole, and directs our attention away from a consideration of the diversities within popular culture itself... Likewise, formulating the question in terms of a conflict between elite and popular culture ... distracts us from considering the degree of interaction between the cultural worlds of the educated and the humbler ranks of society...[4]

This critique of the bipolar model is most firmly associated with the work of the French historian Roger Chartier, who explicitly rejects 'the popular' in favour of what he terms 'fluid circulations, practices shared by various groups, and blurred distinctions'. 'When on the one hand, the concept of popular culture obliterates the bases shared by the whole of society and when, on the other, it masks the plurality of cleavages that differentiate cultural practices, it cannot be held as pertinent to a comprehension of the forms and materials that characterise the cultural universe of societies in the modern period.'[5] Thus we need to take into account not only shared cultural values – 'collective culture' – but also a multiplicity of cultural divisions: regional and local, town vs. country, religious, gender, age, and occupational. Power is not ignored in this new history of popular culture, but the division between dominant and subordinate is not a primary unit of analysis or a structural principle. To adapt Louis Montrose, the older model of ideology is replaced by one that is 'heterogeneous and unstable, permeable and processual'.[6]

The term which Chartier favours to encapsulate this new approach is 'appropriation'. The objective of the historian is to focus

---

3. B. Scribner, 'Is a history of popular culture possible?', *History of European Ideas* 10 (1989), 175–91; M. Rubin, *Corpus Christi: the Eucharist in Late Medieval Culture* (Cambridge, 1991), esp. introduction; T. Harris (ed.), *Popular Culture in England, c. 1500–1850* (London, 1995), esp. ch. 1: T. Harris, 'Problematising popular culture'.

4. Harris, 'Problematising popular culture', pp. 4–5.

5. R. Chartier, *The Cultural Uses of Print in Early Modern France* (Princeton, 1987), pp. 3–5. See also, his 'Popular culture: a concept revisited', *Intellectual History Newsletter* 15 (1993), 3–13, repr. as 'Popular appropriations: the readers and their books', in R. Chartier, *Forms and Meanings* (Philadelphia, 1995), ch. 4.

6. L. Montrose, *The Purpose of Playing: Shakespeare and the Cultural Politics of the Elizabethan Theatre* (Chicago, 1996), p. 12. His prologue, 'Texts and histories', is particularly useful.

on a belief, action, or object, and to examine the uses to which it was put – in other words, the various ways in which it was handled culturally. The starting point for analysis is the text, ritual, artefact, practice, or belief rather than the social category or stratum. It is an approach 'that concentrates on differentiated uses and plural appropriation of the same goods, the same ideas, and the same actions'.[7]

Let us return to Burke to make clear the differences in approach. Burke's point of departure for cultural analysis is the anthropological distinction between the 'great' and 'little' traditions:

> Applying this model to early modern Europe, we can identify the great tradition easily enough. It includes the classical tradition, as it was handed down in schools and universities . . . and some intellectual movements which are likely to have affected only the educated minority – the Renaissance, the Scientific Revolution of the seventeenth century, the Enlightenment. Subtract all this from the culture of early modern Europe, and what residue is left? There are folksongs and folktales; devotional images and decorated marriage-chests; mystery plays and farces; broadsides and chap-books; and, above all, festivals . . .[8]

It is important to be aware that Burke stresses the ways in which this model is threatened by cultural overlap and divisions at the popular level. It is easy to forget just how path-breaking his study was. One of his themes is the inequality of the traffic between the traditions. The elite participated in popular culture: 'popular culture was everybody's culture'. They were 'bi-cultural', 'amphibious'. But the people did not participate in elite culture. Although the elite would later withdraw (see below), 'the crucial cultural difference in early modern Europe . . . was that between the majority, for whom popular culture was the only culture, and the minority, who had access to the great tradition but participated in the little tradition as a second culture.'[9] Burke's other allowance is for multiplicity at the popular level: there were 'many popular cultures or many varieties of popular culture'.[10]

Some might argue that the starting point for analysis makes no difference. Both the bipolar and cultural appropriation models permit overlap and multiplicity. However, the moment of departure is vital because it privileges, and sets agendas. To return to Burke's model, quoted above, quite apart from precluding any popular contributions to the Renaissance, Scientific Revolution, and Enlightenment (massive questions in themselves), it categorises the popular as a

---

7. Chartier, *Cultural Uses*, p. 6.   8. Burke, *Popular Culture*, p. 24.
9. Ibid., p. 28.   10. Ibid., pp. 29–58 (quote on p. 29).

residual cultural form, equates cultural forms and practices with a given social level, and prioritises the elite/popular divide. Whatever the later modifications or clarifications, bipolarity fixes the conceptual boundaries. The model of appropriation, on the other hand, will go directly to the form – let us say, chapbooks or festivals – or to a particular example without assuming prior social categorisation. This mode of analysis may indeed find that a polarity (of some sort) applies, but it will be more attuned to multiple uses and less likely merely to confirm something that has already been decided.

Chartier's analysis is not without its problems. The search for commonality, in less subtle hands, could easily distort or erase important social or cultural cleavages. The effect of stressing multiplicity can be identical, though obviously for different reasons. In Chapter 1 we saw that Michel Foucault's stress on the 'polyvalence of discourses' can only be followed so far. While we can accept his rejection of 'a world of discourse divided between accepted discourse and excluded discourse, or between a dominant discourse and a dominated one', and endorse his thesis of 'a multiplicity of discursive elements that can come into play in various strategies',[11] there is a sense in which we must have it both ways. There are dominances amidst the multiplicity: we saw that gender fractured Foucault's sexual mosaic.

A further problem with the concept of appropriation is that it is superficially dynamic but potentially static: once an item, idea, or an action has been appropriated, it is no longer the 'same' item, idea, or action. If we use the methodology associated with appropriation – and this book suggests that we should – it is crucial that this use is accompanied with a recognition of culture as *process*.[12] The motion of culture, culture as change, is the particular contribution of the historian.

II

The dialectic of containment and resistance has dominated studies of popular culture.[13] One influential approach has been to see the

11. M. Foucault, *The History of Sexuality: Volume 1: An Introduction* (London, 1978), p. 100.

12. Scribner, 'Popular culture', pp. 180, 186.

13. Hall, 'Notes', pp. 228–9, 232–3. They dominate his analysis too. See also L.W. Levine, 'The folklore of industrial society: popular culture and its audiences', *American Historical Review* 97 (1992), 1369–99; and the debate – around the same poles – which follows his paper, with contributions by R. Kelley, N.Z. Davis, T. Jackson Lears, and Levine's response: *American Historical Review* 97 (1992), 1400–30.

early modern period in terms of gentry hegemony. The hegemonic group maintains its position by dominating the organisations which shape ideas: the institutions of religion, the law, education, politics, and communication. Edward Thompson has outlined this process for the eighteenth century, and it can apply to the early modern period as a whole, although the principal institutions of domination will vary.[14] Hegemony determines the parameters of the possible, inhibiting the development of social, political or cultural alternatives to the given. It is an ongoing process, an impulse to domination, a striving for control never complete. As a theory of historical analysis, hegemony accounts for class rule, compliance, and the limitations to resistance – but it also recognises that resistance did exist. Thompson's metaphor for the socio-cultural structure of the eighteenth century is one of a 'field of force', with the aristocracy and gentry at one pole, plebeians at the other, the middling sort oscillating between the two, and with the hegemony of the gentry determining the limits of the field.[15]

Thompson's analysis can still be read profitably as a demonstration that the exercise of class power and resistance to the exercising of that power are central to early modern society, what he called the theatre of gentry hegemony and the counter-theatre of the poor, 'class struggle without class'. However, one problem with his view of early modern England, it is becoming increasingly clear, is that it did not sufficiently recognise the field-of-force power of the middling sort, who cannot be so simply subsumed in yet another bipolar frame.[16] These vaguely defined and historically contingent groups, ranging from lower-level merchant families and those of prosperous yeomen down to wealthier tradesmen, craftsmen, and husbandmen, were prominent and assertive socially, politically, economically, and culturally.[17] They are certainly ubiquitous in this

14. See Reay, 'Popular culture in early modern England', in Reay (ed.), *Popular Culture*, pp. 17–20.

15. E.P. Thompson, 'Patrician society, plebeian culture', *Journal of Social History* 7 (1974), 382–405; E.P. Thompson, 'Eighteenth-century English society: class struggle without class?', *Social History* 3 (1978), 133–65. His argument was restated in his book, *Customs in Common* (London, 1991), ch. 2: 'The patricians and the plebs' (a massive eighty pages).

16. Harris, 'Problematising popular culture', pp. 16–18; P. King, 'Edward Thompson's contribution to eighteenth-century studies. The patrician–plebeian model re-examined', *Social History* 21 (1996), 215–28.

17. For the middling sort, see P. Earle, *The Making of the English Middle Class: Business, Society and Family Life in London, 1660–1730* (London, 1989); T.B. Leinwand, 'Shakespeare and the middling sort', *Shakespeare Quarterly* 44 (1993), 284–303; J. Barry and C. Brooks (eds), *The Middling Sort of People: Culture, Society and Politics in England, 1550–1800* (London, 1994), esp. J. Barry, 'Introduction'; M.E. Hunt, *The Middling Sort: Commerce, Gender, and the Family in England, 1680–1780* (Berkeley, 1996).

book. They were producers, sellers, employers, and (though they rarely worked for others) workers. They provided theatre players and the bulk of theatre audiences.[18] They serviced England's urban renaissance in late seventeenth- and early eighteenth-century provincial towns.[19] They were consumers, and not just of print; indeed, they formed the core of a precocious early modern English consumer culture.[20] They invested in empire.[21] They were indispensable, as we have seen, in the operation and administration of the law and government at the parish level – male activity, it should be noted, often made possible by the household work of wives and children. They forced the political and religious pace of the English Revolution.[22] They were active in eighteenth-century political life.[23] In a sense, *they* were 'the people', the constituted political voice of the nation. Kathleen Wilson has demonstrated that the extra-parliamentary political culture which emerged in the print, coffee-house, and club cultures of the eighteenth-century provincial town, forged by party conflict, imperialism, and patriotism, was largely masculine and middling-sort.[24]

Whether the prominence of this social grouping was converted into wider cultural expression is a different matter. It could be maintained that the middling sort did develop a type of composite culture: community-based, mainly urban, fashioned by the common (male) experience of apprenticeship, advanced literacy, reformed religion, political activism, trading networks, and steeped in patriotism and belief in the value of commerce.[25] Margaret Hunt

18. Montrose, *Purpose of Playing*, p. 208.
19. P. Borsay, 'The English urban renaissance: the development of provincial urban culture c. 1680–c. 1760', *Social History* 5 (1977), 581–603; P. Borsay, *The English Urban Renaissance: Culture and Society in the Provincial Town 1660–1770* (Oxford, 1989); K. Wilson, *The Sense of the People: Politics, Culture and Imperialism in England, 1715–1785* (Cambridge, 1995), ch. 1.
20. See J. Brewer and R. Porter (eds), *Consumption and the World of Goods* (London, 1993), esp. chs 9 (C. Shammas, 'Changes in English and Anglo-American consumption from 1550 to 1800'), and 10 (L. Weatherill, 'The meaning of consumer behaviour in late seventeenth- and early eighteenth-century England'); P.D. Glennie and N.J. Thrift, 'Consumers, identities, and consumption spaces in early-modern England', *Environment and Planning A* 28 (1996), 25–45. (I owe this last reference to Mark Dawson.)
21. Wilson, *Sense of the People*, p. 56.
22. B. Manning, *The English People and the English Revolution 1640–1649* (London, 1976).
23. N. Rogers, 'The middling sort in eighteenth-century politics', in Barry and Brooks (eds), *Middling Sort*, ch. 6.
24. Wilson, *Sense of the People*.
25. Barry, 'Introduction', J. Barry, 'Bourgeois collectivism? Urban association and the middling sort', and S. D'Cruze, 'The middling sort in eighteenth-century Colchester: independence, social relations and the community broker', all in Barry and Brooks (eds), *Middling Sort*, are particularly helpful here. See also, Wilson, *Sense of the People*; Hunt, *Middling Sort*.

has argued that a middling-sort, commercial culture had developed by the eighteenth century.[26] But we must guard against replicating the same kind of cultural homogeneities for this 'group' that we are challenging elsewhere.[27] The point is that this variegated group – comprising 20 to 40 per cent of early modern English house-holds[28] – disrupts neat bipolarities.

The languages of early modern social description are also reveal-ing. Keith Wrightson has discovered that 'a language of "sorts"' was in common use by the end of the sixteenth century. Society was divided into the 'better' or the 'richer' sorts, aligned against the 'poorer', 'meaner', or 'common' sorts of people. This bipolar classification may appear to support Thompson's patrician/plebeian field of force, but it was a flexible category used to distinguish the *middling sorts* from those below them on the social hierarchy. That is, the binary surface of the language of sorts disguised more varied uses. By the end of the seventeenth century, as a result of civil war action and discourse, the term 'middle sort' had been added to the repertoire of social description.[29] By the 1750s, the end of our period, descriptions were well on their way to the tripartite termino-logy of class.[30] In short, there is linguistic support for the interpos-ing of the middling sort in Thompson's field of force.

None of this is to deny that elite–plebeian polarities did exist. Daniel Defoe experienced the cultural extremes of Tunbridge Wells and the lead mining communities of Derbyshire. Wells was a place where 'company and diversion is . . . the main business of the place' and where 'those people who have nothing to do any where else, seem to be the only people who have anything to do at Tunbridge'. He was dazzled by the rich clothing, jewels, beautiful women, 'liberty of conversation', and profusion of good food. 'In a word, Tunbridge wants nothing that can add to the felicities of life, or that can make a man or woman compleatly happy, always provided they have money.'[31] Contrast this with his description of a Derbyshire lead miner:

26. Hunt, *Middling Sort*.

27. P. Earle, 'The middling sort in London', in Barry and Brooks (eds), *Middling Sort*, ch. 5, discusses the vagueness of the category.

28. Barry, 'Introduction', p. 3; Wilson, *Sense of the People*, p. 57.

29. K. Wrightson, 'Estates, degrees, and sorts: changing perceptions of society in Tudor and Stuart England', in P.J. Corfield (ed.), *Language, History and Class* (Oxford, 1991), ch. 2; K. Wrightson, '"Sorts of people" in Tudor and Stuart England', in Barry and Brooks (eds), *Middling Sort*, ch. 1.

30. P.J. Corfield, 'Class by name and number in eighteenth-century Britain', in Corfield (ed.), *Language*, ch. 5.

31. D. Defoe, *A Tour through the Whole Island of Great Britain* (London, 1974 edn.), Vol. 1, pp. 126–7.

the man was a most uncouth spectacle; he was cloathed all in leather, had a cap of the same without brims, some tools in a little basket which he drew up with him, not one of the names of which we could understand but by the help of an interpreter. Nor indeed could we understand any of the man's discourse so as to make out a whole sentence; and yet the man was pretty free of his tongue too.

'[W]e that saw him ascend *ab inferis*, fancied he look'd like an inhabitant of the dark regions ... who was just ascended into the world of light.' Defoe and his companions gave the man some money, the equivalent of the profits of three days' work, and reflected upon how fortunate they were not having to 'get our bread thus, one hundred and fifty yards underground, or in a hole as deep in the earth as the cross upon St. Paul's cupolo is high out of it'.[32] The assumptions and interactions of class cram such accounts. When Defoe and his company talked to the wife of a lead miner, she addressed one of the men as 'your worship' and impressed on them how 'contented' she and her family were. She cried when they gave her money.[33]

And yet Defoe and the miner with the recently acquired cash ended up in the same alehouse! Cultural separation was not total. Defoe's anatomy of Sturbridge Fair, the greatest fair 'in the world', provides one final example of the cultural contours that I am trying to convey. It was a regional fair, held every August or September, near Cambridge, but drawing concourses of people from London and all over the nation. Thus there were wholesalers from London, rendezvousing with their chapmen; clothiers from Yorkshire and Lancashire; brewers from the north, buying hops from the south; and wool-buyers from East Anglia. There was iron and brass ware from Birmingham; tools and knives from Sheffield; glassware and stockings from Nottingham and Leicester; and fabrics from the west. Coaches and boats ferried people backwards and forwards from Cambridge and other towns.

This city of booths, tents, and temporary warehouses offered trade and entertainment to every social group. Defoe said that the wholesale dealers, who had their own square of booths, could sell a combined 'one hundred thousand pounds worth of woollen manufactures' in less than a week. But there were considerable numbers of smaller traders too:

It is impossible to describe all the parts and circumstances of this fair exactly; the shops are placed in rows like streets, wherof one is call'd

32. Ibid., Vol. 2, pp. 164–5.   33. Ibid., Vol. 2, pp. 162–3.

Cheapside; and here, as in several other streets, are all sorts of trades, who sell by retale, and who come principally from London with their goods; scarce any trades are omitted, goldsmiths, toyshops, brasiers, turners, milleners, haberdashers, hatters, mercers, drapers, pewtrers, china-warehouses, and in a word all trades that can be named in London; with coffee-houses, taverns, brandy-shops, and eating houses, innumerable, and all in tents and booths, as above.

The 'meaner sort of people' also flocked to the fair, lodging in stables and barns in the surrounding communities. As the whole-sale trade concluded, the gentry arrived 'from all parts of the county round'; 'and tho' they come for their diversion; yet 'tis not a little money they lay out; which generally falls to the share of the retailers . . . and some loose coins, they reserve for the puppet-shows, drolls, rope-dancers, and such like'. Finally, on the last day, a horse fair was held with foot and horse races 'to divert the meaner sort of people only'.[34] Although the role of gender is unclear, we have a cultural mix. The contours of social differentiation are ever-present – in Defoe's account as well as in the events he is describing – but a simple elite/popular inscription would obscure more variegated interaction and representation. And this is what we have encountered in chapter after chapter in this book.

III

The social plurality of early modern England makes it likely that culture was experienced in a variety of ways. We have seen that youth appear again and again in our discussion. In fact a recent history of youth in the century before 1640 keeps slipping into a general social history of the period: there are few topics which do not relate to youth.[35] Although it is unlikely that there was a developed youth culture in the early modern period, in the way that we would understand the term, there is much evidence of youth interaction and socialisation, particularly in festivity and ritual.[36] The insubordination of the young, Paul Griffiths has shown, was an important component of early modern English culture.[37] We do not need merely to rely on the complaints of their elders.

34. Ibid., Vol. 1, pp. 80–5.

35. I have in mind P. Griffiths, *Youth and Authority: Formative Experiences in England 1560–1640* (Oxford, 1996).

36. I.K. Ben-Amos, *Adolescence and Youth in Early Modern England* (New Haven, 1994), ch. 8; Griffiths, *Youth and Authority*, esp. ch. 3; R. Hutton, *The Stations of the Sun: a History of the Ritual Year in Britain* (Oxford, 1996), pp. 414–15.

37. Griffiths, *Youth and Authority*.

When historians write of the participation of youth in festivity, they are often referring to male youth. Early modern cultures were also heavily gendered in ways which historians are only beginning to explore.[38] *The Pinder of Wakefield* (1632) is a good example of this gendering. The book is about George Greene, from Wakefield, the son of a husbandman. He is 'captain' or leader of a group of hard-drinking young men, craftsmen and tradesmen, who frequent the local alehouse and engage in manly acts – the pamphlet is very masculinist in tone. As its full title promises, it consists of a series of jokes and stories, including combat and friendship with Robin Hood and his men: 'Being the merry History of . . . the lusty Pinder of the North. Briefly shewing his manhood and his brave merriments amongst his boone Companions . . . With the great Battel fought betwixt them him and Robin Hood, Scarlet and little John, and after his living with them in the Woods.' George is a popular hero, 'our second Saint George for England', a fellow of good cheer, frequenter of wakes, weddings, may poles and sports. He stands for liberality, hospitality, good fellowship, and wit. He is a trickster and an admirer of other tricksters, whether it is putting fish-hooks in a pocket to catch a pickpocket or using a trussed cat as a shield. George is well liked by the community, and, indeed, is an enforcer of a certain kind of popular morality: punishing upstarts, Puritans, troublesome characters forever taking their neighbours to court, and robbers. Some of this morality is heavily gendered, for one of his roles is as a champion of dominated husbands. He organises a riding to mock a woman who had beaten her husband, and is credited with being the inventor of the cucking stool used against scolding wives!

George and his male companions are always wrestling and cudgeling. They are 'proper fellowes', 'brave lads', 'bonny bulchins', 'lusty sturdy', 'stout' fellows who conduct themselves 'stoutly' and 'stiffely' and do 'brave deedes', laying about their opponents 'so manfully'. He is gracious in victory; after a Midsummer pitched battle between the men of Wakefield and the men of Halifax and Kendal, they all embrace, those injured are patched up, and George spends all the twenty marks prize money, a considerable sum, to

38. For important initiatives, see P. Crawford, *Women and Religion in England 1500–1720* (London, 1993); S.D. Amussen, 'The gendering of popular culture in early modern England', in Harris (ed.), *Popular Culture*, ch. 3; A. Fletcher, *Gender, Sex and Subordination in England 1500–1800* (London, 1995); S.D. Amussen, ' "The part of a Christian man": the cultural politics of manhood in early modern England', in S.D. Amussen and M.A. Kishlansky (eds), *Political Culture and Cultural Politics in Early Modern England* (Manchester, 1995), ch. 9; and L. Gowing, *Domestic Dangers: Women, Words, and Sex in Early Modern London* (Oxford, 1996).

drink 'merrily' in reconciliation. The languages of masculinity in the *Pinder* read strangely to a modern reader. After the fight with George, Robin Hood says:

> Come I pray thee George, live with me in the woods/and what pleasure the woods can afford thou shalt have it to the full. Oh there is delight for a King . . . it is a Palace of pleasure. Come, deny me not man, . . . in woods wee'l hawke, hunt, wee'l dance and sing, ride, run, with all delights whatsoever, come I will not bee denyed man. Quoth George, Robin Hood thou hast almost perswaded me, because I know thou lovest a man, and of thy prowesse I have heard before. Nay, quoth little John, thou shalt have also one hundred more lusty brave fellowes to thy companions. I, quoth Scarlet, those that will not shrink, but drinke and sing, and merrily trowle the bowle. God-a-mercy my brave sparkes, come all wee are friends: come lusty Robin Hood . . . With that there was much imbracing betwixt George his Soldates and Robin Hood, Scarlet and little John wonderfull to behold . . .[39]

We could debate the homoeroticism of this extract, yet there is little doubting that if the protagonists had been female the language would have been totally different.

We saw how it is impossible to discuss early modern sexualities without considering the different experiences of male and female. As we saw in Chapter 1, gender far outweighed considerations of elite/popular in the axes of the cultures of sex. Male sexual jealousy and obsession with cuckoldry, an over-representation of male control to be found at all levels of society, betrayed a common insecurity: what Mark Breitenberg has described as 'anxious masculinity'.[40] For while women were subordinate in early modern society – in every possible sphere – it was, to use Susan Amussen's apposite term, a 'limited subordination'.[41] The irony is that the cultural expression of this limitation – almost of necessity – took highly exaggerated forms.

IV

England was also a nation of 'local cultural contrasts'.[42] There was a diversity of experience, whether we are referring to the geographies

---

39. E.A. Horsman (ed.), *The Pinder of Wakefield* (Liverpool, 1956), p. 69.
40. M. Breitenberg, 'Anxious masculinity: sexual jealousy in early modern England', *Feminist Studies* 19 (1993), 377–98.
41. Amussen, 'Gendering of popular culture', p. 51.
42. D. Underdown, 'Regional cultures? Local variations in popular culture during the early modern period', in Harris (ed.), *Popular Culture*, ch. 2.

of riots, literacy, religious experience, illegitimacy, or the regional variants of festive drama. This regional pluralism comprises the urban–rural differences encountered in most areas of popular culture. It includes the peculiarities of the wider regions of north, south, east, and west mentioned in every chapter. But it also involves more localised cultures: the civic cultures of London or Bristol;[43] the ritual peculiarities of particular towns or villages; or the customs and folklore associated with distinctive local economies.

The fissures of regionalism are represented nowhere more vividly than in the observations of outsiders. The inhabitants of the fens were 'a kind of people according to the nature of the place where they dwell rude, uncivill, and envious to all others whom they call *Upland-men*: who stalking on high upon stilts, apply their mindes, to grasing, fishing and fowling'. The draining of their watery environment, it was said, would bring mental as well as material reclamation:

> There shall a change of Men and Manners be;
> Hearts, thick and tough as Hydes, shall feel Remorse,
> And Souls of Sedge shall understand Discourse,
> New hands shall learn to Work, forget to Steal,
> New leggs shall go to church, new knees shall kneel.[44]

Daniel Defoe's *Tour . . . Through the Whole Island of Great Britain* (1724–6) is littered with regional encounters. He saw the fishing fair of Yarmouth, beginning on Michaelmas Day and lasting throughout October, with 'the land cover'd with people, and the river with barks and boats, busy day and night, landing and carrying off the herrings'.[45] He noted the material culture of wrecking, visible all along the Norfolk coast from Winterton to Cromer, where 'country people had scarce a barn, or a shed, or a stable' that was not built from the wrecks of ships.[46] He wrote scathingly of the Charlton Horn Fair (in Kent),

> the rudeness of which I cannot but think, is such as ought to be suppress'd . . . The mob indeed at that time take all kinds of liberties, and the women are especially impudent for that day; as if it was a day that justify'd the giving themselves a loose to all manner of indecency and immodesty, without any reproach, or without suffering the censure which such behaviour would deserve at another time.[47]

43. Compare P. Burke, 'Popular culture in seventeenth-century London', and J. Barry, 'Popular culture in seventeenth-century Bristol', in Reay (ed.), *Popular Culture*, chs. 1 and 2 respectively.
44. W. Camden, *Britannia* (1637), and S. Fortrey, *Narrative* (1685), quoted in H.C. Darby, *The Draining of the Fens* (Cambridge, 1956), pp. 23, 90.
45. Defoe, *Tour*, Vol. 1. p. 66.   46. Ibid., Vol. 1, p. 71.   47. Ibid., Vol. 1, p. 97.

He struggled with west country dialect: 'tho' the tongue be all meer natural English, yet those that are but a little acquainted with them, cannot understand one half of what they say'.[48]

V

Once the bipolar approach to popular cultures has been unpicked, several other orthodoxies of popular cultural historical studies collapse. An influential frame is to see the early modern world as a turning point, a crisis in elite–popular relations. Robert Muchembled is the most extreme proponent of this view, arguing that in France in the sixteenth and seventeenth centuries state and church instituted a 'cultural revolution', 'cultural invasion', or 'cultural conquest', a systematic repression of an older popular culture. This cultural war was conducted on a number of fronts – indeed impacted on every aspect of popular culture in what Muchembled describes, rather graphically, as 'constrained souls and subjected bodies'.[49] 'The Catholic Counter Reformation and the absolute State, between 1550 and 1750 for the most part, pooled all their efforts to construct a new type of man' (the gendered language is Muchembled's).[50] A sense of sin was inculcated. Sexual and bodily matters were treated with new decorum. Values of hierarchy and obedience were inscribed. The boundaries of the sacred and the profane were redrawn. Magical practices were suppressed. The impact of this acculturation was profound: 'Popular culture is one of history's losers: shattered by the far-reaching cultural revolution between the end of the Middle Ages and the contemporary age, like all losers, it has left few traces ... This mutilation was easily accomplished, what is more, since popular culture was essentially oral, and its adversaries wielded the formidable weapon of writing.'[51] When popular culture had been 'eclipsed', a new 'mass' culture was offered as consolation in the form of popular literature (i.e. the French chapbook).

Although his analysis is by no means as schematic and mechanistic as Muchembled's, Peter Burke has provided a wider European framework for a very similar process, what he has termed 'the reform of popular culture', the 'systematic attempt by members of the elite ... to reform the culture of ordinary people'. Burke writes

---

48. Ibid., Vol. 1, p. 219.   49. Muchembled, *Popular Culture*, p. 5.
50. Ibid., p. 233.   51. Ibid., p. 1.

of reform rather than conquest, and he sees elite withdrawal as an important component of the process. Yet his time-frame is very similar to that of Muchembled:

> In 1500 . . . popular culture was everyone's culture; a second culture for the educated, and the only culture for everyone else. By 1800, however, in most parts of Europe, the clergy, the nobility, the merchants, the professional men – and their wives – had abandoned popular culture to the lower classes, from whom they were now separated, as never before, by profound differences in world view.[52]

These models find little support in this book. Such popular cultures are empty of agency. Whether being moulded, conquered, repressed, transformed, shattered, or merely reformed, recoiled from, or 'trickled down' upon, popular culture appears as a passive rather than an active entity. They are 'reduced to a childlike state', 'submissive'.[53] They are not the popular cultures of this book.

Nor is the chronology of much utility. As Chartier has observed, popular culture is viewed as perpetually in a state of momentous transformation: in the medieval period, the early modern period, the nineteenth century, the late twentieth century. In our period alone, historians claim climactic suppressions and divergences between popular and elite in the 1640s (Underdown), by 1660 (Wrightson), from the end of the seventeenth century (Borsay), by 1750 (Muchembled), by 1800 (Burke), and from 1750 to 1850 (Robert Malcolmson).[54] The precise nature of that divergence varies too. Burke, we have seen, refers to reform and withdrawal; Muchembled to conquest. Wrightson and David Levine have suggested that village elites, including the middling sort, distanced themselves from the poor and attempted to control and reform the more unruly aspects of popular culture,[55] whereas Peter Borsay's thesis is of social emulation drawing a section of middle-class society into a new urban elite and creating cultural differentiation of a different kind: 'a widening cultural gap . . . between polite society and the majority of ordinary people, and with it the transformation of an inclusive traditional culture into an exclusive popular one'.[56] To quote Chartier,

52. Burke, *Popular Culture*, pp. 208, 234, 270.
53. Muchembled, *Popular Culture*, p. 234.
54. For most of these historians, see above. For Wrightson, see K. Wrightson, *English Society 1580–1680* (London, 1982), p. 227. For Malcolmson, see R.W. Malcolmson, *Popular Recreations in English Society 1700–1850* (Cambridge, 1973), chs 6–7.
55. K. Wrightson and D. Levine, *Poverty and Piety in an English Village: Terling, 1525–1700* (Oxford, 1995 edn).
56. Borsay, *English Urban Renaissance*, ch. 11 (p. 285 for quote).

Historiographically speaking, therefore, the fate of popular culture seems forever to be stifled, inhibited, and abraded, but at the same time ever to be reborn out of its decay. This indicates, perhaps that the true problem is not to identify the decisive moment of the disappearence of popular culture, but rather to consider for each epoch how complex relations were developed between forms imposed (more or less forcibly) and established practices (sometimes allowed to blossom and sometimes restrained).[57]

In other words, cultural reform was always on the agenda – reform from below as well as from above – and popular cultures were perpetually being reshaped and reshaping themselves. The best way of viewing this is as a state of continued dynamic process rather than as a series of crescendos and abrupt caesuras.

It is not my intention to deny the historical nature of the popular cultures which we have been traversing. We have continually noted changes over time. However, there are two points which should be made in connection with this change (and the models above). One is that while we may detect change, even transformation, in one cultural sphere, this should not be converted immediately into evidence for wider cultural alteration. The other is that cultural continuities are just as important. Perhaps continuity is the wrong word to indicate the subtle re-forming and retaining which proceeded amidst change, but it is a useful counter to notions of dramatic metamorphosis.

VI

There are numerous instances of overlap between popular and elite (if we persist in using these terms), examples of 'shared' and 'common' cultures. In the chapters above, we have seen gentry implicated in anti-enclosure rioting and charivaris, consuming popular print, and participating in folk drama and libellous rhymes. When a Bath gentlewoman was ridiculed in 1614–15 in a rhyme sung in tavern, inn, and alehouse – 'Theres none compares with Muddy Mall, That plays the whoore from springe to fall . . . [I]f you have golde she showes her arsse, [i]f you have none shee burnes your tarse' – most of those accused of disgracing her name were members of the gentry. One of their number had openly ridiculed

---

57. Chartier, *Forms and Meanings*, p. 86.

the woman's husband (as a cuckold) in the marketplace, in front of the servants of butchers and tanners.[58]

David Underdown has recently sketched out the intersections of the political cultures of early modern England, found in 'a common stock of familiar ideas and metaphors about household and commonwealth: the patriarchal state, the body politic, the divine origins of monarchy and hierarchy'. Although he sees the English Revolution as a watershed, leading to division and divergence (bipolarity again!), the period before 1640 saw a 'common political language' shared by gentry and plebeian, and revealed in the ideologies of custom and rights, notions of masculinity and the place of women in society, belief in witchcraft, widespread anti-popery, and Protestant nationalism.[59]

However, observations about shared cultures will only get us so far. For common beliefs could mask a multiplicity of different emphases and applications. Notions of honour applied to all social levels in early modern England, but the meanings of reputation differed significantly according to gender and rank. Male libertinism was a mark of gentility in some circles. The stigma of female unchastity could be modified, if not overridden, by the high social status of the woman concerned. Even aspersions of cuckoldry, 'normally the most serious slur on a man's sexual worth', Faramerz Dabhoiwala has explained, 'could be flattened by the weight of one's social reputation'.[60] The action that women took to protect their reputation, Laura Gowing has suggested, also reflected their social position. Those of middling and lower status worked actively to protect their honour, using the law to guard their names or speaking vociferously to defend their reputations. 'For higher status women . . . the ideology of passivity had more purchase.' Indeed, if they spoke out loudly, this 'use of Tongue' (as a libel of a gentleman's wife mocked) was confirmation of alleged dishonour and lack of gentility.[61] Defoe described early eighteenth-century society

58. J. Stokes (ed.), *Records of Early English Drama: Somerset, Vol. 1 The Records* (Toronto, 1996), pp. 22–6.

59. D. Underdown, *A Freeborn People: Politics and the Nation in Seventeenth-century England* (Oxford, 1996), esp. pp. 10–12, 128–9 (quote on p. 12). See also, the excellent survey by John Walter, 'The commons and their mental worlds', in J. Morrill (ed.), *The Oxford Illustrated History of Tudor and Stuart Britain* (Oxford, 1996), ch. 10.

60. F. Dabhoiwala, 'The construction of honour, reputation and status in late seventeenth- and early eighteenth-century England', *Transactions of the Royal Historical Society* 6 (1996), 201–13 (quote on p. 204).

61. L. Gowing, 'Women, status and the popular culture of dishonour', *Transactions of the Royal Historical Society* 6 (1996), 225–34 (quotes on pp. 226, 231).

as one in which 'character' and 'reputation' was layered by gender and class. He thought 'the making havoc of the characters of inno- cent women' more likely among upper-class men than women, but that the likelihood of slander bore an inverse relationship to social position and level of civilisation:

> slander is a meanness below persons of honour and quality, and to do injustice to the ladies, especially, is a degree below those who have any share of breeding and sense: On this account you may observe, 'tis more practis'd among the citizens than among the gentry, and in country towns and villages, more than in the city, and so on, till you come to the meer *canail*, the common mobb of the street, and there, no reputation, no character can shine without having dirt thrown upon it every day . . .[62]

It is with the meanings and uses of shared values that we are most concerned, then, rather than the surface hints at commonality. The belief in the influence of the stars on human affairs provides another example.[63] Astrology was a genuinely popular belief system. Astrological almanacs sold in their hundreds of thousands, and the most successful astrologers were seeing between 1,000 and 2,000 people a year. Astrology's attraction lay in the systematic way in which it viewed everything: explaining, predicting, from the defeat and death of a king to minor thefts or medical ailments. It was compatible with Christianity, indeed reinforced providential ways of viewing the universe. 'God's will was writ large in the heavens, and astrology provided the interpretative methodology.'[64] Yet astrology was a multiple entity. There were many astrologies and many uses of it. One of its forms was 'judicial astrology', a 'prognostic art' with its own cryptography and 'symbolic language system', decoded so lovingly by Ann Geneva.[65] This was the form closely associated with healing. But there were other types. Patrick Curry places 'judicial astrology' midway in his hierarchy, between the high astrology of natural philosophers (natural astrology), and more general, less

---

62. Defoe, *Tour*, Vol. 1, pp. 127–8.

63. For astrology, see K. Thomas, *Religion and the Decline of Magic* (Harmondsworth, 1973), chs 10–12; B. Capp, *Astrology and the Popular Press: English Almanacs 1500– 1800* (London, 1979); A. Chapman, 'Astrological medicine', in C. Webster (ed.), *Health, Medicine and Mortality in the Sixteenth Century* (Cambridge, 1979), ch. 8; P. Curry, *Prophecy and Power: Astrology in Early Modern England* (Cambridge, 1989); A. Geneva, *Astrology and the Seventeenth Century Mind: William Lilly and the Language of the Stars* (Manchester, 1995).

64. Geneva, *Astrology*, p. 264.   65. Ibid., pp. 4, 9.

systematic, beliefs in the influence of the stars – what he terms popular astrology.[66] 'Popular' is perhaps the wrong term, for it implies that judicial astrology was not as widely held. However, the observation about variety holds: astrological beliefs were widely shared, but 'different social groups adopted and adapted them for very different purposes; and therein lies their meaning and interest'.[67]

The combination of diversity amidst shared values can be demonstrated for another area of early modern culture not covered in any detail in this book: medicine. There is a consensus among medical historians that rather than a clear division between high and low or learned and popular there 'was a spectrum of medical knowledge shared by the population as a whole'.[68] The early modern medical marketplace contained a diverse group of healers: physicians, surgeons, and apothecaries, the ancestors of our modern-day medical hierarchy who were a minority group in that society; midwives; itinerant healers and drug sellers; cunning folk; clergymen; people in the community with some area of expertise (e.g. blacksmiths or sow gelders who practised medicine on humans as well as animals); members of the gentry; and self-medicators. And these practitioners drew on an eclectic but widely shared range of beliefs and techniques: astrology, herbal medicine, humoralism (restoring the balance of the body's fluids, usually by blood-letting or purging), and folk medicine (imitative magic, transference, the use of formulas or charms – astrological and religious).[69]

Obviously medicine had its social and educational contours. The size of fees – the lowest costing the weekly wage of a labourer – and the nature of the medical advice literature would indicate that the middle and upper levels of society were better able to consult

66. P. Curry, 'Astrology in early modern England: the making of a vulgar knowledge', in S. Pumfrey, P.L. Rossi, and M. Slawinski (eds), *Science, Culture and Popular Belief in Renaissance Europe* (Manchester, 1991), ch. 12.

67. Ibid., p. 285.

68. L.M. Beier, *Sufferers and Healers: the Experience of Illness in Seventeenth-century England* (London, 1987), p. 4.

69. See H.J. Cook, 'The medical marketplace of London', in his *The Decline of the Old Medical Regime in Stuart London* (Ithaca, NY, 1986), ch. 1; R. Sawyer, 'Patients, healers and disease in the southeast midlands, 1597–1634' (University of Wisconsin-Madison, Ph.D., 1986), chs 3–5; Beier, *Sufferers and Healers*; M. Pelling, 'Medical practice in early modern England: trade or profession?', in W.R. Prest (ed.), *The Professions in Early Modern England* (London, 1987), ch. 4; J. Henry, 'Doctors and healers: popular culture and the medical profession', in Pumfrey, Rossi, and Slawinski (eds), *Science*, ch. 9; A. Wear, 'The popularization of medicine in early modern England', in R. Porter (ed.), *The Popularization of medicine 1650–1850* (London, 1992), ch. 1.

the higher levels of the medical profession and to purchase practical advice (including instructions relating to surgery).[70] Ronald Sawyer has shown that the level of consultation provided by the healer Richard Napier varied with the social status of the patient – i.e. their facility to interact and engage intellectually as well as their ability to pay.[71] The triumvirate of physician, surgeon, and apothecary also presented a self-image of hierarchy and superiority. Physicians had Latin and Greek, university training, and knowledge of classical, medieval, and early modern medical texts. A surgeon could speak contemptuously of an illiterate craftsman who claimed to be able to heal eyes without even knowing what an eye was, 'of what members or parts it is composed'.[72] And yet these boundaries and self-representations collapsed constantly. Physicians were amazingly eclectic in their approaches, drawing on the panoply of folk as well as classical remedies. The elite sought out cunning folk. The poor did visit surgeons and physicians; poor relief covered emergencies. Everyone engaged in self-medication. Medical ideas circulated widely: early modern drama, for instance, is suffused with the assumptions and languages of humoralism.[73] In the words of Roy Porter, 'The picture is . . . one of pluralism and . . . interchange of ideas and information. Vital necessity meant that healing practices transcended educational and class barriers.'[74]

Perhaps it is at the individual level that we can best see the process of continual negotiation at work in early modern culture. Samuel Pepys was a middling man rapidly establishing himself at the gentry level. As a naval bureaucrat, he moved in gentry circles. He recorded parliamentary affairs, court gossip, meetings and meals with royalty and aristocrats. He kept a now famous diary – itself, as Mark Dawson has shown, a product of its writer's position, a 'social ledger', 'an exercise in social accounting', recording Pepys's upwardly mobile performance (and the reactions and evaluations of

70. For fees, see I. Loudon, 'The nature of provincial medical practice in eighteenth-century England', *Medical History* 29 (1985), 1–32. For books, see P. Slack, 'Mirrors of health and treasures of poor men: the uses of vernacular medical literature of Tudor England', in Webster (ed.), *Health*, ch. 7; P.K. Wilson, 'Acquiring surgical know-how: occupational and lay instruction in eighteenth-century London', in Porter (ed.), *Popularization of Medicine*, ch. 2.

71. Sawyer, 'Patients', pp. 300–11. It is a pity that this invaluable thesis has never been published.

72. Beier, *Sufferers and Healers*, pp. 38–9.

73. Henry, 'Doctors and healers', pp. 198–9.

74. R. Porter, 'The people's health in Georgian England', in Harris (ed.), *Popular Culture*, p. 125.

others) on a social and cultural stage.[75] He acquired a massive library: about 500 books in the 1660s (the period covered by his famous diary), and some 3,000 volumes by the time of his death in 1703. Although he did not always comprehend everything that he read – of Descartes he noted, 'I understand not, nor think he did well that writ it, though a most learned man' – he could spend 55s. on a book and fine binding, and owned an impressive range of scientific, religious, philosophical, political, and historical works.[76] And this expensively bound library, kept in Pepys's study along with his collection of scientific instruments, was a conscious representation of gentility and gentlemanly scholarship.[77]

However, Pepys was also familiar with the milieu of the alehouse and fair. After flageolet (flute) lessons, consultation with his bookbinder, and a visit to Whitehall, he could move – in a single day – from watching brawling butchers and watermen in the Southwark Bear Garden ('It was pleasant to see, but that I stood in the pit and feared that in the tumult I might get some hurt') to 'a turn or two' in the park at St James ('it being a most sweet day').[78] In the words of Dawson, 'Pepys's experience as conveyed by the Diary sees him moving across a broad cultural spectrum which encompassed the cultural worlds of both social inferiors and superiors.'[79] Pepys and gentry companions went to Bartholomew Fair to see acrobats, a dancing horse, and puppet plays. Lady Castlemaine, the King's mistress, was there in 1667, watching the puppet show, 'Patient Griselda'.[80] But the picture is not one of a common culture, for the diary shows a continual process of cultural discrimination, of acceptance and rejection, participation and non-participation, of appropriation and (what Dawson terms) 'dis-appropriation'. Pepys complained about the presence of 'citizens' and 'mean people' at the stage plays at Christmas. Southwark Fair was 'very dirty' and the puppet play he saw there an 'idle thing'. He was ashamed to be seen going into an alehouse in Shoe Lane. Ironically, Pepys's massive collection of ballads and chapbooks (used in this book and numerous other studies of early modern popular culture) was part of this

75. M.S. Dawson, 'Pepysian texts and the exploration of early modern English culture' (University of Auckland, M.A., 1997), ch. 1 (quotes on pp. 48, 70).

76. For Descartes, see R. Latham and W. Matthews (eds), *The Diary of Samuel Pepys*, 11 vols (London, 1970–83), Vol. 9, p. 401.

77. Dawson, 'Pepysian texts', ch. 2.

78. Latham and Matthews (eds), *Diary of Samuel Pepys*, Vol. 8, pp. 237–9: 27 May 1667.

79. Ibid., p. 153.

80. Latham and Matthews (eds), *Diary of Samuel Pepys*, Vol. 8, p. 409 (for Castlemaine); ibid., Vol. 9, pp. 293, 299, 301.

very discrimination. They were catalogued in his library as '*Vulgaria*': he was distancing himself as he collected and classified.[81]

The newer approaches to popular culture(s) do not provide the neat explanations and models of the older historiography. The picture that we have is one of shared but variegated cultures, of multiple uses, and conditional change. This book supports notions of multiple uses. We have seen the multiple meanings of festive drama and ritual. As Miri Rubin once put it, people never 'experience ritual from a unitary position . . . *communitas* is dissolved as soon as the sweat evaporates off the brow of the ritual performer'.[82] Another important (and linked) theme has been one of cultural fluidity and hybridity. We saw the fusion of the different discourses and traditions of witchcraft. We noted the interaction and compromise involved in the history of religions in England during the early modern period. We have explored the complicated margins of literacy and orality, including what I have termed the orality of print. The purpose is not to negate the social configuration in the patterns of early modern culture which we have been tracing; indeed, we have allowed for those more heavily inscribed. However, the argument is that although the elite–popular division was important, it no longer carries the expositive force that it once did.

VII

Historians – especially authors of textbooks – are appropriators too: of the past, and of the work of fellow historians and others. Students (and historians) have to be aware that histories (representations of the past) are always provisional. They tell us as much about the agendas of their historians as they do about the subjects of their studies. Diane Purkiss has demonstrated that it was not only the villagers and townspeople of early modern England who projected their fantasies onto the witch. Certain types of feminist, modern-day witches, and academic historians have (variously) been 'at play in the fields of the past'.[83] Purkiss met a witch who had heard of

81. Dawson, 'Pepysian texts', ch. 3. It should be said that Dawson is a little more wedded to the elite–popular distinction than I am.

82. Rubin, *Corpus Christi*, p. 2.

83. D. Purkiss, *The Witch in History: Early Modern and Twentieth-century Interpretations* (London, 1996). See her withering analysis in chs 1–3 (Part 1). As no doubt Purkiss would realise, her interpretations of witchcraft in the remainder of the book represent yet another type of projection. ('At play in the fields of the past' is the title of her second chapter.)

Carlo Ginzburg's famous study of the sixteenth-century northern Italian benandanti: the spiritual night battles between white and black witches. She told Purkiss that she herself had been involved in such night battles, most recently 'over the Twyford Down road-works', that white witches had prevented a German invasion during the Second World War, and that 'some book by Clineburg [Ginzburg]' had described the night battles.[84] This is using history in a way that will horrify historians. It represents quintessential appropriation, untrammelled by any rules of evidence. Yet, as Purkiss has argued, mercilessly, influential (male) academic historians – and their successors (through their silences) – have also re-worked the early modern witch in their own image: privileging and suppressing. 'In the hands of historians' the witch had become the primitive, irrational 'other', reinforcing (in counterposition) the scientific rationality of the observer/detective/historian. Gender theory has been ignored in what, until recently, was essentially a history of women uninformed by women's history.[85]

As Michel de Certeau has put it, the terms used by historians of popular culture, including the term popular culture itself, are learned categories, and 'define less the content of a popular culture than the historian's gaze'.[86] Historians have an unavoidable transferential relationship with the past.[87] Carolyn Steedman has argued that this is most pronounced in histories of childhood where historical analysis is bound up with complex emotions and desires, including the unconscious quest for one's own 'lost childhood'.[88] But some historians of popular culture have criticised themselves for romanticising or valorising their subject, feeling a contradiction 'inherent in our penchant for boosting the significance of popular life in the past, while being unable or unwilling to overcome our

---

84. Ibid., p. 44.
85. Ibid., ch. 3: 'The witch in the hands of the historians'. It should be pointed out that there is more than an element of wisdom after the event in Purkiss's critique of the work of Alan Macfarlane and Keith Thomas, and that her work appeared too late to include some recent breaks with the dominant historiography of English witchcraft. Still, her argument is persuasive.
86. See D. LaCapra, *History and Criticism* (Ithaca, NY, 1985), esp. ch. 2: '*The cheese and the worms*: the cosmos of a twentieth-century historian'; M. de Certeau, *Heterologies: Discourse on the Other* (Minneapolis, 1989), ch. 8 (quote at p. 129). De Certeau's article, 'The beauty of the dead', originally appeared in French in 1980 as a response to a series of studies of French popular culture which were published in the 1960s.
87. LaCapra, *History and Criticism*, ch. 3.
88. C. Steedman, *Past Tenses: Essays on Writing Autobiography and History* (London, 1992), p. 201.

distaste for common ways in our own day'.[89] Political battles, allegiances, and desires can be projected onto safe fantasies about the past. De Certeau has claimed a more sinister relationship between past and present, where historically the study of popular culture has been intrinsic to the very act of its repression, and where idealisation, objectification, and classification have been a means of historical erasure. Seeing popular culture perpetually as the other, viewed from the hierarchical vantage point of learned culture, silences alternative possibilities.[90]

Like the cultures they describe, and try to explain, histories are perpetually in flux and always contestable. Whatever our impetus to capture, or evoke, however skilful we are at our craft (and perhaps we are the most dangerous when we are most evocative) we are never going to 'recapture' any past. The most that historians can ever provide is constructed, and always shifting, glimpses. We began the chapter on early modern witchcraft with an example of animal metamorphosis and Robert Darnton's statement about unravelling a joke or a ritual which we do not get, to unpick an alien belief system. The real jest is that we never get the joke. We can explore the intellectual and social frameworks which made witch-hunting possible, yet we cannot quite comprehend the seventeenth-century Newcastle women who thought that Dorothy Stranger could transform herself into a cat. Just as we never really 'get' Darnton's 'great cat massacre' (despite his considerable style), the appropriately named Stranger remains a stranger.[91] Infuriatingly, as our knowledge increases, witchcraft becomes more rather than less opaque. We have to reconcile ourselves to the fact that, whatever the beauty of the chase, there are some quarries we will never apprehend.

Moreover, we should recognise that we are involved in many different hunts. As the new historicist Louis Montrose has expressed it, our comprehensions of the past are shaped by our own social, cultural, historical, and institutional dispositions. 'As scholars, we

89. G. Strauss, 'The dilemma of popular history', *Past and Present* 132 (1991), 144. See also, the debate between W. Beik and G. Strauss, 'The dilemma of popular history', *Past and Present* 141 (1993), 207–19.

90. See de Certeau, *Heterologies*, ch. 8.

91. For an interesting discussion of Darnton's book, see R. Chartier, 'Text, symbols, and Frenchness', *Journal of Modern History* 57 (1985), 682–95; R. Darnton, 'The symbolic element in history', *Journal of Modern History* 58 (1986), 218–34; D. LaCapra, 'Chartier, Darnton, and the great symbol massacre', *Journal of Modern History* 58 (1988), 95–112; J. Fernandez, 'Historians tell tales: of Cartesian cats and Gallic cockfights', *Journal of Modern History* 58 (1988), 113–27; H. Mah, 'Suppressing the text: the metaphysics of ethnographic history in Darnton's great cat massacre', *History Workshop* 31 (1991), 1–20.

reconstruct the past, but the versions of the past so reconstructed are also the texts that we, as historically sited subjects, have actively fashioned. Thus, a historical criticism that seeks to recover meanings that are in any final or absolute sense authentic, correct, and complete is in pursuit of an illusion.'[92]

VIII

A curious thing has happened – is happening – in modern studies of popular culture: the elision of the past. It is not that the past is ignored, for historical assumptions and judgements are made at every interpretive turn.[93] What I have in mind is the relative neglect – in case studies, cited authorities, discussed methodologies, and theoretical genuflexions – of histories and historians of the period before the late nineteenth century.[94] In a sense, this is hardly surprising. One introductory guide to cultural theory informs us that what the most influential approaches informing studies of popular culture have in common is 'the insistence that whatever else popular culture might be, it is definitely a culture that only emerged following industrialization and urbanization'. Popular culture is a product of modernity. Before this, 'Britain had two cultures: a common culture which was shared by two classes, and a separate elite culture produced and consumed by the dominant classes in society.' [95] It did not have popular cultures. The subject matter of this book, open in front of you, does (did) not exist! Accordingly, Dominic Strinati's recent guide to key texts and theories takes us through chapters on the Frankfurt School, structuralism and semiology, Marxism, feminism, and postmodernism. The index identifies

92. Montrose, *Purpose of Playing*, p. 16.
93. This is the irony of the situation. It is doubly ironic, given what has been termed 'the historic turn' in the humanities and social sciences during the 1990s, although, of course, this turn to history does not necessarily involve historians! See T.J. McDonald (ed.), *The Historic Turn in the Human Sciences* (Ann Arbor, 1996).
94. There are two related issues here: the elision of early modern history, and the elision of all history. The discipline of history was central to what can be seen as early cultural studies, but it was nineteenth- and twentieth-century history: see B. Waites, T. Bennett, and G. Martin (eds), *Popular Culture: Past and Present* (London, 1982); and T. Bennett, C. Mercer, and J. Woollacott (eds), *Popular Culture and Social Relations* (Milton Keynes, 1986). The discussion which follows relates to more recent trends in cultural studies. For the responses of intellectual historians to cultural studies, a separate though not unconnected issue, see *Intellectual History Newsletter* 18 (1996), 3–69: 'Symposium: intellectual history in the age of cultural studies'.
95. J. Storey, *An Introductory Guide to Cultural Theory and Popular Culture* (Athens, Ga., 1993), pp. 16–17.

a 'cultural studies approach' to popular culture; there are entries on 'linguistics, structural', 'literature', and the 'sociology of culture'. But 'historical approaches' does not appear.[96] Such studies, whatever the sophistication of their analyses of the present, collude in the very Leavisite, conservative conception of history and culture they claim to reject:

> What we have lost is the organic community with the living culture it embodied. Folk-songs, folk-dances, Cotswold cottages and handicraft products are signs and expressions of something more: an art of life, a way of living, ordered and patterned, involving social arts, codes of intercourse and a responsive adjustment, growing out of immemorial experience, to the natural environment and the rhythm of the year.[97]

This is not the world we have lost, but the cultural world that we never had.

Even those who consciously smuggle history back into cultural studies are guilty of neglect. Peter Goodall's recent analysis, which explicitly challenges an identified tendency to equate cultural studies with *contemporary* culture and purports to 'restore a longer historical perspective to the study of culture', provides a very brief chapter on the eighteenth and nineteenth centuries and does not go any earlier than that period.[98] While David Chaney, notwithstanding his awareness that many of the supposed qualities of postmodern culture – 'parody/pastiche, depthlessness, allegory, spectacular show, and an ironic celebration of artifice' – have antecedents in earlier popular culture, and despite his location of 'cultural history' firmly on the map of cultural studies, does little to challenge the overall elision.[99]

It would be idiotic to deny that representations of the early modern cultures that we have lost are light years away from the

---

96. D. Strinati, *An Introduction to Theories of Popular Culture* (London, 1995).

97. F.R. Leavis and Denys Thompson quoted in both Storey, *Guide to Cultural Theory*, p. 32, and Strinati, *Theories of Popular Culture*, pp. 43–4. I am not saying that influential strands of cultural studies subscribe to a Leavisite view of the past. But I am claiming that their silence about England's past does nothing to challenge such assumptions, and that their focus on vaguely defined industrialisation and urbanisation, centred in the nineteenth century (in itself oblivious to historians' challenges to modernisation theories), reinforces this type of historical perspective.

98. P. Goodall, *High Culture, Popular Culture: the Long Debate* (Sydney, 1995), pp. xiii–xiv.

99. David Chaney locates cultural history as one of the significant contributions of cultural studies – he spends a couple of pages on E.P. Thompson, and even has a line on the historian of early modern France, N.Z. Davis – yet the stress again is on industrialisation and urbanisation: D. Chaney, *The Cultural Turn: Scene-setting Essays on Contemporary Cultural History* (London, 1994), pp. 50–7, and 204 (for the quote on postmodernism).

consumer cultures of late-twentieth-century popular culture, the images (visual and aural) of advertising, film, TV, clothing, record, photograph, computer, and material possession.[100] No amount of huffing and puffing by historians is going to remove the focus of cultural studies upon the modern. Nor should it.[101] But there is surely room for a little mindfulness that a perspective on the history of culture longer than that of the modern world might have some relevance to interpretations of modernity and postmodernity.[102] Those interested in popular cultures today can surely benefit from an awareness that the complex cultural interactions of the past – transitions, configurations, contestations, resistances: the jostlings of gender, class, race, religion, generation, allegiance to locality and nation – might have explanatory value for the present. Historians can challenge the definition of cultural studies as 'the study of *contemporary* culture'.[103] Practitioners of cultural studies should remedy history's absent presence.

100. My favourite cartographers of recent popular culture are D. Hebdige, *Subculture: the Meaning of Style* (London, 1979); D. Hebdige, *Hiding in the Light: On Images and Things* (London, 1988); J. Fiske, *Understanding Popular Culture* (London, 1989); A. McRobbie, *Postmodernism and Popular Culture* (London, 1994); and F. Mort, *Cultures of Consumption: Masculinities and Social Space in Late Twentieth-century Britain* (London, 1996).

101. See the stimulating recent collaboration between modern historians and others, examining 'the experience of [English] modernity over the last hundred years': M. Nava and A. O'Shea (eds), *Modern Times: Reflections on a Century of English Modernity* (London, 1996).

102. The influence of Mikhail Bakhtin's *Rabelais and His World* is the great exception to this claim: see Fiske, *Understanding Popular Culture*, ch. 4; J. Docker, *Postmodernism and Popular Culture: a Cultural History* (Melbourne, 1994), passim. New historicism is also clearly influential in its explorations of power and gender in the early modern world. See H.A. Vesser (ed.), *The New Historicism* (New York, 1989); L. Montrose, 'New historicisms', in S. Greenblatt and G. Gunn (eds), *Redrawing the Boundaries* (New York, 1992), pp. 392–418. But both these examples, while dealing with the past, are best described as literary studies rather than the work of historians.

103. S. During (ed.), *The Cultural Studies Reader* (London, 1993), p. 1. This is somewhat ironic considering During's awareness, in his introduction, of the importance of both contested histories and historically demonstrated cultural interaction (pp. 22, 25). There are no historians among the more than thirty contributors. The simultaneous neglect and assumption of history permeates another important reader in cultural studies: L. Grossberg, C. Nelson, and P. Treichler (eds), *Cultural Studies* (London, 1992). Note the paucity of papers by historians, and the sometimes awkward reactions to their work: see chs 16 and 33 by Catherine Hall and Carolyn Steedman. However, see C. Mukerji and M. Schudson (eds), *Rethinking Popular Culture: Contemporary Perspectives in Cultural Studies* (Berkeley, 1991), which has a whole section: 'Popular culture in historical studies'. For encouraging signs of another attempt to cross boundaries – from a cultural studies initiative – see the special issue of the journal edited by Meaghan Morris and Stephen Muecke, *UTS Review: Cultural Studies and New Writing* 2 (1996): 'Is an experimental history possible?'

Select Bibliography

Chapter 1 Sexualities

Adair, R., *Courtship, Illegitimacy and Marriage in Early Modern England* (Manchester, 1996).

Amussen, S.D., 'The gendering of popular culture in early modern England', in T. Harris (ed.), *Popular Culture in England, c. 1500–1850* (London, 1995), ch. 3.

Fletcher, A., *Gender, Sex and Subordination in England 1500–1800* (London, 1995).

Foucault, M., *The History of Sexuality: Volume 1: An Introduction* (London, 1978).

Gowing, L., *Domestic Dangers: Women, Words, and Sex in Early Modern London* (Oxford, 1996).

Griffiths, P., *Youth and Authority: Formative Experiences in England 1560–1640* (Oxford, 1996), ch. 5.

Hindle, S., 'The shaming of Margaret Knowsley: gossip, gender and the experience of authority in early modern England', *Continuity and Change* 9 (1994), 391–419.

Hitchcock, T., *English Sexualities, 1700–1800* (New York, 1997).

Ingram, M., 'The reform of popular culture? Sex and marriage in early modern England', in B. Reay (ed.), *Popular Culture in Seventeenth-century England* (London, 1985), ch. 4.

Ingram, M., *Church Courts, Sex and Marriage in England, 1570–1640* (Cambridge, 1987).

Porter, R., and Hall, L., *The Facts of Life: the Creation of Sexual Knowledge in Britain, 1650–1950* (New Haven, 1995).

Zimmerman, S., (ed.), *Erotic Politics: Desire on the Renaissance Stage* (London, 1992).

Chapter 2 Orality, Literacy, and Print

Barry, J., 'Literacy and literature in popular culture: reading and writing in historical perspective', in T. Harris (ed.), *Popular Culture in England, c. 1500–1850* (London, 1995), ch. 4.

Chartier, R., *The Cultural Uses of Print in Early Modern France* (Princeton, 1987).

Cressy, D., 'Literacy in context: meaning and measurement in early modern England', in J. Brewer and R. Porter (eds), *Consumption and the World of Goods* (London, 1993), ch. 15.

Cressy, D., *Literacy and the Social Order: Reading and Writing in Tudor and Stuart England* (Cambridge, 1980).

Fox, A., 'Ballads, libels and popular ridicule in Jacobean England', *Past and Present* 145 (1994), 47–83.

Houston, R.A., *Scottish Literacy and the Scottish Identity: Illiteracy and Society in Scotland and Northern England, 1600–1800* (Cambridge, 1985).

Raven, J., Small, H., and Tadmor, N. (eds), *The Practice and Representation of Reading in England* (Cambridge, 1996).

Spufford, M., *Small Books and Pleasant Histories: Popular Fiction and its Readership in Seventeenth-century England* (London, 1981).

Spufford, M., 'The pedlar, the historian and the folklorist: seventeenth century communications', *Folklore* 105 (1994), 13–24.

Thomas, K., 'The meaning of literacy in early modern England', in G. Baumann (ed.), *The Written Word: Literacy in Transition* (Oxford, 1986), pp. 97–130.

Watt, T., *Cheap Print and Popular Piety 1550–1640* (Cambridge, 1991).

Wurzbach, N., *The Rise of the English Street Ballad, 1550–1650* (Cambridge, 1990).

Chapter 3   Religions

Collinson, P., *The Birthpangs of Protestant England* (London, 1988).

Cressy, D., *Birth, Marriage, and Death: Ritual, Religion, and the Life-cycle in Tudor and Stuart England* (Oxford, 1997).

Duffy, E., *The Stripping of the Altars: Traditional Religion in England c. 1400–c. 1580* (New Haven, 1992).

Durston, C., and Eales, J. (eds), *The Culture of English Puritanism, 1560–1700* (London, 1996).

Haigh, C. (ed.), *The English Reformation Revised* (Cambridge, 1987).

Haigh, C., *English Reformations* (Oxford, 1993).

Hutton, R., 'The English Reformation and the evidence of folklore', *Past and Present* 148 (1995), 89–116.

Hutton, R., *The Rise and Fall of Merry England: the Ritual Year 1400–1700* (Oxford, 1994).

Ingram, M., 'From reformation to toleration: popular religious cultures in England, 1540–1690', in T. Harris (ed.), *Popular Culture in England, c. 1500–1850* (London, 1995), ch. 5.

McGregor, J.F., and Reay, B. (eds), *Radical Religion in the English Revolution* (Oxford, 1986).

Seaver, P.S., *Wallington's World: a Puritan Artisan in Seventeenth-century London* (Stanford, Calif., 1985).

Spufford, M., *Small Books and Pleasant Histories: Popular Fiction and its Readership in Seventeenth-century England* (London, 1981).

Watt, T., *Cheap Print and Popular Piety 1550–1640* (Cambridge, 1991).

Wrightson, K., and Levine, D., *Poverty and Piety in an English Village: Terling, 1525–1700* (Oxford, 1995).

Chapter 4   Witchcraft

Barry, J., Hester, M., and Roberts, G. (eds), *Witchcraft in Early Modern Europe: Studies in Culture and Belief* (Cambridge, 1996).

Briggs, R., *Witches and Neighbours: the Social and Cultural Context of European Witchcraft* (London, 1996).

Clark, S., *Thinking with Demons: the Idea of Witchcraft in Early Modern Europe* (Oxford, 1997).

Gaskill, M., 'Witchcraft and power in early modern England: the case of Margaret Moore', in J. Kermode and G. Walker (eds), *Women, Crime and the Courts in Early Modern England* (London, 1994), ch. 6.

Holmes, C., 'Popular culture? Witches, magistrates, and divines in early modern England', in S.L. Kaplan (ed.), *Understanding Popular Culture* (Berlin, 1984), pp. 85–111.

Holmes, C., 'Women: witnesses and witches', *Past and Present* 140 (1993), 45–78.

Jackson, L., 'Witches, wives and mothers: witchcraft persecution and women's confessions in seventeenth-century England', *Women's History Review* 4 (1995), 63–83.

Macfarlane, A., *Witchcraft in Tudor and Stuart England* (London, 1970).

Purkiss, D., *The Witch in History: Early Modern and Twentieth-century Interpretations* (London, 1996).

Roper, L., *Oedipus and the Devil: Witchcraft, Sexuality and Religion in Early Modern Europe* (London, 1994).

Sharpe, J., *Instruments of Darkness: Witchcraft in England 1550–1750* (London, 1996).

Simpson, J., 'Witches and witchbusters', *Folklore* 107 (1996), 5–18.

Thomas, K., *Religion and the Decline of Magic* (Harmondsworth, 1973).

Chapter 5 Festive Drama and Ritual

Bergeron, D.W., *English Civic Pageantry 1558–1642* (London, 1971).

Borsay, P., '"All the town's a stage": urban ritual and ceremony 1660–1800', in P. Clark (ed.), *The Transformation of English Provincial Towns 1600–1800* (London, 1984), ch. 7.

Bushaway, B., *By Rite: Custom, Ceremony and Community in England 1700–1880* (London, 1982).

Cressy, D., *Bonfires and Bells: National Memory and the Protestant Calendar in Elizabethan and Stuart England* (London, 1989).

Hindle, S., 'Custom, festival and protest in early modern England: the Little Budworth wakes, St Peter's Day, 1596', *Rural History* 6 (1995), 155–78.

Hutton, R., *The Stations of the Sun: a History of the Ritual Year in Britain* (Oxford, 1996).

Ingram, M., 'Ridings, rough music and the "reform of popular culture" in early modern England', *Past and Present* 105 (1984), 79–113.

Malcolmson, R.W., *Popular Recreations in English Society 1700–1850* (Cambridge, 1973).

Phythian-Adams, C., *Local History and Folklore: a New Framework* (London, 1975).

Smuts, R.M., 'Public ceremony and royal charisma: the English royal entry in London, 1485–1642', in A.L. Beier, D. Cannadine, and J.M. Rosenheim (eds), *The First Modern Society* (Cambridge, 1989), ch. 2.

Underdown, D., *Revel, Riot, and Rebellion: Popular Politics and Culture in England 1603–1660* (Oxford, 1985).

Chapter 6 Riots and the Law

Bohstedt, J., 'The moral economy and the discipline of historical context', *Journal of Social History* 26 (1992–3), 265–84.

Brewer, J., and Styles, J. (eds), *An Ungovernable People: the English and their Law in the Seventeenth and Eighteenth Centuries* (London, 1983).

Charlesworth, A. (ed.), *An Atlas of Rural Protest in Britain 1548–1900* (London, 1983).

Griffiths, P., Fox, A., and Hindle, S. (eds), *The Experience of Authority in Early Modern England* (London, 1996).

Hay, D., Linebaugh, P., Rule, J.G., Thompson, E.P., and Winslow, C., *Albion's Fatal Tree: Crime and Society in Eighteenth-century England* (Harmondsworth, 1977).

Neeson, J.M., *Commoners: Common Right, Enclosure and Social Change in England, 1700–1820* (Cambridge, 1993).

Randall, A., and Charlesworth, A. (eds), *Markets, Market Culture and Popular Protest in Eighteenth-century Britain and Ireland* (Liverpool, 1996).

Sharp, B., 'Popular protest in seventeenth-century England', in B. Reay (ed.), *Popular Culture in Seventeenth-century England* (London, 1985), ch. 8.

Sharpe, J., 'The people and the law', in B. Reay (ed.), *Popular Culture in Seventeenth-century England* (London, 1985), ch. 7.

Slack, P. (ed.), *Rebellion, Popular Protest and the Social Order in Early Modern England* (Cambridge, 1984).

Stevenson, J., *Popular Disturbances in England, 1700–1832* (London, 1992 edn).

Thompson, E.P., *Customs in Common* (London, 1991).

Chapter 7   Popular Cultures

Barry, J., and Brooks, C. (eds), *The Middling Sort of People: Culture, Society and Politics in England, 1550–1800* (London, 1994).

Burke, P., *Popular Culture in Early Modern Europe* (London, 1978, repr. 1994).

Chartier, R., *The Cultural Uses of Print in Early Modern France* (Princeton, 1987).

Chartier, R., *Forms and Meanings* (Philadelphia, 1995).

Gowing, L., 'Women, status and the popular culture of dishonour', *Transactions of the Royal Historical Society* 6 (1996), 225–34.

Harris, T. (ed.), *Popular Culture in England, c. 1500–1850* (London, 1995).

Hunt, M.E., *The Middling Sort: Commerce, Gender, and the Family in England, 1680–1780* (Berkeley, 1996).

Kaplan, S.L. (ed.), *Understanding Popular Culture: Europe from the Middle Ages to the Nineteenth Century* (Berlin, 1984).

King, P., 'Edward Thompson's contribution to eighteenth-century studies. The patrician–plebeian model re-examined', *Social History* 21 (1996), 215–28.

Reay, B. (ed.), *Popular Culture in Seventeenth-century England* (London, 1985 and 1988).

Scribner, B., 'Is a history of popular culture possible?', *History of European Ideas* 10 (1989), 175–91.

Underdown, D., *A Freeborn People: Politics and the Nation in Seventeenth-century England* (Oxford, 1996).

Walter, J., 'The commons and their mental worlds', in J. Morrill (ed.), *The Oxford Illustrated History of Tudor and Stuart Britain* (Oxford, 1996), ch. 10.

Index